THEY SAW IT HAPPEN

THEY
SAW IT HAPPEN

*An Anthology
of Eye-witnesses' Accounts of
Events in British History
55 B.C.-A.D. 1485*

Compiled by

W. O. HASSALL

Editor of the Holkham Bible

With a foreword by

E. E. Y. HALES

BASIL BLACKWELL
OXFORD

First Printed 1957
Reprinted 1959
Reprinted 1963
Reprinted 1967
Reprinted 1970
Reprinted 1973

0 631 05210 0 (boards)
0 631 05280 1 (paper)

Printed in Great Britain by
The Camelot Press, Ltd, London and Southampton

FOREWORD

Whatever the meaning of history may be there was once a time when it was not history. It was experience, shared by living people; pain perhaps, or ecstacy, or fear, or just a small deed done well, or badly, or indifferently. Upon these happenings the historians write their gloss, but the first thing is that they happened, and for us the first thing is that they happen again, in our imaginations. Before we interpret we experience; before we judge we feel. When Gibbon sat in the ruins of the Roman Forum and heard the Franciscans at their chanting, the idea came to him of writing his *Decline and Fall of the Roman Empire*; first he felt, then he wrote. We may not write about the past but we can feel it, and when we feel it we live, however briefly, a new life, live again in history, renew a moment that was once, and is no more, yet exists eternally. As Thomas Hardy wrote:

'By briefest meeting something sure is won
> It will have been:
Nor God nor Demon can undo the done,
> Unsight the seen.'

Dr. Hassall, in this volume, enables us to live, in imagination, in the Middle Ages, as Mr. Routh, in the second volume, of the same title, has enabled us to live in the period of the Tudors and the Stuarts. It is a full-blooded and varied life and it extends over a long time, from the coming of the Romans under Julius Caesar to the coming of the Tudors under Henry Tudor. We live with kings and archbishops, with barons and merchants, with Benedictines and Franciscans, with scholars and saints and heretics. We live in a world in which it is perfectly easy to believe in the miraculous removal of a corpse by demons, from the nave of a church, or in the preservation undamaged of Saint Margaret's Gospel book, adorned with jewels and gold, though it had lain lost at the bottom of a river bed (it now lies, more securely, in the Bodleian library). It is a rude and brutal world, in which the body of the first Norman king was squeezed into too small a coffin, so that it burst asunder, the body of the next king was conveyed in a cart, for burial at Winchester, ' the blood dripping from it all the way ', and the son of his successor was shipwrecked and drowned by drunken sailors in the ill-fated White Ship. But behind the violence and the dark deeds shines the light which is the saving grace of the Middle Ages, the light which, though it makes the dark deeds darker still, yet shows where medieval man found his guidance and the source of his genius and strength. From the dates which the chroniclers are so careful to give it seems as though a Feast of Our Lady is always at hand, or just past, as though the Nativity, the Annunciation, or the Assumption, or one of the major Saints' days was never far away. And though we read how Saint Thomas of Canterbury, in Edward Grim's terrible narrative, ' dyed the surface of the virgin Mother Church ' with ' the colours of the lily and the rose ' (his brain and his blood) we also read how the most powerful of medieval kings was ready to do penance for the deed and we know that the pilgrims followed, through the centuries, and from the four corners of the western world.

Yet, for myself, I am grateful for this book less for its reminders of the thundering medieval drama, with its vivid clashes of kings, archbishops and barons, than I am for its intimate glimpses of ordinary people. These are not so easy to come by, in the early Middle Ages, as in later centuries, and one is the more grateful that Dr. Hassall has contrived to include them. How delightful to read Richard de Bury's protests against the way children (and grown-ups) will maltreat even the finest illuminated books: ' . . . Let no crying child admire the pictures in the capital letters, lest he defile the parchment with his wet hand, for he touches instantly whatever he sees. Laymen, moreover, who look in the same way at a book lying upside down as when it is open in its natural way, are wholly unworthy the intercourse of books. . . . Again, a becoming cleanness of hands would add much to books and scholars. . . .' Or there is John Russell's advice to those whose duty it is to give a baron a bath: ' . . . always be careful that the door is shut '. But perhaps the best of all are the dialogues of Aelfric's pupils, in the eleventh century. Dr. Hassall rightly allows them seven pages; they are pages which give us a splendid picture of country life in the reign of Ethelred.

In the course of reading this book we learn many interesting

details—we may not, for instance, have realised that the stone
of which the Oxford colleges and Windsor castle were built
came from a quarry at Wheatley only recently disused. We learn
about the high spirits of the populations of the growing towns,
of their riots, their miracle plays, their wrestling matches. But
the delight of the stories lies in particular people, in the person
who saw it happen, or in the person who suffered because it
happened. We are captivated not so much by the miracle plays
or the wrestling matches themselves as by the poor Prioress of
Clerkenwell who 'prays [Our Lord the King] that he will to
provide and order a remedy because the people of London lay
waste and destroy her corn and grass by their miracle plays and
wrestling matches so that she has no profit of them.'

The players and the wrestlers having departed the corn lies
flat, and what was grass is now bare dust.

The Prioress saw it happen. And so can we.

                                        E. E. Y. HALES.

CONTENTS

INTRODUCTION

Many important people and many important events are not described in this book, for it has seemed better to include passages which give intimate details at some length rather than to crowd the canvas with too many figures. Sometimes the original source has been given for some well-known tale like that of Canute and the waves, sometimes I have included incidents in themselves trivial, but illustrative of everyday life in town or country. This has meant omissions, for every page spent on one thing means a page less spent on another.

Too many dynasties and even too many kingdoms are covered in this volume, with its span of fifteen centuries, for it to rival in scale the admirable Tudor anthology of Mr. Routh. On p.p. xxii and xxiii parallel chronological tables give the framework into which the post-Conquest passages fit; but it is sincerely hoped that if this book is used in schools as well as for pleasure Messrs. Blackwell will not be blamed if some unfortunate child has to learn this table.

The Sources

Those who wish to read about the chief characters of British History will be able to do so by consulting the abridged *Dictionary of National Biography*. A full account, with valuable references to the sources on which the incidents in each life are based, is to be found in the unabridged edition in the larger libraries. For details about events and the original sources which tell us about them the bibliographies in the *Cambridge Medieval History* are invaluable.

Scottish readers should use the valuable collections of source material compiled by J. Stevenson, A. O. Anderson and W. C. Dickinson, G. Donaldson and I. A. Milne and must pardon the emphasis in this volume on London, Oxfordshire and Norfolk. These areas were richer and more peaceful in the fourteenth century than was the north, so that more documents survive in and about them, from which as a local resident, I have been able to choose.

It was customary for medieval writers to copy pieces from earlier authors; so this work, as a work of shreds and patches, scissors and paste, has something in common with a medieval chronicle—except that it does not start with the Creation or the mythical Brutus who came from Troy to found Britain just as Aeneas came to Italy. Often a later writer incorporated in his compilation pieces which previous writers in their turn had borrowed. Thus a medieval chronicler tends to be most useful and original in the concluding sections of his work, when he is narrating events contemporary with himself or at least repeating what his elders have told him.

Sometimes a chronicler of contemporary events is not an eyewitness but reports what he has heard. Such accounts may be ill-informed hearsay, of value only as an echo of rumours current at the time and giving no real glimpse of the scenes that were transacted, but sometimes second-hand accounts, such as Bede's story of Coifi, have obviously been recorded from the vivid reports of eyewitnesses. Vast as are the medieval sources from which to draw they are not so vast as those for later periods, and it is sad that there is no eyewitness account of the Saxon landings, although we have an account of the first Roman invasion in the words of the Roman general himself.

It is not necessary to believe what one reads because it is written contemporaneously. Indeed, not even an owner of a newspaper would feel sufficiently loyal to his friends or rivals as to suggest that the public should accept the verbal accuracy of the reports printed in other newspapers, even British twentieth-century ones. Medieval writers were often propagandists with axes to grind, their statistical ideas were wild, and they had a lively faith in the reality of demons which few nineteenth-century editors of their works shared. If we are only to believe eye-witnesses we may doubt the Battle of Hastings, but we should be committed to accept as true much which those who claim to respect evidence would dismiss as superstition.

This is not a ' source book '. It does not display specimens of the sources of British History as such, for many important sources are not exemplified though sometimes several long passages are included from the writings of a single authority.

The passages are chosen mainly because they give vivid impressions of past periods, such as one might expect if a newspaper could send a special correspondent into the Day before Yesterday. But, of course, such a correspondent would see with the eyes of our generation and in the light of the events which have occurred between Then and Now. The writers here quoted were only familiar with the intellectual climate and interests of their own generation.

Some of the passages are chosen to illustrate events and activities important in their time, or of outstanding interest to our generation; others are chosen because they are so graphic that they insist upon their own inclusion. No claim is made that they all tell the truth, and none tell the whole truth. For it must be repeated, a contemporary does not necessarily know better than his descendants. In our own day two nations have been seen to revise their ideas of Hitler and Stalin, for contemporaries who must earn their living often write as those who pay them wish.

Many source books exist, and in many ways are being superseded by the monumental series of *English Historical Documents* arranged in periods, with a large volume by a leading expert for each, now published by Eyre and Spottiswoode. For those who wish to study particular localities for their own sake, or draw from local instances to illustrate national history, there are the lengthening series of the local archaeological and record societies. These heroically continue regular publication in many counties, in spite of rising costs and the extinction of the class which supported them as a duty to a county. For those who wish to locate printed examples of particular kinds of documentary sources, such as manor court rolls or taxation returns, the British Records Association has published two pamphlets which analyse by type the record publications of England, and Scotland and Wales. Of less importance to general readers, students and teachers, but perhaps most important of all for the historical research worker, are the ever-increasing number of official publications about the contents of the Public Record Office. Her Majesty's Stationery Office prints a list of these, but their use requires much time with access to a great library.

The raw materials for medieval history are either literary ones, such as the chronicles preserved in the British Museum, the Bodleian Library and other collections which have been built up by benefaction or purchase; or record ones. ' Records ', as contrasted with chronicles, are documents produced in the course of administrative or other business, with no historical purpose in the minds of their makers. The greatest concentration of these is in the Public Record Office, where Domesday Book is preserved not as a treasured acquisition but as a business record filed on behalf of the Exchequer.

The British Museum and the Public Record Office have on display amazing selections of the really important literary and record sources for history. They show the main documents which tell the story of national history. For local history an attempt has been made by the Oxfordshire Record Society to show in facsimile specimens of the chief types of document, of use for the study of the history of one typical small locality, Wheatley.

Some small selections from medieval texts have long been available for scholars, but of these the Select Charters of Bishop Stubbs is too specialized for most people outside a university. Guy Carleton Lee, *Leading Documents of English History together with Illustrative Material in Contemporary Writers and a Bibliography of Sources*, 1900, is printed in English as a concession to those whose Latin is defective, but its exclusive value lies in its great constitutional and legal documents which furnish the framework of our national development.

This book has a less serious but more exciting purpose. It does not profess to display key documents or types of source; it is rather an attempt to enable an imaginative reader to listen to voices from the past. This is an ambitious aim. For there are gaps in our sources, some of them seem to the modern age long-winded, and none are written in modern English or for modern eyes.

TRANSLATIONS

English translations from Old English are as necessary to most modern Britons as were translations from Latin to the subjects of King Alfred. The Scottish vernacular, not to mention Welsh, is hard for a modern Englishman to understand, though to a Scot I suspect it might seem better to omit it than to print it in the less colourful language of the south. In any case *The Bruce* of Barbour, the father of Scottish Literature, though the main Scottish source for its hero's struggle for freedom, was written six-and-forty years after Robert Bruce's death.

Existing translations have been followed where possible and I am most grateful to those who own various copyrights for permission to use them, but I felt free at times to make minor alterations which it would be pedantic to enumerate. Where alterations are considerable I have said ' translation based on' instead of ' translated by '. Those translations where no acknowledgement is made are my own.

Some of the suggestions for further reading may look puzzling. Sometimes I have not indicated books giving the political and biographical background of one of the selected passages, because sufficient information is often readily available in almost any standard history book. But I have often tried to draw attention to books dealing with some theme which the particular passage suggests. Thus for the famous passage on castles built by lawless barons in the anarchy of Stephen's reign there is no reference to Horace Round's *Geoffrey de Mandeville* but there is a reference to an attractive Batsford book on castles. This is done because we can still visit, or at least see in pictures, the castles built in the times of which we read and of which they were themselves witnesses. Many books important for ' further reading ' are very well worth examining but not for *reading* right through: such are the lavishly illustrated reports of the Historical Monuments Commission, for, if it may be said without offence, the text of these is not readable though the pictures give a display of the Roman and medieval buildings in London which is a revelation alike to those who can walk the streets and those who cannot visit London in person. In country districts the monuments are further apart, but the intelligent study of parish churches evokes exciting lines of thought if inspired and instructed by such works of Mrs. M. D. Anderson and her *Looking for History in English Parish Churches*. Such a book as hers proves that historical works need not be divided into those which are too inaccurate and those which are too dull to recommend to an intelligent reader.

MEDIEVAL BIBLIOGRAPHY

Medieval Chronicles have been studied by T. D. Hardy, *Descriptive Catalogue of Materials relating to the History of Great Britain and Ireland*, Rolls Series, 1862, and the Public Records by V. H. Galbraith, *An Introduction to the Use of the Public Records* 1934. The many works of editors and commentators on early English poets and other writers can be found from the *Cambridge Bibliography of English Literature*, edited by F. W. Bateson, 1940. For particular place-names, often valuable clues to the story of the period of Saxon or Viking settlement, the growing number of county volumes of the Place-Name Society are supplementing F. Ekwall, *The Concise Oxford Dictionary of English Place-Names*, 3rd ed. 1947.

It is a pity that recent medieval studies are inevitably absent from C. Gross, *The Sources of Literature of English History from the Earliest times to about* 1485, 2nd ed. 1915, but since 1937 we have *Writings on British History compiled for the Royal Historical Society*, by A. T. Milne. Many texts of history and literature are edited in the Rolls Series and in the volumes of the Early English Text and Scottish Text Societies.

The monastic history of any area can be worked out from Dugdale's *Monasticon Anglicanum* if no good County History has yet appeared. The Victoria County History gives translations of the section of Domesday Book covering each county published, and for all counties facsimiles were published by the Ordnance Survey Office in the last century.

In general, however, it is only practicable for very few individuals, outside the ranks of professional historians, to indulge in the luxury of medieval historical research, for a knowledge of Latin and access to large libraries are essential. For those who are none the less determined to find out more about the technique of such research there are some very practical articles on such subjects as early handwriting and the use of records in a journal modestly called the *Amateur Historian*.

ACKNOWLEDGEMENTS

Thanks are due to all the translators, editors and publishers listed below. Their names are also repeated in the notes of sources for each extract and in the index. The most indefatigable translator, to whom especial mention is due, is the Reverend J. A. Giles, and this anthology shows what a multitude of valuable translations have been printed by Bohn's Antiquarian Library and David Nutt. All these have very generously allowed reprints to be made. It is a pity that so many of their books are only obtainable occasionally second-hand and that greater numbers are not available in the smaller public libraries.

It would be ungracious to restrict thanks to scholars and publishers protected by copyright, without mentioning the work of early writers and translators. It is good to remember the people they commemorate, and Mr. Routh in Volume II recalled the memory of those who collected and preserved the manuscripts in which the tale is told. Let us also remember the copyists and printers who had made so many early historical works accessible that it was possible before the death of Queen Elizabeth I and the foundation of the Bodleian Library for a private person to possess printed copies of Caesar, Tacitus, Gildas, Bede, Asser, Henry of Huntingdon, William of Malmesbury, Florence of Worcester, William of Newburgh, FitzStephen, Hovenden, Matthew Paris, 'Matthew of Westminster', Froissart, Thomas Walsingham, Philip de Comines, Polydore Vergil, Sir Thomas More and Fabian. All these writers formed part of the historical library used as a working tool and a spiritual inspiration by Chief Justice Coke, champion of the common law against Stuart encroachment, together with volumes of Statutes and Year books and manuscripts like Simeon of Durham and the 'Brut'. After a list of two hundred law books, Sir Edward Coke wrote these words in his library catalogue 'And forasmuch as approved histories are necessary for a iurisconsult, for hee that hath redd them seemed to have lived in those former ages, Histories shall followe in the nexte place.' Presentations from authors and printers made their number even greater than that of his law books, and among them is 'bilious' John Bale's survey of British medieval literature.

As a protestant ex-monk, Bale called Wycliffe the ' Morning Star ', and honoured Henry VIII next after God. He despised the old wives' tales in Felix of Croyland and Eadmer, hates Dunstan's passion for celibacy and More's repute as a popish martyr, and commended John Trevisa's exposure of monastic faults. Bale disliked historical whitewash and agreed with Gildas and *Proverbs* that those who commend the wicked and report the righteous are accursed. But the discovery of truth across the centuries can be as exciting as bitter controversy or clever paradox, and all can unite with Bale in his appreciation of Richard of Holy Trinity, Aldgate, faithfully describing the sights of town, and country, and crusade; and Froissart writing down what he saw and heard as the familiar of Edward III and Philippa of Hainault without approving the one-sidedness which let him repeat Trivet's strictures on the pomposity of the Archbishop Peckham, while suppressing his verdict on his underlying kindliness of heart.

Lastly I must thank three private owners of manuscripts; Lord Macclesfield, Major the Hon. S. Stonor, and especially Lord Leicester, the heir of Sir Edward Coke's library, who has allowed me to make many excerpts from his muniments and library at Holkham. That library contained until recently the Holkham Bible Picture Book, now displayed in the British Museum, a series of coloured drawings made about 1330 by an English layman for a Preaching Friar. These show many detailed scenes of medieval life, often more instructive than those which are better known. A facsimile edition by the Dropmore Press is available in the larger libraries, but black-and-white photographs of individual pages are available from the Courtauld Institute. Averil Hassall's reproductions from this on the endpapers portray medieval people even better than the original by eliminating misleading detail: thus in depicting a dyer's apprentice a young servant (from another page) is substituted for the haloed figure of the infant Christ which is over idealized.

Apologies are due to many modern scholars whose editions have not been quoted, and even more to the memory of medieval writers of outstanding merit like Hemingburgh, Rishanger, and Trivet. The omission of ' John de Mandeville ' is deliberate.

He claims to have seen personally things which he copied out of earlier writers, and as the most popular medieval vernacular writer he has his honour. Attractive passages from other writers are also excluded if their authenticity is doubtful.

The compiler and the publisher wish to thank the following for permission to reproduce copyright material; full details of which are given elsewhere:

G. Bell and Sons, Ltd., for extracts from *Bohn's Antiquarian Library*.

California University Press for an extract from *Philobiblon*, translated by A. Taylor.

Cambridge University Press for extracts from *Social Life in Britain from the Conquest to the Reformation*, by G. G. Coulton; and excerpts from *Eddi's Life of St. Wilfrid*, by B. Colgrave, and *Educational Charters and Documents*, 598 to 1909, by A. F. Leach.

Jonathan Cape, Ltd., for a passage from *The Autobiography of Giraldus Cambrensis*, edited by H. E. Butler.

Chatto and Windus, Ltd., for an extract from *John Russell's Book of Nurture* (The Babees Book), edited by E. Rickert.

The Clarendon Press for extracts from Plummer's edition of *Bede*, and from *A Sourcebook of Welsh History*.

Columbia University Press for a passage from Rickert's translation of Geoffrey le Baker's *Chaucer's World*.

The Hon. Cymmrodorion Society for extracts from *The Ruin of Britain*, and *De Nugis Curialium*.

Eyre and Spottiswoode, Ltd., for extracts from *English Historical Documents* series.

The Historical Association for extracts from their leaflets.

Lincoln Record Society for an extract from one of their volumes.

Longmans Green and Co., Ltd., for an extract from *England before the Norman Conquest*, by R. W. Chambers.

Methuen and Co., Ltd., for a passage from *Archaeology of Roman Britain*, by R. G. Collingwood.

T. Nelson and Sons, Ltd., for extracts from *The Deeds of Stephen* by K. Potter; *The Course of the Exchequer*, edited and trans. by C. Johnson; and *A Source Book of Scottish History*, by Donaldson and Milne.

Oxfordshire Record Society for passages from their publications.

Oxford University Press, and Captain M. Butler-Bowdon, for an extract from the *Book of Margery Kempe*.

Public Record Office and Her Majesty's Stationery Office for an extract from the Calendar of Patent Rolls.

B. Quaritch and Co., Ltd., for an extract from *The Manor Farm and the Boke of Husbandry*, by E. H. Cripps Day.

The Royal Historical Society for extracts from the publications of the Camden Society.

The Selden Society for extracts from their publications.

The Royal Society of Literature for extracts from *The Chronicle of Adam of Usk*, by E. Thompson, and *Chronicon*, edited Thompson.

The Institute of Historical Research for an extract from the *Victoria County History of Warwickshire*.

The Board of Celtic Studies, University of Wales, Cardiff, for an extract from their *History of Law*, No. XI, 1952.

English Kings

William The Conqueror
25.12.1066—9.9.1087
William Rufus
26.9.1087—2.8.1100
Henry Beauclerc
5.8.1100—1.12.1135
Stephen
26.12.1135—25.10.1154
Henry ii
19.12.1154—6.7.1189
Richard The Lion Heart
3.9.1189—6.4.1199
John Lackland
27.5.1199—19.10.1216
Henry iii
28.10.1216—16.11.1272
Edward i, Longshanks
20.11.1272—7.7.1307
Edward of Carnarvon
8.7.1307—20.1.1327
Edward iii
25.1.1327—21.6.1377
Richard of Bordeaux
22.6.1377—29.9.1399
Henry iv, Bolingbroke
30.9.1399—20.3.1413
Henry v, of Monmouth
21.3.1413—31.8.1422
Henry vi
1.9.1422—11.4.71
Edward iv
4.3.1461—9.4.83
Edward v
9.4.1483—25.6.1483
Richard iii, Crouchback
26.6.1483—22.8.1485

Archbishops and Bishops

Stigand 1043–1070
Odo of Bayeux 1049–97
Lanfranc of Bec 1070–89
Anselm of Bec 1093–1109
Ranulf Flambard 1099–1128
Nigel of Ely 1133–1169
Theobald 1139–61
Henry Murdac 1147–53
Thomas Becket 1162–70
Geoffrey Ridel 1174–89
Hubert Walter 1189–1205
William Longchamp 1189–97
Peter des Roches 1205–38
Stephen Langton 1207–1228
Edmund Rich 1234–40
Robert Grosseteste 1235–53
Boniface of Savoy 1245–70
John Pecham 1279–92
Robert Winchelsey 1294–1313
Walter Reynolds 1308–27
Richard de Bury 1335–45
Simon Islip 1349–66
William of Wykeham 1367–1404
William Courtenay 1370–1396
Thomas Arundel 1374–1414
Richard le Scrope 1386–1405
Henry Chichele 1408–43
John Stafford 1425–52
William Alnwick 1426–49
Robert Neville 1427–57
Thomas Bourchier 1435–86
William of Waynflete 1447–86
Richard Beauchamp 1449–81
Thomas Kemp 1450–89
George Neville 1427–57
Thomas Rotherham 1468–1500

Significant dates

	Scotland
33 Cluniac foundations 1066–1154	Malcolm iii
The North devastated 1069–70	1058–93
Domesday Book 1086	Donald Bane
Robert Duke of Normandy 1087–1134	1093–7
Crypt of Canterbury built 1096–1107	Duncan ii
68 Cistercian foundations 1100–1216	1094
179 Augustinian *ditto* 1100–1216	Edgar
Matilda Empress of Henry 1114–67	1097–1107
Eleanor wife of Henry ii 1152–1204	Alexander i
Government reforms 1158–89	1107–24
R. Glanville Justiciar 1180–9	David i
Third Crusade 1189–92	1124–53
Richard in prison 1292–4	Malcolm iv
Pope Innocent iii 1198–1216	1153–65
De Burgh Justiciar 1215–43	William i
Royal Minority 1216–32	1165–1214
300 Friaries founded 1216–1350	Alexander ii
Westminster Abbey rebuilt 1245–69	1249–86
Simon de Montfort active 1248–67	Margaret
Edwardian Legislation 1275–90	1286–90
Welsh Castles built 1276–83	John Balliol
Eleanor Crosses built 1291–4	1292–6
Roger Mortimer rules 1326–30	Robert i
Philippa of Hainault Queen 1328–71	1306–29
English win in France 1337–60	David ii
John of Gaunt 1340–90	1329–71
The Black Prince 1343–76	Robert ii
The Black Death 1348–9	1371–90
' Piers Plowman ' written 1362–92	Robert iii
Sir Henry Percy, Hotspur 1364–1403	1390–1406
John Wicliffe active 1369–84	James i
' Canterbury Tales ' written 1387–1400	1406–37
French win in France 1389–75	James ii
English win in France 1415–29	1437–60
French win in France 1430–53	James iii
All Souls College built 1438–41	1460–88
Eton College built 1441–59	
Margaret of Anjou Queen 1445–82	
King's College Chapel built 1446–1515	
The ' Kingmaker ' Earl of Warwick 1449–71	
Wars of the Roses 1455–85	
Caxton at Westminster 1477–91	

THE ROMANS ARRIVE, 55 B.C.

Julius Caesar attacked Britain because the tribesmen helped their conquered kinsmen across the Channel to resist subjection.

Source: Caesar, *Commentaries on the Gallic War*, book 4, an account by the best informed man present. He writes in the third person.

Further Reading: C. and J. Hawkes, *Prehistoric Britain*, Pelican Books, 1949. Grahame Clark, *Prehistoric England*, Batsford, 1940. V. Gordon Childe, *Prehistoric Scotland*, Historical Association Pamphlets, no. 115, 1940. Ian Richmond, *Roman Britain*, Britain in Pictures Series, 1947. *Transactions* of local archaeological societies.

The build of the warships apparently sprung a surprise on the natives and, as their greater manoeuvrability was obvious, Caesar ordered them to draw away from the transports. He had them rowed up to a station on the enemy's exposed flank from which our barrage of slings, artillery and arrows might force their withdrawal. Our men reaped considerable benefit from these tactics. The build of the ships, the dash of the oars and the novel type of barrage demoralized the natives. They halted and actually beat a slight retreat. Our men had come to a standstill mainly because of the depth of water; but the standard-bearer of the Tenth legion prayed to the gods for a blessing on the legion. 'You must jump for it, fellows,' he shouted, 'unless you mean to let them get the Eagle. I for one shall do my duty to my country and my captain.' He roared this out and plunged overboard to carry his Eagle towards the other side. At this, our men encouraged one another not to let a thing like that happen and leapt overboard to a man. Those on the ships within sight followed suit in a general advance.

Fighting was tough on both sides. My men could not keep in line, get a firm foothold or keep to their own standards. Each man joined the nearest unit irrespective of his ship and chaos reigned. The enemy knew the lie of the shoals and when they saw from the beach isolated groups disembarking they made a mounted charge and attacked them in their difficulties. These they outnumbered and surrounded, while their comrades raked the main party with an enfilade. Caesar assessed the situation and had both the boats of the warships and the sloops packed

with soldiers to help wherever he saw need. Our men reached the
land and were there reinforced by all those behind.

Then came the assault which routed the enemy, but we could
not follow up satisfactorily as the cavalry had failed to hold its
course and make the island. The enemy lost the day. As soon as
they could stop bolting they sent a peace delegation to Caesar.
Commius, the Atrebatian, came along with it. It was he whom
Caesar had sent to Britain to bring that general's instructions;
but they had seized him as soon as he stepped ashore and clapped
him in irons. The outcome of our victory was his release. In
sueing for peace they attributed this outrage to the lower classes
and asked him to let it pass as an act of their folly. Caesar
protested at their unprovoked aggression after they had taken it
upon themselves to send a delegation over to the continent to
make peace with him. Yet he forgave their folly and demanded
hostages. Some they delivered on the spot but promised to
send for the others from up-country in a few days. Meanwhile
they demobilized the tribesmen, and the chiefs came in from all
quarters to surrender themselves and their countries to Caesar.
Thus peace was made within four days of the landing in Britain.

The seventeen ships with the cavalry left the upper harbour
with a gentle breeze. They were nearing Britain and had been
sighted from the camp when a squall got up. It was impossible
to keep on course and some were swept back to their starting
point while others scudded westwards to the lower part of the
island and were in jeopardy. These anchored, but began shipping
water and had to make for the continent through the stormy
night.

Now it was a full moon and we did not realize that this
generally means high tides there; so the tide began to swamp
the invasion craft which Caesar had beached while the storm
battered the transports in the roads and there was nothing we
could do about it. There were many wrecks and the other ships
were put out of commission by the loss of cables, anchors, etc.
Inevitably the army was affected, for no other vessels were available for their withdrawal, there was no tackle for refitting and
there was no commissariat for the winter as it was assumed they
would winter in Gaul.

The British princes had met to fulfil Caesar's demands but they saw how the land lay and held a congress. They knew the Romans were without cavalry, ships or food and as the camp was small they supposed that the expedition was insignificant—for Caesar had brought over the combat troops without the supply train. Their best plan seemed revolt, a denial of food, etc. to us, and a prolongation of the campaign into the winter. If our army should be beaten and return no more, they believed that no one would ever again come to Britain with hostile intent. Their new plot was to filter out of the camp and to begin an unobtrusive mobilization.

Caesar did not yet know their intentions; but the naval disaster and the failure of hostages to arrive led him to anticipate the sequel and he began to prepare for the worst. He had daily requisitions of corn brought in from the farms, took the timber and brass of the worst wrecks to refit the other ships, and ordered essential replacements from the continent. Twelve ships were lost, but the supreme efforts of the soldiers thus made the others able to serve.

Meanwhile the Seventh legion was out on a routine foraging mission without any thought of action as there were still people on the farms and traffic in and out of the camp. Suddenly the guards at the gate reported to Caesar an exceptional quantity of dust where the legion had gone. Caesar rightly sensed a new native stratagem. He told the two duty cohorts to follow him and the other two to relieve them, and the rest to arm and follow at once. After a short march he saw his troops pressed by the enemy almost to breaking point with the legion undeployed and subject to cross-fire. For the corn had been reaped in every district except one and the enemy had guessed they would go there and had prepared an ambush by night in the woods. Our men were scattered, busy reaping with arms piled, when the attack began. They killed some, put the others into confusion and surrounded them with both cavalry and chariots.

A chariot fight is like this: first they scour the field shooting and this often breaks the line just with the fear of the horses and the din of wheels. When they have infiltrated among the cavalry units they jump down and fight as infantry. Meanwhile the drivers withdraw a bit to wait where they can quickly escape to base if compelled by weight of numbers. Thus they show the dash of cavalry and the steadiness of infantry in action. Daily drill teaches them the habit of checking their steeds even in full career down a steep slope, of lightning turns and of running along the pole, standing on the yoke and getting back quickly into the chariot.

Caesar brought help in the nick of time to our men for they were dismayed by such novel tactics. . . .

THE BRITONS, 54 B.C.

Source: Caesar, *Commentaries on the Gallic War*, book 5.

Further Reading: R. G. Collingwood and J. N. L. Myres, *Roman Britain* (Oxford History of England), 1949.

The inhabitants of the hinterland claim to be natives of the island but the Belgae colonized the coastal fringe attracted over by war and loot. These mostly retain the names of their original states although they stayed in Britain after the war and settled as farmers. The population is large with many buildings which follow practically the Gallic style. Cattle are numerous and they use brass or iron rings of fixed weights for currency. Tin occurs in the midlands, and a little iron near the coast. They import bronze. Varieties of timber are as in Gaul, except beech and fir. They have a taboo against eating hare, cock or goose, but rear them for sport. It is more temperate than Gaul and winter milder. . . . The inhabitants of Kent are the most civilized as it is maritime and their customs are much like the Gallic. Inland, corn is little grown, but they live on milk and meat and wear skins. Most Britons are dyed with blue woad and this makes them look fiercer as warriors. They have long hair and shave everywhere except their heads and moustaches. . . .

CAESAR'S SECOND INVASION, 54 B.C.

The Thames formed a natural barrier. Later, London Bridge was built at the point nearest the sea where a bridge could be constructed. On it were to converge the straight roads which marked the lines of advance of Caesar's successors when the conquest of Britain was seriously undertaken in A.D. 43.

Source: Caesar, *Commentaries on the Gallic War*, book 5.

Further Reading: Ordnance Survey, *Roman Britain*, latest edition. Illustrated Regional Guides to Ancient Monuments, H.M. Office of Works, 1935–9. *Antiquity*, edited quarterly. I. A. Richmond, *Roman Britain* (Pelican), 1963.

. . . Caesar knew their intentions and advanced into the Cassivelaunus country to the river Thames. It has only one ford, a difficult one. On arriving he saw the enemy posted in strength on the opposite bank. Sharp stakes were fixed in front to fortify it and there were others under water hidden by the stream, as he learnt from prisoner-of-war and escaper reports. Caesar sent the cavalry forward and ordered the foot to follow directly behind; but the advance was so rapid and enthusiastic, although the water was up to the men's necks, that the enemy could not hold the legions, and their cavalry quitted the banks and turned tail.

As has been said, Cassivelaunus pinned no hope on battle and had released most of his forces except for some 4,000 charioteers. His method was to observe our route, and retire a little from the line of march using impenetrable hides and woods. Along our proposed route he used to force the livestock and peasantry from the fields into the woods; and when our cavalry ranged the fields to plunder and ravage better, he would dispatch charioteers by tracks and paths out of the woods with which he was familiar to engage our horse giving them real cause for alarm. This hazard limited their range and resulted in Caesar prohibiting distant patrols from the column and only allowing punitive expeditions within the area practicable for the infantry.

Meanwhile the Trinobantes approached Caesar with promises of submission and obedience. They were almost the strongest state in those parts and from it had come the youthful Mandubratius to Caesar in Gaul to throw himself on his protection.

His father Imanuentius had got power in that state but had been killed by Cassivelaunus and he himself had fled for his life. They wanted Caesar to shield Mandubratius from Cassivelaunus and to send someone to take charge of their state and rule it. Caesar required forty hostages and supplies for the troops, and sent them Mandubratius. They obeyed with alacrity and sent hostages in full and the supplies.

He put the Trinobantes under his protection and ordered them to be spared the violence of his soldiery; and the Cenimagni, Segenitaci, Ancalites, Bibroci and the Cassi opened negotiations and surrendered. He learnt from them that the town of Cassivelaunus [near St. Albans] was in the vicinity behind a shield of woods and marshes and that here there was a big concentration of men and beasts. Now the Britons call it a town when they have fortified an impenetrable wood with a rampart and a moat where they generally rally to avoid a hostile incursion. He came there with the legions and found a place admirably fortified by the adaptation of topographical advantages but decided to assault it from two sides. The enemy stood for a short while but could not hold our attack and hurried out of the other side of the town. A great stock of cattle was found there and many of the enemy were killed or captured in the pursuit.

Meanwhile Cassivelaunus sent emissaries to Kent, which we mentioned before as next the sea, where there were four kings, Cingetorix, Carnilius, Taximagulus and Segonax. He told them to mass, to attack our naval camp and storm it. They came to the camp but our men made a sortie inflicting many fatal casualties and even capturing the noble general Cingetorix and withdrew without loss. Cassivelaunus heard about this engagement. He had sustained heavy losses, his country had been ravaged and he had been badly shaken by the defection of the tribes; so he sent Caesar delegates by Commius the Atrebatian to discuss surrender. Caesar wanted to winter on the continent because of sudden revolts in Gaul and the summer was almost over. He saw that the affair might well be protracted so he demanded hostages and fixed what annual tribute should be paid to Rome. He absolutely forbade Cassivelaunus to take reprisals on Mandubratius or the Trinobantes.

BOUDICCA REVOLTS, A.D. 61

Claudius began the serious conquest of Britain in A.D. 43 and Nero was too occupied elsewhere to attend to British affairs. The Romans conquered the lowland area and reached the Severn, the Dee and the Humber. Inefficiency led to local corruption, financiers like the philosopher Seneca called in the money which they had lent to the Roman traders who followed the legions to sell the luxuries of Romanized life, and gross injustice led to a revolt. Boudicca [Boadicea] burnt London and massacred its inhabitants—everywhere in the city a layer of ash remains to testify to the work of her desperate native followers, and cartloads of bones in Spitalfields are accompanied by skulls which resemble those of Italians of the period.

Source: Tacitus, *Annals*, book xiv. Tacitus was son-in-law of Agricola, who had fought against the rebels. Tacitus makes acute comments on recent politics.

Further Reading: A. R. Burn, *Agricola and Roman Britain*, 1953.

Prasutagus, King of the Iceni, was remarkably rich and he made the Emperor co-heir with his two daughters in .the hope that this would preserve his home and kingdom from wrong. The opposite happened, for officers plundered his kingdom and their minions plundered his home as if it were a prize. They scourged his queen, Boudicca, and dishonoured her daughters. As if they had been given the whole district they disinherited the Icenian chiefs and treated the royal family as slaves. This disgrace and fear of worse with degradation to provincial status drove them to arms, and the Trinobantes were stirred to revolt. Any others whose spirits were unbroken by slavery made a secret conspiracy to recover liberty; for they bitterly hated the retired soldiers, who had come to the new colony at Colchester and driven them out of their homes and lands, calling them captives and slaves, with the active support of the soldiers who sympathized with their circumstances and enjoyed the prospect of plunder. The temple of Claudius seemed to them a citadel of unending servitude, and under the cloak of religion its priests were squandering the fortunes of all. It seemed to them easy to uproot a colony which was quite unfortified—for our government had hardly troubled about defence, being more interested in comfort than practical needs.

For no apparent reason the statue of Victory at Colchester

fell backwards as if in defeat. Women went mad and screamed
that the End was at hand. Strange groans were heard in the
Council and cries in the theatre. There was an inverted mirage
of the colony in the Thames estuary. The tide flowed red like
blood and things like human corpses were left by the tide. Such
portents encouraged the Britons and demoralized the veterans.
Suetonius was far away so they begged help from Catus Decianus,
the procurator. He sent only 200 half-armed men and there was
a handful of men in the town. They simply relied on the protection of the temple; they were hindered by those who knew
about the underground movement and upset any plans; they did
not fortify themselves with any rampart or moat, nor did they
withdraw the elderly and the females so that the men of fighting
age could put up a defence by themselves. The barbarian hordes
surrounded them, caught as ill prepared as if they were in full
enjoyment of peace. The rest of the town was taken at once and
set ablaze. The soldiers were crowded into the temple and it
was stormed after a siege of two days. The triumphant Britons
met Petilius Cerialis, in command of the Ninth legion, as he was
hurrying to the rescue, overwhelmed him and annihilated the
infantry. Cerialis escaped to his defences with the cavalry. The
procurator Catus embarked in terror for Gaul at this disastrous
outburst of the anger of a province which his own rapacity had
reduced to violence.

Suetonius made a bold dash for London through enemy
country. It was not entitled a colony but the number of traders
and stores there made it important. There he hesitated whether
he should not make a stand, but he saw how few soldiers were
available and had ample proofs of the check received by Petilius'
daring, so he decided that he must sacrifice one town to win the
war. He did not listen to miserable prayers for help but gave the
signal to march, taking all who could accompany him. Those
who were kept back by sex, age or the attractions of the place all
perished. It was the same sad story at Verulamium [St. Albans],
for the barbarians did not wait to reduce the various forts and
garrisons on the way, but in their lust for spoil and dislike of
trouble they preferred what was a richer prize for themselves and
less defensible by us. It is said that seventy thousand citizens

and collaborators were killed in the places mentioned. They did not take prisoners or sell them at all, but it was the sword, the gibbet, the cross or the flames as if they knew they would have to pay retribution but were taking their revenge meanwhile and could brook no delay.

ROMANIZATION OF BRITAIN

The influence of Mediterranean life on Britain was increased by the occupation of the country by Rome and the building of roads. People began to live in the Roman way more in the lowlands than in the wilder highlands. Along the roads came not only the legions but Christian missionaries. The Roman army had returned in A.D. 43, nearly a century after Caesar's expeditions, and the revolt of Boudicca was in vain.

Source: Tacitus, *Agricola*. The life of a Roman governor, with an account of the people and geography of Britain, its recent history, and Agricola's campaigns, written by his own son-in-law. If Tacitus had not written a work which happens to have survived in two fifteenth-century manuscripts, Agricola would hardly be remembered except as a name inscribed on a leaden pipe of A.D. 79 found at Chester. Agricola penetrated to central Scotland where some of his forts have been excavated. He became governor in A.D. 78.

Further Reading: F. Haverfield, *The Roman Occupation of Britain*. Revised ed. G. Macdonald, 1924. Jessie Mothersole, *In Roman Scotland*, 1927. Sir George Macdonald, *The Roman Wall in Scotland*, 1934.

Scattered and unlettered as the people were, they were prone to war. So that they should become used to peace and quiet, he [Agricola] encouraged them in private and helped them in public to build temples, market-places and houses, by praising the willing and chiding the backward. Thus competition for honour achieved the work of compulsion. Furthermore he instructed the sons of chiefs in the liberal arts and gave preference to the natural talents of the Britons over the industry of the Gauls, so that people who had only recently despised the Latin tongue began to covet a knowledge of rhetoric. Then even our mode of dress was held in respect and *togas* were often to be seen. Gradually they were seduced by the demoralizing influences of luxury—colonnades, baths and elegant parties. This was called civilization by the naive, while it was really an aspect of imperialist domination.

ROMAN INSCRIPTIONS

Over two thousand inscriptions record the words which were carved to perpetuate the thoughts of those who lived in Roman Britain. Formal inscriptions on tombs and altars are supplemented by intimate remarks scribbled on potsherds by literate workmen.

(1) *Source*: A. R. Burn, *The Romans in Britain*: *an Anthology of Inscriptions with translations and a running commentary*, Blackwell 1932. pp. 64-5, 76, 82, 88, 95, 120, 143, 145, 163 and 211.

1. A London tavern's address scratched on a jug.
    London; next door to the temple of Isis.

2. A potter.
    Clementinus made this box-tile.

3. Stamps for four proprietary eye tonics.
    Gaius Valerius Amandus' Vinegar-lotion for running eyes.
    Gaius Valerius Amandus' Drops for dim sight.
    Gaius Valerius Valentinus' Poppy-ointment after an attack of inflammation of the eyes.
    A mixture for clearing the sight.

4. A veteran.
    Julius Valens, Veteran of Legion II Augusta, lived 100 years. Julia Secundina his wife and Julius Martinus his son had this made.

5. A wife of Bath.
    To the Gods of the Underworld. Gaius Calpurnius Receptus, Priest of the Goddess Sul [of Bath], lived for seventy-five years. Calpurnia Trifosa, his freedwoman and wife, set up this stone.
    [At the temple of Sul there were perpetual fires fed by coal.]

6. Foreign cults on Hadrian's wall, built A.D. 122-7.
    Aurelius Juvenalis [dedicates this] to the Mother-Goddesses of his own land over the sea.
    To the holy god Silvanus, the Huntsmen of Banna [dedicate this].

7. Wall of Antoninus Pius, built A.D. 140-2.
    For the Emperor Caesar Titus Aelius Hadrianus Antoninus Pius, Father of his Country, Legion II Augusta built [this wall] for a space of four miles and six hundred and fifty-two paces.

8. A slaves' union.

[The grave] of Hardalio. The Club of his fellow-slaves set this up to their well-deserving comrade.

9. A Caermarthenshire King of ' King Arthur's ' period.

In memory of Voteporix the Protector.

(2) *Source*: R. G. Collingwood, *The Archaeology of Roman Britain* Methuen 1930, pp. 174–6, where some of the above are quoted with facsimiles of no. 1 above and no. 1 below.

1. Curse, on a metal tablet from the Temple at Lydney.

To the God Nodens. Silvianus has lost a ring, and dedicated half [its value] to Nodens. Among those who are called Senicianus, permit no health until he bring it to the temple of Nodens.

2. Remarks of workers recorded on tiles.

Primus has made ten tiles.

Enough!

Austalis has been going off on his own every day this fortnight.

3. Remark underneath an illegible scrawl on a wall.

For shame!

THE LAST ROMAN, Fifth Century

Source: Gildas, *The Ruin of Britain*, translated by Hugh Williams, in Cymmrodorion Record Series no. 3, 1899. Gildas is a turgid and almost unintelligible writer, concerned with history and contemporary events only so far as they show how God punishes the sins of the Britons. He is not concerned with virtue or success and has nothing to say about the heavily armoured horsemen of the later Roman Empire rallying under King Arthur to repel the heathen. Apart from the growing body of archaeological evidence and the early entries in the Anglo-Saxon Chronicle, we have a few fascinating Saxon poems. Of these Professor R. K. Gordon has printed an anthology in translation in *Everyman's Library*, 1954. Perhaps the oldest English poem is ' Widsith ', composed in the seventh century, which tells of the many heroic peoples visited by the minstrel in a period when peoples were on the move as we learn from place-names and the patterns of the ornaments and weapons found by archaeologists.

Further Reading: E. T. Leeds, *The Archaeology of the Anglo-Saxon Settlement*, 1913.

They [the invaders] first landed on the eastern side of the island, by the invitation of the unlucky king, and there fixed their sharp talons, apparently to fight in favour of the island, but alas! more truly against it. Their motherland, finding her first brood thus successful, sends forth a larger company of her wolfish offspring, which sailing over, join themselves to their bastard-born comrades. From that time the germ of iniquity and the root of contention planted their poison amongst us, as we deserved, and shot forth into leaves and branches. The barbarians being thus introduced as soldiers into the island, to encounter as they falsely said, any dangers in defence of their hospitable entertainers, obtain an allowance of provisions, which, for some time being plentifully bestowed, stopped their doggish mouths. Yet they complain that their monthly supplies are not furnished in sufficient abundance, and they industriously aggravate each occasion of quarrel, saying that unless more liberality is shown them, they will break the treaty and plunder the whole island. In a short time, they follow up their threats with deeds.

For the fire of vengeance, justly kindled by former crimes, spread from sea to sea, fed by the hands of our foes in the east, and did not cease, until, destroying the neighbouring towns and lands, it reached the other side of the island, and dipped its red and savage tongue in the western ocean. . . . So that all the columns were levelled with the ground by the frequent strokes of the battering-ram, all the husbandmen routed, together with their bishops, priests, and people, whilst the sword gleamed, and the flames crackled around them on every side. Lamentable to behold, in the midst of the streets lay the tops of lofty towers, tumbled to the ground, stones of high walls, holy altars, fragments of human bodies, covered with livid clots of coagulated blood, looking as if they had been squeezed together in a press; and with no chance of being buried, save in the ruins of the houses, or in the ravening bellies of wild beasts and birds. . . . Some, therefore, of the miserable remnant, being taken in the mountains, were murdered in great numbers; others, constrained by famine, came and yielded themselves to be slaves for ever to their foes, running the risk of being instantly slain, which truly was the greatest favour that could be offered them: some others passed beyond the seas with loud lamentations instead of the voice of exhortation. . . .

That they should not be utterly destroyed, they take up arms and challenge their victors to battle under Ambrosius Aurelianus. He was a man of unassuming character, who, alone of the Roman race, chanced to survive in shock of such a storm (as his parents, people undoubtedly clad in the purple, had been killed in it), whose offspring in our days have greatly degenerated from their ancestral nobleness. To these men, by the Lord's favour, there came victory.

From that time, the citizens were sometimes victorious, sometimes the enemy. . . . This continued up to the year of the siege of Badon Hill, and of almost the last great slaughter inflicted upon the rascally crew. And this commences, a fact I know, as the forty-fourth year, with one month now elapsed; it is also the year of my birth. But not even at the present day are the cities of our country inhabited as formerly; deserted and dismantled, they lie neglected until now, because, although wars with foreigners have ceased, domestic wars continue.

DESTRUCTION OF BRITAIN, Sixth Century

Saint Gildas the Wise was born in the year of the battle of Mount Badon (496) and yielding to the pressure of friends he wrote a gloomy and rhetorical account of the wickedness of the British kings and the triumphs of the Saxons.

Gildas regarded the Saxon victory as God's punishment for Celtic depravity, and the victors took his words as a justification for Teutonic excesses.

Source: *The Works of Gildas*, translated by J. A. Giles in *Six Old English Chronicles*, Bohn's Antiquarian Library, 1885, p. 309.

Further Reading: G. H. Wheeler, ' Gildas de Excidio Britanniae, Chapter 26 ', *English Historical Review*, lvi, 1941. Edition with translation by Hugh Williams, in Cymmrodorion Record Series, no. 3 (London, 1899):

A vague rumour suddenly as if on wings reaches the ears of all, that their inveterate foes were rapidly approaching to destroy the whole country, and to take possession of it, as of old, from one end to the other. But yet they derived no advantage from this intelligence. . . . A pestilential disease mortally affected the foolish people, which, without the sword, cut off so large a

number of persons, that the living were not able to bury them.
. . . A council was called to settle what was best and most
expedient to be done, in order to repel such frequent and fatal
irruptions and plunderings of the above-named nations.

Then all the councillors, together with that proud tyrant
Gurthrigern (Vortigern), the British king, were so blinded, that,
as a protection to their country, they sealed its doom by inviting
in among them (like wolves into the sheep-fold), the fierce and
impious Saxons, a race hateful both to God and men, to repel
the invasions of the northern nations. Nothing was ever so
pernicious to our country, nothing was ever so unlucky. What
palpable darkness must have enveloped their minds—darkness
desperate and cruel! Those very people whom, when absent,
they dreaded more than death itself, were invited to reside, as
one may say, under the selfsame roof.

THE CONVERSION OF NORTHUMBRIA, 627

The story of King Edwin's council has the ring of an eyewitness
account. It is preserved in Bede's world famous *Ecclesiastical History
of the English Nation*. Bede's literary career began about 700. The
preface of his history discusses the various sources he used for different
parts of his work, and as he was a monk of Jarrow and was encouraged by his learned abbot it is natural to read that his Northumbrian
church history from the time of the conversion was not based on one
source but on the faithful testimony of many witnesses who knew or
remembered. Bede was the first historian to date events by the year
of Our Lord. King Alfred was the first of many translators.

Source: Translated from *Venerabilis Baedae Opera Historica*.

Further Reading: *Bede: his Life, Times and Writings*, ed. A. Hamilton
Thompson, Oxford, 1935. R. W. Chambers, ' Bede ', *Proceedings
British Academy*, xxii, 1936. ' Bede of Jarrow ' in E. S. Duckett, *Anglo-
Saxon Saints and Scholars*, New York 1947. W. G. Collingwood,
Northumbrian Crosses of the Pre-Norman Age (London, 1927).

The king listened [to Paulinus] and replied that he wished
to receive the faith as explained and that it was his duty. He
would discuss it with his chief friends and advisers so that if
they agreed they should all be consecrated together in Christ,
the Fountain of Life. Paulinus consented and he acted accord-

ingly. He asked each of the wise men at a council his views on the New Teaching and Preaching of a novel religion.

Coifi answered before any of his subordinate priests: ' Examine, O King, this preaching, yourself, but I am telling the whole truth when I confess that I find our former beliefs are unprofitable and useless. None of your subjects was more meticulous than I in the worship of our gods but many had more royal favours than I with more promotion and they gain their ends more; but if the gods were any good they would back up me as I served them better. If, therefore, reflexion leads you to consider the New Preaching of greater virtue and efficacy, let us accept them with no more ado.'

Another noble saw his wisdom and added: ' The life of man, O King, compared with the time of which we know not, is like the flight of a sparrow through the hall. There you sit at meat with your chieftains and servants in winter time with a fire blazing in the midst and rain and storm blustering outside and in it flies through one door and quickly out of the other. While it is within it is not touched by the winter storm, but after a little while of calm it vanishes from your sight into the winter again. Thus we see the life of man for a span, but what came before or what follows after we know not. If the New Teaching brings surer knowledge, surely it should be followed.' The other elders and counsellors of the king were prompted by God to speak likewise.

Coifi asked to hear Paulinus more carefully on his God. The king commanded and he did this and when he had listened he cried ' I long knew that our religion was meaningless, for the more I sought truth therein the less I found it. Now I make public confession that truth shines in this preaching and can give us life, salvation and eternal bliss. I propose, O King, that we straightway curse and burn the shrines and altars which we have honoured without profit.' To cut a long story short, the king publicly licensed the mission of Paulinus, renounced his idolatry and accepted Christianity. He asked the Chief Priest who should first desecrate the altars and shrines of the idols with their precincts and he replied ' I. Who better than I who ignorantly worshipped them, for an example to all by the wisdom God has

given me?' Spurning superstition he straightway asked the king
for arms and a stallion. He mounted and rode to destroy the idols.
It had been unlawful for a priest to carry arms or ride, save on
a mare. With sword girded, he grasped a lance, mounted the
king's stallion and hurried to the idols. The mob gazed and
thought him possessed. Without a pause he charged to the shrine,
cast in his lance and desecrated it. Glad in the knowledge of the
true God he bade his comrades burn the shrine and its precincts.
The very spot is still shown, near York. . . .

SYNOD OF WHITBY, 664

On this occasion it was decided that Britian should follow the
customs of the Roman, not of the native Celtic church.

Source: Eddi's *Life of St. Wilfrid*, ebited and translated by B.
Colgrave. *The Life of Bishop Wilfrid by Eddius Stephanus*, Cambridge,
1927, p. 21. Bede says that Eddi had been invited from Kent by
Wilfrid as a singing master and the author refers to himself as one of
two singers brought to Northumbria by Wilfrid. He writes as a
partisan but he was an eyewitness. Bede gives another contemporary
account of this important meeting between the leaders of the Celtic
and Roman churches.

Further Reading: A. J. Mason, *The Mission of St. Augustine to
England according to the Original Documents*, Cambridge 1897. E. S.
Duckett, *Anglo-Saxon Saints and Scholars*, New York 1947. M. Deanes-
ley, *A History of the Medieval Church*, 590–1500, 6th ed., 1950.

On a certain occasion in the days of Colman, bishop of York
and metropolitan, while Oswiu and Alhfrith his son were
reigning, the abbots and priests and men of all ranks in the order
of the Church gathered together in a monastery called Whitby,
in the presence of the holy mother and most pious nun Hilda, as
well as of the kings and two bishops, namely Colman and Agilbert,
to consider the question of the proper date for the keeping of
Easter—whether in accordance with the British and Scottish
manner and that of the whole of the northern district, Easter
should be kept on the Sunday between the fourteenth day of the
moon and the twenty-second, or whether the plan of the
apostolic see was better, namely to celebrate Easter Sunday
between the fifteenth day of the moon and the twenty-first. The
opportunity was granted first of all to Bishop Colman, as was

proper, to state his case in the presence of all. He boldly spoke in reply as follows: ' Our fathers and their predecessors, plainly inspired by the Holy Spirit as was Columba, ordained the celebration of Easter on the fourteenth day of the moon, if it was a Sunday, following the example of the Apostle and Evangelist John " who leaned on the breast of the Lord at supper " and was called the friend of the Lord. He celebrated Easter on the fourteenth day of the moon and we, like his disciples Polycarp and others, celebrate it on his authority; we dare not change for our fathers' sake, nor do we wish to do so. I have expressed the opinion of our party, do you state yours.'

Agilbert the foreign bishop and Agatho his priest bade St. Wilfrid, priest and abbot, with his persuasive eloquence explain in his own tongue the system of the Roman Church and of the apostolic see. With his customary humility he answered in these words: ' This question has already been admirably investigated by the three hundred and eighteen most holy and learned fathers gathered together in Nicaea, a city of Bithynia. They fixed amongst other decisions upon a lunar cycle which recurs every nineteen years. This cycle never shows that Easter is to be kept on the fourteenth day of the moon. This is the fixed rule of the apostolic see and of almost the whole world, and our fathers, after many decrees had been made, uttered these words: "he who condemns any one of these let him be accursed." '

Then, after St. Wilfrid the priest had finished his speech, King Oswiu smilingly asked them all: ' Tell me which is greater in the kingdom of heaven, Columba or the Apostle Peter? ' The whole synod answered with one voice and one consent: 'The Lord settled this when he declared: " Thou art Peter and upon this rock I will build my Church and the gates of hell shall not prevail against it. And I will give thee the keys of the kingdom of heaven; and whatsoever thou shalt bind on earth shall be bound in heaven; and whatsoever thou shalt loose on earth shall be loosed in heaven." '

The king wisely replied: ' He is the porter and keeps the keys. With him I will have no differences nor will I agree with those who have such, nor in any single particular will I gainsay his decisions so long as I live.'

So Bishop Colman was told what he must do, should he reject the tonsure and the Easter rule for fear of his fellow-countrymen, namely he must retire and leave his see to be taken by another and a better man. Thus indeed he did.

BRITISH RESISTANCE TO MERCIA, Eighth Century

The reference to demons reminds us that there are more witnesses to the existence of the Devil than of many human historical characters. Offa (d. 796) made Mercia supreme and built a dyke to keep out the Welsh (704–709).

Source: From the *Life of St. Guthlac* by Felix, who claims to repeat what friends of Guthlac told him, translated by D. Whitelock in *English Historical Documents*, c. 500–1042, Eyre and Spottiswoode, 1955, p. 711.

Further Reading: F. M. Stenton, *Anglo-Saxon England*, Oxford, 1943, 2nd ed., 1947, R. H. Hodgkin, *A History of the Anglo-Saxons*, 2 vols. Oxford, revised ed. 1952. C. W. Jones, *Saints' Lives and Chronicles in Early England*, Ithaca, New York 1947

Thus it happened in the days of Cenred, king of the Mercians, when the Britons, the dangerous enemies of the Saxon race, were oppressing the nation of the English with war, pillage and devastation of the people, that on a certain night at the time of cockcrow, as the man of blessed memory, Guthlac, was devoting himself according to his wont to vigils and prayers, he was suddenly, as he supposed, overcome by sleep, and seemed to hear the shouts of a raging crowd. Then, in less time than it takes to tell it, roused from a light sleep, he went outside the little cell in which he was sitting, and standing, pricking up his ears, he recognized the words that the crowd were saying and that British hosts were approaching his cell. For in former vicissitudes of other times, he had been an exile among them, long enough to be able to understand their sibilant speech. They strove without delay to enter the house across the swamp, and almost at the same moment he saw all his buildings on fire, with the flame rising above them; him too they caught, and began to lift him up aloft on the sharp points of their spears. Then truly the man of God at length plainly perceived the thousand-fold shapes of the deceitful enemy with his thousand-fold wiles, and chanted as if with prophetic mouth the first verse of the 67th psalm: 'Let God arise.' When they heard this, all the hosts of demons, in less time than it takes to tell it, vanished at that same moment like smoke from his sight.

KING ALFRED, 849-901

Alfred rightly lives in popular memory as the model English king, and legend only does justice to his extraordinary virtues, for he was deliverer from the heathen Danes, lawgiver, teacher, saint and king.

Source: Asser, monk of St. David's, *Of the Deeds of Alfred*, translated by E. Conybeare, *Alfred in the Chroniclers*, 1900, p. 105. Asser came to Alfred's court in 884. His account breaks off in 893.

In the year 877, the Heathen, as autumn-tide drew on, in part sat them down at Exeter, and in part went back to raid in Mercia. Day by day the number of the miscreants [*perversi*] grew ever larger, so that were thirty thousand slain in one day others would take their place twice-fold. Then bade Alfred make barks [*cymbas*] throughout the realm, and keels [*galeas*], that is long ships, that he might meet the foes in sea-fight, as they came in. Therein embarked he adventurers [*piratos*] and let them keep the water-way [*vias maris*]. But himself hied he with all speed to Exeter, where the Heathen were wintering, and shut them up in that city, and besieged them. On his seamen also laid he strait command, that they should suffer no supplies to reach the foe by way of the Narrow Seas [*in parte freti*].

Then met there his seamen 120 ships, laden with armed warriors, coming to the help of their kinsfolk [*concivium*]. And when the King's officers found ships thus filled with Heathen warmen, then leapt they to arms, and boarded the savages like men. But the Heathen, who now for nearly a month had been wave-tossed and ship-worn, vainly returned the onset. So that in a moment their line of battle was shattered [*lacerata*], and sunken in a place called Swanwich; and they perished one and all. . . .

In the year of the Incarnation 878, the 27th [really the 30th] of the age of Alfred, the oft-mentioned host left Exeter, and came unto Chippenham, a town-royal in the left [North] of Wiltshire [Wiltunscyre], on the east bank of the river which in British is called Avon, and there they wintered. And many of the country-folk drave they, by force of arms, and through need and fear, to sail beyond seas, and, for the most part, brought they under their sway all that dwelt in that land.

At the same time Alfred, with a few of his lords, and some warriors also, dwelt in the woods and fens [*gronnosa*] of Somerset—a life of sore trouble and unrest. For he had nought whereon to live save only what he might carry off, either by force or stealth, from the Heathen; or even from the Christians who had bowed to their sway. . . .

ALFRED'S NAVY

Alfred revived the forgotten seafaring traditions of the English, in order to defend the shore from the Danes.

Source: *Anglo-Saxon Chronicle*, translated by E. Conybeare, Alfred in the Chroniclers, E. S. Stock, 1900, pp. 123, 125, 130. It was Alfred who had the chronicle shaped and in his reign it becomes a contemporary narrative of stirring event.

Further Reading: A. T. Mahan, *The Influence of Sea Power on History*, 1890. Publications of the Navy Records Society. *Anglo-Saxon Chronicle*, translated by G. N. Garmonsway, Everyman's Library, 1923.

875 . . . And that summer did King Alfred put out to sea with a ship-force, and fought against seven ship-crews. And one of them he took, and the rest he put to flight. . . .

882. . . And King Alfred put to sea with his ships, and fought with four ship-crews of Danish men. And two of them he took, and all on board were slain. And two yielded them to him; and sore broken and wounded were they ere that yielding. . . . And, from Kent, King Alfred sent his fleet unto East Anglia. So soon as they came into Stour-mouth then met them 16 pirate ships; and they fought therewith, and took the ships, one and all, and slew the ship-men. And even as they wended homeward with the spoil there met them a great fleet of pirates, and that very day fought them. And the Danish men won that day. . . .

897 . . . Then bade King Alfred that long ships be built against the 'esks'; and they were full-nigh twice as long; some had sixty oars, some more; both swifter were they, and steadier, and eke higher than the other. Neither like the Danish were they shapen, nor the Frisian, but so as seemed him to be most worth.

[Describes subsequent engagements.]

KING ALFRED ON EDUCATION

Source: King Alfred's prose preface to his translation of Gregory's
Pastoral Care. Translated by R. W. Chambers, *England before the
Norman Conquest*, University of London intermediate source-books of
history, no. vii, Longmans 1926, pp. 222–5.

Further Reading: K. Sisam, ' The Publication of Alfred's Pastoral
Care ' in *Studies in the History of Old English Literature*, 1953, pp. 140–7.
C. Plummer, *The Life and Times of Alfred the Great*, Oxford, 1902.
B. A. Lees, *Alfred the Great, the Truth Teller*, New York 1915.

King Alfred bids greet bishop Waerferth with his words
in loving and friendly wise: and I would have thee know that it
has come very often into my mind, what wise counsellors there
were of old throughout England, both spiritual and lay; and
how happy were those times then throughout England; and how
the kings who had the authority over the folk obeyed God and
his messengers; and they both maintained peace, and morals,
and authority within their kingdom, and also extended their
borders; and what good success they had both with warfare
and with wisdom; and also the spiritual orders, how eager they
were both in teaching and in learning, and in all the services
they owed to God; and how strangers came hither to this land
in search of wisdom and learning; and how we now must get
these things from abroad, if we are to have them. So utterly was
learning fallen off in England that there were very few on this
side of the Humber who could understand their service-books in
English, or translate even a letter from Latin into English: and
I ween that there were not many beyond the Humber. So few
were there of them that I cannot remember even a single one
south of the Thames when I succeeded to the Kingdom. Thanks
be to Almighty God that we have now any supply of teachers.
And so, I bid thee to do as I believe that thou thyself dost wish,
that thou rid thyself of the cares of this world, as often as thou
canst, that thou mayest apply the wisdom which God has given
thee, wherever thou canst. Bethink thee what temporal punish-
ments came upon us, in that we neither loved wisdom ourselves
nor suffered other men to have it: we loved the name of Christian
only, and very few of us loved the Christian virtues.

When I called all this to mind, then I remember also how I
had seen, before it was all harried and burnt up, how the churches

throughout all England stood filled with treasures and books.
And there was also a great multitude of God's servants, but they
could make very little use of the books, because they were not
written in their own speech. As if they had said: ' Our fore-
fathers, who held these places before us, loved wisdom, and
through wisdom they got wealth, and left it to us. Here their
track may still be seen, but we cannot follow it up, and so we
have lost both the wealth and the wisdom, because we would not
bend our minds to following the track.'

Then, when I remembered all this, I wondered greatly
concerning men of wise and good counsel who of old were
throughout England, and had learned all these books fully, that
they would turn no part of them into their own tongue. But
then I soon made answer to myself and said: ' They did not
ween that ever men would become so reckless, and learning so
fall away; it was from deliberate purpose that they abstained from
doing it, and wished that there should be greater wisdom
here in this land, as we knew more tongues. . . .'

Therefore it seems better to me, if it seems also to you that
we too should turn into the tongue which we can all understand
certain books which are most necessary for all men to know;
and that we bring it about (as we very easily may, with God's
help, if we have peace) that all the youth which now is in England
of freemen who have wealth enough to be able to apply themselves to it, be set to learning, so long as they are good for no
other business, till the time that they can well read anything
written in English; let those, who are to be taught further, and
set apart for a higher office be taught further in Latin.

When I remembered how the knowledge of Latin had
before this fallen away throughout England, and yet many could
read what was written in English, then I began, among the other
diverse and manifold cares of this kingdom, to turn into English
the book which is called in Latin *Pastoralis* and in English
Shepherd's Book, sometimes word by word, sometimes sense by
sense, as I learnt it from Plegmund my archbishop, and from
Asser my bishop, and from Grimbold my mass-priest, and from
John my mass-priest. And when I had learnt it, as best I could
understand it, as I could most clearly interpret it, I turned it into
English; and to every bishopric in my kingdom will I send one. . . .

ST. DUNSTAN, CRAFTSMAN AND ARTIST, 924-88

St. Dunstan, Abbot of Glastonbury, with St. Aethelwold, Abbot of Abingdon, led a monastic revival of the Benedictine Order in the middle of the tenth century, at a time when England had been demoralized by the Danish raids.

English needlework was famous.

Source: Life of St. Dunstan, edited by W. Stubbs, *Memorials of St. Dunstan*, pp. 3–52 and transla.ed by Dorothy Whitelock in *English Historical Documents*, c. 500–1042, 1955, p. 827. This is the oldest life and is dedicated to Aelfric, Archbishop of Canterbury, 995–1005. The author twice claims to have witnessed what he related but he must have been writing at least seventeen years after St. Dunstan's death.

Further Reading: D. T. Rice, *English Art*, 871–1100, 1952. J. Armitage Robinson, *The Times of St. Dunstan*, Oxford 1923. G. Baldwin Brown, *The Arts in Early England*, 6 vols., 1903–37. W. Oakeshott, *The Sequence of English Medieval Art*, London 1950. F. Wormald, *English Drawings of the Tenth and Eleventh Centuries*, 1952.

Among his sacred studies of literature he also diligently cultivated the art of writing that he might be sufficient in all things; and the art of harp-playing, and skill in painting likewise; and, so to speak, he excelled as a keen investigator of all useful things. On this account a certain noble woman called Aethelwynn called him to her on one occasion with a friendly request to design her a stole for the divine service with divers figures, which she could afterwards diversify and adorn with gold and gems. When he came to her for this work, he usually brought with him his *cythera*, which in the native language we call ' harp ', that he might at times delight himself and the hearts of his listeners in it. Then one day after dinner, when he and the aforesaid woman returned with her workwomen to the said work, it happened by a marvellous event that this same harp of the blessed champion, hanging on the wall of the chamber, rang out a melody of jubilation of its own accord, without anyone touching it, with a clear sound in the hearing of all. For it rang out and played the melody of this anthem, and continued chanting the melody right through to the end: ' Let the souls of the saints who followed the steps of Christ rejoice in the heavens; and because they shed their blood for his love, they shall reign with

Christ for ever.' And when they heard it, he and the aforesaid woman and all her workwomen were terrified, and completely forgetting the work in their hands, gazed at one another in astonishment, marvelling greatly what new warning that miraculous act might prefigure.

TRIAL BY ORDEAL

This method of trial and trial by combat were instituted on the assumption that God would intervene to support the innocent. Athelstan (died 27 October 940) was Alfred's grandson and could be called the first king of all the English. He not only temporarily united them but even claimed all Britain. In 934 the Scots with Norse allies challenged him unsuccessfully at *Brunanburb*. William of Malmesbury writing about 1125 says he was of middle height and slender, ' his hair, as we have ourselves seen from his relics, flaxen, beautifully mingled with gold threads.'

Source: Laws of King Athelstan.

Further Reading: *Ancient Laws and Institutes of England, ed.* W. Thorpe, 1840. At all periods laws are an important source of historical information. H. C. Lea, *Superstition and Force, Essays on the Wager of Law, The Wager of Battle, The Ordeal, Torture*, Philadelphia 3rd ed. 1878.

See the description of *Brunanburb* in the Anglo-Saxon Chronicle of which the best translation is the most accessible, by G.N.Garmonsway in Everyman's Library, 1953.

And concerning the ordeal we enjoin by command of God, and of the archbishop, and of all bishops: that no man come within the church after the fire is borne in with which the ordeal shall be heated, except the mass-priest, and him who shall go thereto: and let there be measured nine feet from the stake to the mark, by the man's feet who goes thereto. But if it be water, let it be heated till it low to boiling. And be the kettle of iron or of brass, of lead or of clay. And if it be a single accusation, let the hand dive after the stone up to the wrist; and if it be threefold, up to the elbow. And when the ordeal is ready, then let two men go in of either side; and be they agreed that it is so hot as we before have said. And let go in an equal number of men of either side, and stand on both sides of the ordeal, along the church; and let these all be fasting, and abstinent from their wives on that night; and let the mass-priest sprinkle holy water over them all, and let each of them taste of the holy water, and give them all the book and the image of Christ's rood to kiss: and let no man mend the fire any longer when the hallowing is begun; but let the iron lie upon the hot embers till the last collect: after that, let it be laid upon the ' stapela ' [pile]; and let there be no other speaking within, except that they earnestly pray to Almighty God that he make manifest what is soothest. And let him go thereto; and let his hand be enveloped, and be it postponed till after the third day, whether it be foul or clean within the envelope. And he who shall break this law, be the ordeal with respect to him void, and let him pay to the king cxx. shillings as ' wite '. . . .

AELFRIC'S PUPILS, 1005

The people here portrayed following their country callings remained much the same for centuries. For them the Norman Conquest meant the substitution of the native upper class by an aristocracy of ' Frenchmen ' who called sheep and kine ' mouton ' and ' beef ' when the meat reached the halls of the consumers. In each century changes, such as the building of windmills in the thirteenth century, altered life, but town and country were much closer together, and the pattern of life was to receive its rudest shocks with the modern invention of internal combustion engines to reduce distance and banish horses.

Source: *Colloquies* of Aelfric, Abbot of Eynsham, amplified by a pupil. These dialogues were written in English and Latin, to teach Latin by practice in conversation. The method remained popular for centuries and has left pictures of daily life cast into the form now adopted in many broadcasting programmes to make a talk more interesting by the use of a compère to pose questions. Aelfric was the biographer of St. Aethelwold, who probably taught him at Abingdon Abbey and transferred him to Winchester. He became Abbot of Cerne and later of Eynsham. Anglicans from 1566 onwards reprinted his writings because they believed he supported their views on transubstantion. He is mostly omitted from Migne's *Patrologia*, but is regarded as orthodox by the *Catholic Encyclopaedia*.

Further Reading: Dorothy Whitelock, *The Beginnings of English Society*, Pelican Book 1952. M. and C. H. B. Quennell, *Everyday Life in Anglo-Saxon, Viking and Norman Times*, 1926.

Boys. We boys ask you, sir, to teach us to talk properly as we are ignorant and speak badly.

Master. What do you want to say?

B. We do not mind so long as it is correct. . . .

M. Will you accept beatings while learning?

B. That is better than to stay ignorant. But we know you have mercy and will not give us more strokes than we make you.

M. . . . What is your work?

B. I am a professed monk and sing seven times daily with the brothers and attend to reading and song. But I want to learn Latin conversation extra.

M. What do these comrades of yours know?

B. Some are ploughmen, others shepherds, cowherds, with huntsmen, fishermen, fowlers, merchants, shoemakers, salters and local bakers.

M. Well ploughman, how do you set about it?

Ploughman. O sir, I work too much. I go out first thing chasing the oxen to the field and yoke up for the plough. It's never so sharp a season that I dare lie in for fear of my master. But I yoke the oxen and fix the ploughshare and coulter and every day I must plough a whole land or more.

M. Have you a mate?

P. I have a child to goad up the oxen and he is hoarse with cold and shouting.

M. What more in the day's work?

P. A lot. I must fill the mangers with hay, and water the oxen and carry out the dung.

M. Oh, it is a great work!

P. Yes, because I am not a free man.

M. Well, shepherd? Have you any work?

Shepherd. Yes. First thing I drive my sheep to pasture and stand over them, summer and winter, with dogs so that wolves don't eat them, and I lead them back to the cotes and milk them twice a day and move their cotes too, and make cheese and butter and do not let the master down.

M. Cowherd, what is your job?

B. O sir, much work. When the ploughman unyokes the oxen I lead them to pasture and stand over them all night on watch against thieves and again first thing I hand them over to the ploughman, well fed and watered.

M. Is that one of your set?

B. Yes.

M. Do you know anything?

B. I know one art.

M. What sort?

Huntsman. I'm a huntsman.

M. Whose?

H. The king's.

M. How do you follow your art?

H. I make my nets and put them in a good spot, and set my dogs on to chase wild animals so that they fall into the nets and are caught and I kill them in the nets.

M. Must you have nets to hunt?

H. I can do it without too.

M. How?

H. I follow the wild deer with swift hounds.

M. What kind of wild deer do you get?

H. I catch hart, boar, fallow deer, roe and sometimes hare.

M. Were you out to-day?

H. No, as it's Sunday but I was yesterday.

M. What did you bag?

H. Two harts and one boar.

M. How?

H. I took the harts in nets and killed the boar.

M. How did you dare kill the boar?

H. The hounds brought him to me and I faced him and killed him with a sudden move.

M. You really were brave.

H. A huntsman shouldn't be a coward for different sorts of game lie in the woods.

M. What do you do with your venison?

H. I give the king the whole bag as I am his huntsman.

M. What does he give you?

H. He gives me good clothes and food and sometimes a horse or a ring to encourage me.

M. What is your trade?

Fisherman. I'm a fisherman.

M. What do you earn?

F. Food, clothes and money.

M. How do you get fish?

F. I go aboard and put my nets in the river and cast a hook and lines and take what I catch.

M. What if the fish are nasty?

F. I throw those back and keep the good ones.

M. Where do you sell your fish?

F. In town.

M. Who buys them?

F. The townsfolk. I can't catch as many as I could sell.

M. What sort of fish do you catch?

[F. Lists kinds of fish.]

M. Why don't you fish in the sea?

F. I do, but seldom as it's a long sail to the sea.

M. What do you catch at sea?

[F. Lists more fish.]

M. How would you like to catch a whale?

F. I wouldn't.

M. Why not?

F. It's risky. It's safer on the river than joining a whaling fleet.

M. Why?

F. Because I like catching fish that I can kill. . . .

M. But many whalers escape and get a good price.

F. Yes, but I'm not that sort of man.

M. What do you say, fowler, how do you catch fowl?

F. With nets, snares, lime [etc.]

M. Have you a falcon?

F. Yes.

M. Do you know how to train them?

F. Yes. What good would they be otherwise?

H. Give me a falcon.

F. Gladly, if you give me a swift hound. What sort do you want, big or little?

H. Big.

M. How do you feed falcons?

F. They feed themselves in winter and me, and in spring I let them fly to the wood and I take the chicks in autumn and tame them.

M.   Why do you let them escape?

F.   Because I don't want to feed them in summer as they eat too much.

M.   Many do feed the trained ones through the summer so as to have them ready again.

F.   Yes, but I don't want so much work as I know how to catch not only one but more as well.

M.   What say you, merchant?

Merchant.   I claim to be useful to the king and the authorities and the wealthy and to the whole population.

M.   How?

Merchant.   I go aboard ship with my wares and sail abroad and sell, and buy valuables which aren't found here and import them at great risk from oversea and sometimes suffer shipwreck with the loss of all my capital and only escape by the skin of my teeth.

M.   What sort of imports do you bring?

Merchant.   Purple, silk, jewels, gold, assorted clothing, dyes, wine, oil, ivory, latten, brass, tin, sulphur, glass, etc.

M.   Do you propose to sell them at cost price?

Merchant.   No. Or what would I be paid for my work? But I like to sell them dearer than I bought them abroad so that I get some return to keep myself and my wife and son.

M.   Well, shoemaker, what useful work do you do for society?

Shoemaker.   My craft is really useful and essential.

M.   How?

S.   I buy hides and fells and work them up with my skill and make different sorts of footwear, slippers, clogs, boots, bottles, bridles, horse-trappings, flasks, leather bottles, spur-leathers, halters, wallets and pouches. None of you could get through the winter without my skill.

M.   O salter, what is your line good for?

Salter.   Much, to all of you. None of you would enjoy good meals without it.

M.   How?

S.   Everyone likes a taste of salt at meals. Who stores his cellars or cupboards without my skill? Dairy produce goes bad on you unless I'm on guard, and you don't like vegetables without me.

M. Well, baker? What is your trade good for? Can we live without you?

Baker. For a while, but not long or well. Every table seems empty without me and without bread every dish seems revolting. I strengthen the heart of man and am the staff of life. The little ones don't like leaving me out either.

M. What of the cook? Is his job essential?

Cook. If you expel me from your college you'll have to chew your vegetables green and your meat raw. You can't have rich soup without my aid.

M. We don't care about you, you're not indispensable, for we can boil and roast for ourselves.

C. If you turn me out and do this you will all be slaves and there won't be a master among you. What's more, you won't eat without me.

M. Well, monk, you who spoke before, here I've tried that your companions are good and really useful. Who are these?

Boy. I have smiths, blacksmiths, a goldsmith, a silversmith, a coppersmith, a woodworker and many other workers in various trades.

M. Have you any wise counsellor?

B. Of course. How could our assembly be managed without a counsellor?

M. Well, wise one, which art seems to you the chief one?

Counsellor. In my view the service of God has first place, as the Gospel says, First seek the Kingdom of God. . . .

M. And which of the workaday arts is first?

C. Farming, for the ploughman feeds us all.

Blacksmith. Where would he get his share and coulter or even his goad without my craft? Where would the fisherman get his hook, the shoemaker his awl or the tailor his needle? Isn't it from my labour?

Counsellor. True, but we would rather stay at the ploughman's than with you. For he provides bread and ale. But you only give us in your shop iron sparks, the din of thundering hammers and the puffing of the bellows.

Woodworker. Don't you all need me for I make houses, various kinds of container and ships for you?

Blacksmith. How can you make such a claim, woodworker? For you couldn't make a single hole without me.

Counsellor. Comrades and skilled workers! Stop arguing and keep calm. In skill each of you is necessary to the other. We always come round to the ploughman who provides food for man and beast. I advise all workers to concentrate on their own crafts. For the one who loses his skill is lost himself. Priest or monk, civilian or soldier, do your work well. Be what you are, for it is a shame for a man not to want to be himself and what he ought to be.

M. Boys, how do you like that speech?

B. Well enough, but your talking is too deep and grown-up. Talk on our level so we understand.

M. Why do you work so hard at lessons?

B. So as not to be dumb beasts who only know grass and water.

M. What is your aim?

B. To be wise.

M. Wisdom? Do you want to be sharp and quick, cunning, astute, glib—but with evil minds inside. . . .?

B. No, that's not wisdom. . . .

M. . . . What have you done to-day, boy?

B. Much. Last night when I heard the alarm I got up out of bed, went to church and sang nocturne with the brethren. Then we sang the martyrology and lauds, then prime and the seven psalms with litanies and first mass, then tierce and the mass for the day, then we sang sext and ate and drank and slept and got up again and sang nones and now we are here with you ready to hear what you tell us.

M. When do you want to sing vespers and compline?

B. At the proper time.

M. Have you been thrashed to-day?

B. No. I was careful.

M. What about the rest?

B. Why ask me? I daren't tell tales. Each one knows whether or not he had a beating.

M.　What do you eat in the day?

B.　Meat, for I am still subject to the rod and still a novice.

M.　What else?

B.　Vegetables, eggs, fish, cheese, butter, beans and everything clean, with thankfulness.

M.　You are a great eater to eat everything laid.

B.　I'm not so hungry as to eat everything at one meal.

M.　How?

B.　Sometimes I eat this, sometimes that, soberly, like a monk, not greedily, for I'm no glutton.

M.　What do you drink?

B.　Ale, if there is any, otherwise just water.

M.　Don't you drink wine?

B.　I can't afford that and wine isn't a drink for boys but for wise old men.

M.　Where do you sleep?

B.　In the dormitory with the brethren.

M.　Who calls you for nocturnes?

B.　Sometimes I hear the bell and get up. Sometimes my master gives me a rude awakening with his stick.

M.　Good boys and clever learners, your teacher tells you to keep the Commandments and behave decently everywhere. Walk reverently when you hear the church bells and go into prayers, bow humbly to the holy altars, stand in good order, sing together, ask forgiveness of your sins and go out without playing the fool to the cloister or the classroom.

CHARMS

Charms for health and finding what was lost were popular. Charms are still advertised for sale to readers of Science Fiction, but they are more commercial.

(1) *Source*: O. Cockayne, *Leechdoms, Wortcunning and Starcraft of Early England*, Rolls Series 1864, i, 391.

TO RECOVER CATTLE

A man must sing when one hath stolen any one of his cattle. Say before thou speak any other word. Bethlehem was hight the borough, wherein Christ was born: it is far famed over all earth. So may this deed be in sight of men notorious, per crucem Christi. Then pray three times to the east, and say thrice, May the cross of Christ bring it back from the east; and *turn* to the west, and say, May the cross of Christ bring it back from the west; and to the south, and say thrice, May the cross of Christ bring it back from the south; and to the north, and say, The cross of Christ was hidden and has been found. The Jews hanged Christ, they did to him the worst of deeds; they concealed what they were not able to conceal. So never may this deed become concealed. Per crucem Christi.

FOR THE SAME

If cattle be taken away privily; if it be a horse, sing this over his foot shackles, or over his bridle. If it be another sort of cattle, sing over the hoof track, and light three candles and drip the wax three times into the hoof track. No man will be able to conceal it. If it be other goods, then sing it on the four sides of thee, and first sing it looking up. Peter, Patrick, Philip, Mary, Bridget, Felicitas; in the name of God, and the church; he who seeketh, findeth.

FOR A STITCH

Write a cross of Christ, and sing over the place this thrice, Longinus miles lancea ponxit dominum et restitit sanguis et recessit dolor.

(2) *Source*: G. Storms, *Anglo-Saxon Magic*, The Hague 1948, nos. 29 and 35.

Against Stomach-ache.

Against stomach-ache and pain in the abdomen. When you see a dungbeetle throw up earth, catch it between your hands together with the heap. Wave it vigorously with your hands and say three times:

Remedium facio ad ventris dolorem.

Then throw away the beetle over your back and take care that you do not look after it.

When a man's stomach or abdomen pains him, catch the belly between your hands.

He will soon be better.

For twelve months you may do so after catching the beetle.

Against Dysentery.

This letter was brought by an angel to Rome, when they were
sorely afflicted with dysentery. Write this on parchment so
long that it can go round the head, and hang it on the neck of
the man who is in need of it.

He will soon be better.

Ranmigan. adonai. eltheos. mur. O ineffabile. Omiginan.
midanmian. misane. dimas. mode. mida. mamagartem. Orta
min. sigmone. beronice. irritas. venas quasi dulaþ. fervor.
fruxantis. sanguinis. siccatur. fla. fracta. frigula. mirgul. etsihdon.
segulta. frautantur. in arno. midoninis. abar vetho. sydone multo.
sacculo. pp. pppp sother sother.

Misere. mei deus deus mini deus mi.

A Ω N Y Alleluiah,   Alleluiah.

CANUTE, 1017-35

Canute died on 12 November 1035. As a youth he was a cruel
enemy to Ethelred, cutting off the hands, ears and noses of English
hostages, but after he succeeded Edmund as King of England in 1017
he reigned as a native king and treated England as the chief of his
realms.

Source: Henry of Huntingdon, *History of the English*, is the authority
for the story of Canute and the waves. He wrote between 1125 and
1130, but the story may have been an oral tradition.

Canute reigned for twenty years. He died at Scaftesbith
[Shaftesbury] and was buried at Winchester in the old monastery.
A few facts about his reign should be briefly told, for never
before him was there a king in England of such greatness. For
he was lord of all Denmark, all England, all Norway and at the
same time of Scotland. Over and above the number of the wars
in which he was so glorious, he did three handsome and magnificent acts. Firstly, he married his daughter [Gunhild] to the
Roman emperor [Henry III] with indescribable riches. Secondly,
on his path to Rome [1031] he paid money and reduced by as
much as a half all those evil exactions called tolls and pontages

on the road which leads to Rome through France. Thirdly at the very summit of his power, he ordered his throne to be set on the seaside when the tide was rising. He addressed the mounting waters ' You are under my sway as is the land no which is my throne and there has never been anyone who has resisted my rule without being punished. I therefore command you not to rise on to my land and you are not to dare to wet the clothes or limbs of your master.' The sea rose in the usual way and wetted the feet and legs of the monarch without showing any respect. The king accordingly leapt up and said: ' Know all inhabitants of earth, that vain and trivial is the power of kings nor is anyone worthy of the name of king save Him whose nod heaven and earth, and sea obey under laws eternal.' King Canute therefore, never again set the golden crown upon his neck but set it for ever above an image of the Lord which is nailed to a cross, in honour of God the great king. By His mercy may the soul of King Canute rest in peace.

DUTIES OF BOORS, BEE-KEEPERS AND SWINE-HERDS, Eleventh Century

This description does not apply, the writer warns us, to all districts, and in process of time the services due became more and more commuted for money payments. See p. 125.

Source: *Rights and Ranks of People*, translated in D. Douglas and G. W. Greenaway, *English Historical Documents* 1042–1189, Eyre and Spottiswoode 1953, pp. 814–5.

Further Reading: F. W. Maitland, *Domesday Book and Beyond*, ed. 1921. P. Vinogradoff, *The Growth of the Manor*, ed. 1920.

The boor's duties are various, in some places heavy and in others light. On some estates the custom is that he must perform week-work for 2 days in each week of the year as he is directed, and 3 days from the Feast of the Purification to Easter. If he perform carrying service he need not work while his horse is out. At Michaelmas he must pay 10 pence for *gafol* [rent], and at Martinmas 23 sesters [measures] of barley, and 2 hens, and at Easter a young sheep or 2 pence. And he must lie from Martinmas to Easter at his lord's fold as often as it falls to his

lot; and from the time when ploughing is first done until Martinmas he must each week plough 1 acre, and himself present the
seed in the lord's barn. Also [he must plough] 3 acres as boon-
work ['voluntary' unpaid labour], and 2 for pasturage. If he
needs more grass, let him earn it as he may be permitted. Let
him plough 3 acres as his tribute land and sow it from his own
barn, and pay his hearth-penny. And every pair of boors must
maintain 1 hunting dog, and each boor must give 6 loaves to the
herdsman of the lord's swine when he drives his herd to the
mast-pasture. On the same land to which the customs apply a
farmer ought to be given for his occupation of the land 2 oxen,
1 cow, 6 sheep and 7 acres sown on his rood of land. After
that year let him perform all the dues that fall to him, and let
him be given tools for his work and utensils for his house. When
death befalls him let the lord take charge of what he leaves.

The estate law is fixed on each estate: at some places, as I
have said, it is heavier, at some places, also, lighter, because not
all customs about estates are alike. On some estates a boor must
pay tribute in honey, on some in food, on some in ale. Let him
who has the shire always know what are the ancient arrangements
about the estate and what is the custom of the district.

About the bee-keeper. A bee-keeper if he hold a swarm
which is subject to payment must pay what is appointed on that
estate. Amongst us it is appointed that he should give 5 sesters
of honey as tax: in some estates a greater tax is due. Also at
certain times he must be ready for many sorts of work at his
lord's pleasure besides boon-work and the cutting of corn when
ordered and the mowing of meadows. And if he will be provided
with land he must be provided with a horse so as to give it to
supply his lord with a beast of burden or to go with his horse
himself, whichever he is directed. And many things must a
man of such condition do: I cannot recount them all now. When
death befalls him let his lord take charge of what he leaves unless
there should be anything free.

A swine-herd at pay ought to pay for his animals that are
to be slaughtered according to the amount fixed on the estate.
On many estates it is fixed that he pay every year 15 swine for
killing, 10 old and 5 young. Let him have himself whatever he

raises beyond that. On many estates a more severe due is incumbent on the swine-herd. Let each swine-herd take care that after the slaughter of his swine he prepare them properly and singe them: then he will be well entitled to the perquisites. Also he must be—as I said before about the bee-keeper—always ready for every sort of work, and provided with a horse at the lord's need.

A slave swine-herd and a slave bee-keeper after death are liable to one and the same law.

DEATH OF THE WITCH OF BERKELEY, 1065

This story illustrates the reality of devils in the medieval world. At the castle which was later built at Berkeley in Gloucestershire occurred the horrible murder of Edward II in 1327.

Source: William of Malmesbury, *Chronicle of the Kings of England* translated by J. A. Giles, Bohn's Antiquarian Library 1847, p. 230.

At the same time something similar occurred in England, not by divine miracle, but by infernal craft; which when I shall have related, the credit of the narrative will not be shaken, though the minds of the hearers should be incredulous; for I have heard it from a man of such character, who swore he had seen it, that I should blush to disbelieve.

There resided at Berkeley a woman addicted to witchcraft, as it afterwards appeared, and skilled in ancient augury: [. . . and of bad character]. On a certain day, as she was regaling, a jackdaw, which was a very great favourite, chattered a little more loudly than usual. On hearing which the woman's knife fell from her hand, her countenance grew pale, and deeply groaning, ' This day,' said she, ' my plough has completed its last furrow; to-day I shall hear of, and suffer, some dreadful calamity.' While yet speaking, the messenger of her misfortunes arrived; and being asked, ' why he approached with so distressed an air ', ' I bring news,' said he, ' from that village,' naming the place, ' of the death of your son, and of the whole family, by a sudden accident.' At this intelligence, the woman, sorely afflicted, immediately took to her bed, and perceiving the disorder rapidly approaching the vitals, she summoned her surviving children, a monk, and a nun, by hasty letters; and, when they arrived, with faltering voice, addressed them thus: 'Formerly, my children, I constantly administered to my wretched circumstances by demoniacal arts: I have been the sink of every vice, the teacher of every allurement: yet, while practising these crimes, I was accustomed to soothe my hapless soul with the hope of your piety. Despairing of myself, I rested my expectations on you; I advanced you as my defenders against evil spirits, my safe-guards against my strongest foes. Now, since I have approached the end of my life, and shall have those eager to punish, who lured me to sin, I entreat you by your mother's breasts, if you have any regard, any affection, at least to endeavour to alleviate my torments; and, although you cannot revoke the sentence already passed upon my soul, yet you may perhaps rescue my body, by these means: sew up my corpse in the skin of a stag; lay it on its back in a stone coffin; fasten down the lid with lead and iron; on this lay a stone, bound round with three iron chains of enormous weight; let there be psalms sung for fifty nights, and masses said for an equal number of days, to allay the ferocious attacks of my adversaries. If I lie thus secure for three nights, on the fourth day bury your mother in the ground; although I fear, lest the earth, which has been so often burdened with my crimes, should refuse to receive and cherish me in her bosom.' They did their utmost to comply with her injunctions: but alas! vain were pious tears, vows, or entreaties; so great was the woman's guilt, so great the devil's violence. For on the first two nights, while the choir of priests was singing psalms around the body, the devils, one by one, with the utmost ease bursting open the door of the church, though closed with an immense bolt, broke asunder the two outer chains; the middle one being more laboriously wrought, remained entire. On the third night, about cock-crow, the whole monastery seemed to be overthrown from its very foundation, by the clamour of the approaching enemy. One devil, more terrible in appearance than the rest, and of loftier stature, broke the gates to shivers by the violence of his attack. The priests grew motionless with fear, their hair stood on end, and they became speechless. He pro-ceeded, as it appeared, with haughty step towards the coffin, and calling on the woman by name, commanded her to rise. She replying that she could not on account of the chains: ' You shall be loosed,' said he, ' and to your cost: ' and directly he broke the chain, which had mocked the ferocity of the others, with as little exertion as though it had been made of flax. He also beat down the cover of the coffin with his foot, and taking her by the hand, before them all, he dragged her out of the church. At the doors appeared a black horse, proudly neighing, with iron hooks projecting over his whole back; on which the wretched creature was placed, and, immediately, with the whole party, vanished from the eyes of the beholders; her pitiable cries, however, for assistance, were heard for nearly the space of four miles. No person will deem this incredible, who has read St. Gregory's Dialogues. . . .

THE NORMAN CONQUEST, 1066

Source: *The Anglo-Saxon Chronicle*, ed. J. A. Giles, Bohn's Antiquarian Library, 1881.   There is no eyewitness account of the Battle of Hastings and the long account by Ordericus Vitalis is more vivid than the contemporary ones.   The most fascinating and important record is the Bayeux Tapestry.

Further Reading: F. Barlow, *The Feudal Kingdom of England*, 1042–1216, 1955. Doris M. Stenton, *English Society in the Early Middle Ages*, 1954.

Then came William Earl of Normandy into Pevensey, on the eve of St. Michael's mass: and soon after they were on their way, they constructed a castle at Hastings port.   This was then made known to King Harold, and he then gathered a great force, and came to meet him at [the hoary apple-tree]; and William came against him unawares, before his people were set in order.   But the king nevertheless strenuously fought against him with those men who would follow him and there was great slaughter made on either hand.   There was slain King Harold, and Leofwin the earl, his brother, and Girth the earl, his brother, and many good men; and the Frenchmen had possession of the place of carnage, all as God granted them for the people's sins.   Archbishop Aldred and the townsmen of London would then have child Edgar for king, all as was his true natural right: and Edwin and Morcar vowed to him that they would fight together with him. But in that degree that it ought ever to have been forwarder, so was it from day to day later and worse; so that at the end all passed away. This fight was done on the day of Calixtus the pope [14 Oct. 1066]. And William the earl [duke] went afterwards again to Hastings, and there awaited to see whether the people would submit to him. But when he understood that they would not come to him, he went upwards with his army which was left to him, and that which afterwards had come from over sea to him; and he plundered all that part which he over-ran, until he came to Berkhampstead. And there came to meet him Archbishop Aldred [of York], and child Edgar, and Edwin the earl, and Morcar the earl, and all the chief men of London; and then submitted, for need, when the most harm had been done: and it was very unwise that they had not done so before; since God would not better it, for our sins: and they delivered hostages, and swore oaths to him; and he vowed to them that he would be a loving lord to them: and nevertheless, during this, they plundered all that they over-ran. Then, on mid-winter's day, Archbishop Aldred consecrated him king at Westminster; and he gave him a pledge upon Christ's book, and also swore, before he would set the crown upon his head, that he would govern this nation as well as any king before him had at the best done, if they would be faithful to him. Nevertheless, he laid a tribute on the people, very heavy. . . .

AFTER HASTINGS, 1066

Source: William of Poitiers, ' The Deeds of William, Duke of the Normans and King of the English ', translated by D. C. Douglas and G. W. Greenaway, *English Historical Documents*, 1042–1189, Eyre and Spottiswoode 1953, p. 229. Written about 1071 by a Norman soldier who became chaplain of the Conqueror. There is no account of the battle by one who fought in it, but William gives a well-informed intimate account which forms a vivid commentary on the pictures in the Bayeux Tapestry.

Further Reading: Ordericus Vitalis, *Ecclesiastical History*, translated by T. Forester, Bohn's Antiquarian Library, 4 vols. 1853–6.

It would have been just if wolves and vultures had devoured the flesh of these English who had rightly incurred their doom, and if the fields had received their unburied bones. But such a fate seemed cruel to the duke, and he allowed all who wished to do so to collect the bodies for burial. Then, having arranged for the honourable interment of his own men, he left Hastings in charge of a brave commander, and proceeded to Romney, where he punished at his pleasure those who had previously killed some of his men after a struggle.

Then he marched to Dover, which had been reported impregnable and held by a large force. The English, stricken with fear at his approach, had confidence neither in their ramparts nor in the natural strength of the site, nor in the number of their troops. This castle is situated on a rock adjoining the sea, and it is raised up by nature and so strongly fortified that it stands like a straight wall as high as an arrow's flight. Its side is washed by the sea. While the inhabitants were preparing to surrender unconditionally, our men, greedy for booty, set fire to the castle, and the greater part of it was soon enveloped in flames. The duke, unwilling that those who had offered to surrender should suffer loss, gave them a recompense in money for the damage of the castle and their property; and he would have severely punished those who had started the fire if their numbers and base condition had not prevented their detection. Having taken possession of the castle the duke spent eight days adding new fortifications to it.

Owing to the foul water and bad food his knights were there stricken with severe dysentery, and many were brought by weakness almost to the point of death. But this adversity did not daunt the duke. [Then Canterbury surrenders and the duke too has dysentery but will not delay.]

SAXONS AND NORMANS IN NORMAN EYES

Source: William of Malmesbury, *Acts of the Kings*, translated by J. A. Giles, Bohn's Antiquarian Library, 1847.

Further Reading: Sir F. Stenton, *The First Century of English Feudalism*, 1932. D. M. Stenton, *English Society in the Early Middle Ages*, 1066–1307, Pelican Book, 1951.

In fine, the English at that time wore short garments reaching to the mid-knee; they had their hair cropped; their beards shaven; their arms laden with golden bracelets; their skin adorned with punctured designs. They were accustomed to eat till they became surfeited, and to drink till they were sick. These latter qualities they imparted to their conquerors. . . .

[The Normans] live in large edifices with economy; envy their equals; wish to excel their superiors; and plunder their subjects though they defend them from others; they are faithful to their lords though a slight offence renders them perfidious. They weigh treachery by its chance of success, and change their sentiments with money. They are, however, the kindest of nations, and they esteem strangers of equal honour with themselves. They also intermarry with their vassals. They revived, by their arrival, the observances of religion, which were everywhere grown lifeless in England. You might see churches rise in every village, and monasteries in the towns and cities, built after a style unknown before. . . .

KILLING ENGLISHMEN NO MURDER

Source: Richard fitz Nigel, ' Dialogue of the Exchequer ', 1177-9, translated by D. C. Douglas and G. W. Greenaway, *English Historical Documents*, 1042-1189, Eyre and Spottiswoode 1953, p. 523. Richard, Bishop of London, was treasurer of the Exchequer, c. 1160-98, his office having been bought for him by his father, the Bishop of Ely, another Exchequer official.

Further Reading: F. Pollock and F. W. Maitland, *History of the English Law before the time of Edward I*, 2nd ed. 2 vols. Cambridge 1898. W. S. Holdsworth, *History of English Law*, 12 vols. 1922-38. R. L. Poole, *The Exchequer in the Twelfth Century*, Oxford 1912.

Master . . . Next, *murdrum*, properly speaking, is the concealed death of a man where the slayer is unknown. For *murdrum* means the same as ' concealed ' or ' hidden '. Now in the primitive state of the kingdom, after the Conquest, the remnant of the conquered English secretly laid ambushes for the Normans whom they distrusted and hated, and far and wide, in woods and remote places, when opportunity presented itself, they slew them in secret. When, to avenge their deaths, the monarchs and their ministers had for some years taken violent measures against the English with various refinements of torture, and yet the latter had not altogether ceased their attacks, at length the following plan was devised, namely that the hundred in which a Norman was found slain in this way—no evidence being found as to the identity of the slayer—should be condemned to pay into the Treasury a large sum of tested silver; some indeed to the extent of thirty-six pounds, others forty-four pounds, according to the different localities and the frequency of homicide. It is said that this was done so that the imposition of a general penalty might make it safe for wayfarers, and each man might hasten to punish so great a crime and to hand over to justice the man by whose fault such an enormous indemnity was imposed on the whole neighbourhood. You must know that those who sit round the Exchequer table are exempt from these charges, as we have said above.

Disciple. Ought not the concealed death of an Englishman, like that of a Norman, to be reckoned for *murdrum*?

Master. By the original institution it ought not to be so reckoned, as thou hast heard. But, with the English and Normans dwelling together and alternately marrying and giving in marriage, the races have become so fused that it can scarcely be discerned at the present day—I speak of freemen alone—who is English and who is Norman by race. I except, however, the bondmen, who are called villeins, and are not permitted, if their lords object, to change their status. For this reason invariably, when anyone is found slain in this manner nowadays, it is punished as murder, except in the case of those who can be proved to be of servile status, as we have said.

SACK OF PETERBOROUGH, 2 June, 1070

Even after the Norman Conquest the Northmen remained a menace and indeed the Normans themselves were, by name and origin, Northmen.

Source: *The Anglo-Saxon Chronicle*, translated by J. A. Giles, Bohn's Antiquarian Library 1881, p. 450.

The same year king Sweyn came from Denmark into the Humber, and the people of those parts came to meet him and made an alliance with him, for they believed that he would conquer the land. Then the Danish bishop Christien, and Earl

Osbern, and their Danish retainers, came into Ely, and all the people of the fens joined them, for they believed that they should conquer the whole country. Now the monks of Peterborough were told that some of their own men, namely, Hereward and his train, would pillage the monastery, because they had heard that the king had given the abbacy to a French abbot named Turold, and that he was a very stern man, and that he was come into Stamford with all his French followers. There was, at that time, a churchwarden named Ywar; who took all that he could by night, gospels, mass-robes, cassocks, and other garments, and such other small things as he could carry away, and he came before day to the abbot Turold, and told him that he sought his protection, and told how the outlaws were coming to Peterborough, and he said that he had done this at the desire of the monks. Then early in the morning all the outlaws came with many ships, and they endeavoured to enter the monastery, but the monks withstood them, so that they were not able to get in. Then they set fire to it, and burned all the monks' houses, and all those in the town, save one: and they broke in through the fire at Bolhithe-gate [Bulldyke gate], and the monks came before them and desired peace. However they gave no heed to them, but went into the monastery, and climbed up to the holy crucifix, took the crown from our Lord's head, which was all of the purest gold, and the footstool of red gold from under his feet. And they climbed up to the steeple, and brought down the table [crozier or cope?] which was hidden there; it was all of gold and silver. They also seized two gilt shrines, and nine of silver, and they carried off fifteen great crosses of gold and silver. And they took so much gold and silver, and so much treasure in money, robes, and books, that no man can compute the amount; saying they did this because of their allegiance to the monastery: and afterwards they betook themselves to their ships and went to Ely, where they secured their treasures. The Danes believed that they should overcome the Frenchmen, and they drove away all the monks, leaving only one named Leofwin the Long, and he lay sick in the hospital. Then came the abbot Turold, and eight score Frenchmen with him, all well armed; and when he arrived he found all burnt both within and without, excepting the church itself; and all the outlaws were then embarked, knowing that he would come thither. This happened on the fourth day before the Nones of June [2 June]. Then the two kings, William and Sweyn, made peace with each other, on which the Danes departed from Ely, carrying with them all the aforesaid treasure. When they were come into the midst of the sea, there arose a great storm, which dispersed all the ships in which the treasures were : some were driven to Norway, some to Ireland, and others to Denmark, and all the spoils that reached the latter country, being the table [crozier or cope?] and some of the shrines and crosses, and many of the other treasures, they brought to one of the king's towns called . . . , and laid it all up in the church. But one night—through their carelessness and drunkenness the church was burned and all that was in it. Thus was the monastery of Peterborough burned and pillaged. May Almighty God have pity on it in his great mercy: and thus the abbot Turold came to Peterborough, and the monks returned thither and performed Christian worship in the church, which had stood a full week without service of any kind. When Bishop Egelric heard this, he excommunicated all the men who had done this evil.

OBLATES AND NOVICES SCHOOL AT CANTERBURY, c. 1075

Rules show what was felt to be the ideal life for monks. Less edifying are the reports in Episcopal Visitations of what sometimes happened in some monasteries.

Source: Lanfranc's Constitutions, translated from Wilkins, *Concilia*, by A. F. Leach, *Educational Charters and Documents* 598 *to* 1909, Cambridge 1911, p. 61.

Further Reading: Prof. M. D. Knowles, *The Monastic Order in England*, Cambridge, 1941.

When a boy is to be offered [i.e. made an oblate], let a round tonsure be made on his head, and carrying the host in his hands and the cup with the wine, as the custom is, let him be offered by his parents after the Gospel to the priest who celebrates mass. When the priest has accepted the offering, the aforesaid parents should wrap the boy's hands in the pall with which the altar is covered and part of which hangs down in front, and then the abbot should receive him. After which the said parents . . . should immediately promise that . . . the boy will never leave the order he has accepted. . . . This promise they should make beforehand in writing in the presence of witnesses and afterwards place it on the altar.

The prior ought to make a noise to waken the brethren at such hour in the morning as the boys when they have said their several prayers can see to read in the cloister, and when they begin to read let them for some time read aloud, sitting separate from each other, so that one cannot touch another with his hands or clothes. No child shall dare to make a sign or say a word to another except in the sight and hearing of the master; nor get up from the place in which he sits unless told or given leave to do so. Wherever the children go there should be a master between every two of them. When they pass in front of the brethren they should bow to them, and the brethren remaining seated should do the same. One lantern should serve for two; if there are three, the third should carry a second lantern; if there are more, the same arrangement should be observed. They should not put anything into anyone's hand or take anything from anyone's hand, except in the case of the abbot, the senior prior, or their own master, and that not everywhere but only in proper places, where it cannot or ought not to be otherwise. The precentor, too, when he is in their school may give or take from them a book from which to sing or read. If they are serving at the altar, too, they can give or take as their orders require. They should be flogged in a chapter of their own, as their elders are in the great chapter. When they go to confession they should go to the abbot or prior or those specially assigned for the purpose by the abbot. While one confesses another should sit on the steps, and the master should sit close by outside the chapter-house. If they go into the refectory after the verse which is said before food, or into choir at the hours after the Gloria of the first psalm, they are to go to their places and bow as usual, while their master is to go to the place set apart for those who are tardy: but the boy who waits at the abbot's table is not to have any abstinence from food or drink imposed on him except by the abbot's orders. But if by his orders it is imposed, either he must be pardoned or he must be removed from the abbot's table. In choir, if the abbot is there, no one may strike them, no one order them out except by his direction. When he is away, the precentor may chastise them for things to do with his office, and the prior for other things, in which they behave childishly. Wherever they are, no one except the persons above-mentioned may make signs to them, no one may smile at them.

No one shall go into their school, no one shall speak to them anywhere, unless leave to go in or to talk to them has been given by the abbot or prior. They are never to read or do anything else in bed at midday but to cover themselves up and keep quiet. A monk of more than ordinary gravity and discretion shall be master over the other masters, one who may know how, when he has heard any charge against them, to inflict punishment in moderation on those who are at fault or to let them off. When they go to bed the masters shall stand by them at night with lighted candles until they are covered up.

Young men, whether those who have been brought up in the monastery or those coming in from the outside world who are given in charge to masters, shall be looked after in most things as is before provided with regard to the boys. They shall, as is above said, sit separate from each other; shall never leave the place in which they are kept, except with the monk who has charge of them; . . . [etc.]

DOMESDAY BOOK, 1086

The national survey made in 1086 and printed in 1733–1816 is arranged by the names of those who held land, not by parishes. The original is exhibited in the Museum of the Public Record Office and facsimiles for the entries for each county have been published by the Ordnance Survey. These extracts show how the inquiry was made before the results were digested into the form required. This is shown for Birmingham.

(1) *Source*: Robert of Hereford, a contemporary account printed in W. Stubbs, *Select Charters*, 1929.

Further Reading: F. W. Maitland, *Domesday Book and Beyond*, 1897.

This is the twentieth year of William, King of the English. At his orders a description of all England was made this year in the fields of the various provinces, in the holdings of the various lords, in their fields, in houses, in men both bond and free, both in those living only in cottages and in those having houses and fields, in ploughs, in horses and other beasts, in the service and rent of the land of all. Some commissioners were sent after the others and commissioners were sent into places where they were not known and which they did not know in order to check each other's reports and inform the king of those accused of error. The country was troubled with many disasters arising from the collection of royal finances.

(2) *Source*: Title of the Domesday Inquest for Ely, printed in W. Stubbs, *Select Charters*, 1929.

Further Reading: Professor H. C. Darby, *Domesday Geographies* (1953- in progress).

Here below is written the inquiry into the lands as the barons of the king make it, viz. under the oath of the sheriff of the shire and all the barons and their Frenchmen and all the Hundred, the priest, the reeve, and six villagers of each vill. There follows how the manor is called; who held it in the time of King Edward (the Confessor), who holds it now; how many hides; how many plough teams on the demesne; how many men; how many villeins; how many cotters; how many slaves; how many free men; how many socmen; how much woodland; how much meadow; how much pasture; how many mills; how many fish-ponds; how much is added or lost; how much all was worth then; how much now; how much each free man and socman held there or holds; All this in triplicate; viz. in the time of Edward, and when King William gave it; and how it may be now; and if more can be had than is had.

(3) The writer of the Anglo-Saxon Chronicle for 1085 complained that ' not a single hide, nor one yard of land, nor even—it is shameful to say, but he did not think it a shame to do—an ox, a cow or swine left out of what was entered down.' The entry for a particular place might mislead one, if one forgot that through changes of boundary a modern town would include places not originally within its boundaries and that if several lords had land in one place there would be several entries.

Source: Translation of Warwickshire Domesday in *Victoria History of Warwickshire*, 1904, i, 332.

From W[illiam son of Ansculf] Ricoald holds 4 hides in Bermingeham [Birmingham]. There is land for 6 ploughs. In the demesne is 1, and [there are] 5 villeins and 4 bordars with 2 ploughs. Wood[land] half a league long and 2 furlongs broad. It was and is worth 20 shillings. Ulwin held it freely T.R.E. [Time of king Edward the Confessor].

WILLIAM THE CONQUEROR, d. 7 September 1087

William I was thrown against the pommel of his saddle when his horse leapt a ditch or trod on hot ashes at the sack of Mantes, and died in the sixty-first year of his life, his fifty-third year as duke and his twenty-first year as king. His servants stripped his corpse and departed. A local knight took the body for burial to Caen. Few came to the funeral because of a fire, the ceremony was interrupted by a knight who insisted on receiving compensation for having been defrauded of the site on which the duke and his wife had built the church, and the body burst asunder through being forced into too small a stone coffin. The Norman barons began to act as to each seemed best and ducal garrisons were expelled from castles.

Source: *The Anglo-Saxon Chronicle*, translated by J. A. Giles, Bohn's Antiquarian Library, 1881, p. 461.

If any would know what manner of man king William was, the glory that he obtained, and of how many lands he was lord; then will we describe him as we have known him, we, who have looked upon him, and who once lived in his court. This king William, of whom we are speaking, was a very wise and a great man, and more honoured and more powerful than any of his predecessors. He was mild to those good men who loved God, but severe beyond measure towards those who withstood his will. He founded a noble monastery on the spot where God permitted him to conquer England, and he established monks in it, and he made it very rich. In his days the great monastery at Canterbury was built, and many others also throughout England; moreover this land was filled with monks who lived after the rule of St. Benedict; and such was the state of religion in his days that all that would, might observe that which was prescribed by their respective orders. King William was also held in much reverence: he wore his crown three times every year when he was in England: at Easter he wore it at Winchester, at Pentecost at Westminster, and at Christmas at Gloucester. And at these times, all the men of England were with him, archbishops, bishops, abbots, and earls, thanes and knights. So also was he very stern and a wrathful man, so that none durst do anything against his will, and he kept in prison those earls who acted against his pleasure. He removed bishops from their sees, and abbots from their offices, and he imprisoned thanes, and at length he spared not his own brother Odo. This Odo was a very powerful bishop in Normandy, his see was that of Bayeux, and he was foremost to serve the king. He had an earldom in England, and when William was in Normandy he was the first man in this country, and him did he cast into prison. Amongst other things the good order that William established is not to be forgotten; it was such that any man, who was himself aught, might travel over the kingdom with a bosom full of gold unmolested; and no man durst kill another, however great the injury he might have received from him. He reigned over England, and being sharp-sighted to his own interest, he surveyed the kingdom so thoroughly that there was not a single hide of land throughout the whole, of which he knew not the possessor, and how much it was worth, and this he afterwards entered in his register. The land of the Britons [Wales] was under his sway, and he built castles therein. . . . Scotland also was subject to him from his great strength; the land of Normandy was his by inheritance, and he possessed the earldom of Maine; and had he lived two years longer he would have subdued Ireland by his prowess, and that without a battle. Truly there was much trouble in these times, and very great distress; he caused castles to be built, and oppressed the poor. The king was also of great sternness, and he took from his subjects many marks of gold, and many hundred pounds of silver, and this, either with or without right, and with little need. He was given to avarice, and greedily loved gain.

He made large forests for the deer, and enacted laws therewith, so that whoever killed a hart or a hind should be blinded. As he forbade killing the deer, so also the boars; and he loved the tall stags as if he were their father. He also appointed con-

cerning the hares, that they should go free. The rich complained
and the poor murmured, but he was so sturdy that he recked
nought of them; they must will all that the king willed, if they
would live; or would keep their lands; or would hold their
possessions; or would be maintained in their rights. Alas!
that any man should so exalt himself, and carry himself in his
pride over all! May Almighty God show mercy to his soul, and
grant him the forgiveness of his sins!

ST. MARGARET, d. 1093

St. Margaret was the granddaughter of the English king, Edmund
Ironside, and queen of Malcolm Canmore who succeeded Duncan
as king of Scotland on the defeat of Macbeth in 1054. Malcolm and
Margaret were the parents of Matilda, wife of Henry I.

Source: Turgot, Life of St. Margaret in Ancient Lives of Scottish
Saints, translated by W. M. Metcalfe, Paisley, 1895, pp. 297-321.

Further Reading: Lucy Menzies, St. Margaret, 1925. R. W. Cochran-
Patrick, Medieval Scotland, 1892.

To the honourable and excellent Matilda, Queen of the English,
Forasmuch as you have requested, you have also commanded
me, to present to you in writing the story of the life of your
mother. . . . You are wont to say that in this matter my testimony is especially trustworthy, since you have understood that
by reason of her frequent and familiar intercourse with me I am
acquainted with the most part of her secrets. . . .

She made the King himself most attentive to works of justice,
mercy, almsgiving, and other virtues. From her also he learned
to keep the vigil, of the night in prayer. . . . Also the books
which she used either in her devotions or for reading, he, though
unable to read, used often to handle and examine, and when he
heard from her that one of them was dearer to her than the
others, this he also regarded with kindlier affection, and would
kiss and often fondle it. Sometimes also he would send for the
goldsmith, and instruct him to adorn the volume with gold and
precious stones, and when finished he would carry it to the Queen
as proof of his devotion. The Queen, on the other hand, herself
the noblest gem of a royal race, made the splendour of her

husband's royal magnificence much more splendid, and contributed much glory and honour to all the nobility of the kingdom
and their retainers. For she brought it to pass that merchants
who came by land and sea from divers lands, brought with them
for sale many and precious kinds of merchandise which in
Scotland were before unknown, among which, at the instigation
of the Queen, the people bought garments of various colours,
and different kinds of personal ornaments; so that from that time
they went about clothed in new costumes of different fashions,
from the elegance of which they might have been supposed to
be a new race. She also appointed a higher class of servants for
the King, that when he walked or rode abroad numerous bodies
of them might accompany him in state; and this was carried
out with such discipline that wherever they came none of them
was permitted to take anything from anyone by force; nor did
any of them dare to oppress or injure the country people or the
poor in any way. Moreover, she increased the splendour of the
royal palace, so that not only was it brightened by the different
coloured uniforms worn in it, but the whole house was made
resplendent with gold and silver; for the vessels in which the
King and nobles of the kingdom were served with food and
drink, were either of gold or silver, or were gold or silver plated.
And this the Queen did not because the honour of the world
delighted her, but because she felt compelled to do what the
royal dignity required of her. For when she walked in state clad
in splendid apparel, as became a Queen, like another Esther, she
in her heart trod all these trappings beneath her feet, and bore
in mind that under the gems and gold there was nothing but
dust and ashes.

ST. MARGARET'S GOSPEL

Source: Turgot, *Life of St. Margaret*, translated by W. M. Metcalfe,
Ancient Lives of Scottish Saints, Paisley, 1895.
   The beautiful book mentioned in this story is now in the Bodleian
Library. There is a picture postcard of it.
   Further Reading: E. G. Millar, *English Illuminated MSS.*, 10th–
13th *centuries*, Paris and Brussels 1926.

   She had a book of the Gospels beautifully adorned with jewels
and gold, and ornamented with the figures of the four Evangel-

ists, painted and gilt. The capital letters throughout the volume were also resplendent with gold. For this volume she had always a greater affection than she had for any others she was in the habit of reading. It happened that while the person who was carrying it was crossing a ford, he let the volume, which had been carelessly folded in a wrapper, fall into the middle of the stream, and, ignorant of what had occurred, he quietly continued his journey. But when he afterwards wished to produce the book, he, for the first time, became aware that he had lost it. It was sought for a long time, but was not found. At length it was found at the bottom of the river, lying open, so that its leaves were kept in constant motion by the action of the water, and the little coverings of silk which protected the letters of gold from being injured by the contact of the leaves, were carried away by the force of the current. Who would imagine that the book would be worth anything after what had happened to it? Who would believe that even a single letter would have been visible in it? Yet of a truth it was taken up out of the middle of the river so perfect, uninjured, and free from damage, that it looked as though it had not even been touched by the water. For the whiteness of the leaves, and the form of the letters throughout the whole of the volume remained exactly as they were before it fell into the river, except that on the margin of the leaves, towards the edge, some trace of the water could with difficulty be detected. The book was conveyed to the Queen, and the miracle reported to her at the same time, and she having given thanks to Christ, esteemed the volume much more highly than she did before. Wherefore let others consider what they should think of this, but as for me I am of opinion that this miracle was wrought by our Lord because of his love for this venerable Queen.

ARCHBISHOP ANSELM, 4 December 1093—
21 April 1109

Anselm was a figure of outstanding learning and saintliness whom God called to champion the rights of the church at a time when England was ruled by William Rufus, a brutal tyrant without respect for Christianity. Rufus kept the see of Canterbury vacant in order to enjoy its revenues, and temporarily repenting of his sins on a sick bed he was led by the unanimous demand of bishops and people to appoint Anselm archbishop despite all objections. Soon the king recovered and a quarrel followed which the king laid before a Great Council at Rockingham on 25 February 1095.

Source: Eadmer, *History of Modern Times in England*, translated in D. C. Douglas and G. W. Greenaway, *English Historical Documents 1042–1189*, Eyre and Spottiswoode 1953, pp. 655 and 666.

Eadmer, monk of Christ Church, Canterbury, first met Anselm in 1071 and became his intimate companion as archbishop. His dramatic eyewitness accounts are a leading source for the controversy about Investitures in England. In his Life of Anselm Eadmer says he had just copied out his rough draft from wax tablets when Anselm asked him either to stop or to let him revise the text. Anselm did correct it, but a few days later told Eadmer to destroy the quires on which he had written. Eadmer obeyed—having first copied out the contents of the quires on others. Thus Anselm is better known than any other important medieval character.

(1) Then the king, feeling that all their labour was being expended in vain, bade them all fall at Anselm's feet, whether perchance they might constrain him to give consent. But lo! as they prostrated themselves, he in turn fell on his knees before them and would not budge from his first refusal. At length, incensed against him and vexed at themselves for their irresolution in allowing his objections to defeat their purpose for so long, they raised the cry. ' Bring hither the pastoral staff! the pastoral staff! ' And, seizing his right arm, some of them dragged him forward while others pushed him from behind, and so they forced him struggling to the king's bedside. But when the king held out the staff to him, he closed his fist against it, and would not receive it. The bishops then tried to wrench open his fingers, which he kept firmly fixed in the palm of his hand, in order to place the staff therein. But after some moments spent in this vain endeavour, while Anselm cried out with the pain he was suffering, the index finger which they had succeeded in raising being once more immediately closed by him, finally the staff was placed against his clenched fist and held there by the hands of the bishops. While the crowd shouted ' Long live the bishop! ' and the other bishops, together with the clergy, began to chant in a loud voice the *Te Deum Laudamus*, the elected prelate was

carried rather than led into the church near by, still resisting
with all his might crying out, ' It is naught that you are doing; it
is naught that you are doing.' The formalities of the Church
customary on such occasion having been complied with, Anselm
returned to the king, and thus addressed him, ' I tell thee, my
lord king, that thou wilt not die of this sickness, and therefore
I wish thee to know how easily thou mayst alter what has been
done with me; for I have neither acknowledged nor do I acknow-
ledge its validity.' Having thus said, he withdrew from the royal
chamber and retraced his steps, the bishops together with the
lay magnates escorting him. Turning upon them he upbraided
them in these words, ' Do you realize what you have done? You
have yoked together in the plough the untamed bull and the old
and feeble sheep, and what good will come of it? . . . '

(2) Accordingly a Great Council was held in the church of the
castle [Rockingham] there on the Lord's Day beginning at the
first hour of the day. The king and his associates sat apart,
diligently weaving their designs against Anselm. . . . To this
[speech of Anselm] the king rejoined, ' What the archbishop
says runs wholly counter to my mind; no man shall be mine
who chooses to be his. Wherefore, you, the barons of my realm,
do you also forthwith refuse him all faith and friendship as the
bishops have done, to the end it may be made manifest what
profit he hath gained by maintaining his allegiance to the apostolic
see in contempt of my wishes.' The barons protested, ' We were
never his men and we cannot abjure the fealty we have never
sworn to him. He is our archbishop: he has to govern religion
in this land, and in this respect we, who are Christians, cannot
deny the authority of his office while we live here, especially as
no stain of offence is attached to him to compel us to act otherwise in regard to him.' Smothering his anger, the king bore
with this answer, taking care to refrain from contradicting their
argument openly, lest they should take too great offence. The
bishops, as witnesses of this scene, covered their faces in confusion, for they perceived that the eyes of all men were turned
upon them and that their apostasy was, not without justice,
universally detested. If you had been present there, you might
have heard this or that bishop dubbed now by one man, then by

another, with some nickname, accompanied with exclamations of indignation, such as 'traitor Judas', 'Pilate' or 'Herod', and the like. A little later the king asked them one by one whether they had in fact renounced all submission and obedience to Anselm unconditionally, or only in so far as he claimed it by the authority of the Roman pope. Some gave one answer, others the contrary. Those who professed that they had renounced their duty to their archbishop fully and unconditionally, the king commanded to be seated honourably as his faithful friends and liegemen. But those who dared to affirm that they had refused submission and obedience to Anselm solely in respect of instructions issuing from the pope, he branded as traitors and enemies of his will and, in a paroxysm of rage, ordered them to await sentence of condemnation in a corner of the castle. Thus terror-stricken and doubly covered with confusion, they fled and skulked in a corner of the building. Soon, however, they found the wholesome and familiar counsel on which they were wont to rely; that is to say, they gave a large sum of money and were restored to the king's favour. [After a final quarrel in 1097 Anselm left England.]

DEATH OF RUFUS, 2 August, 1100

The strange and apparently expected death of Rufus ended the reign of a violent barbarian who had no respect for the rights of his followers or of the Church. The New Forest, to which the Norman kings attached much importance as a source of sport, was a suitable setting for his sudden end.

Source: William of Malmesbury, *Chronicle of the Kings of the English*, translated by J. A. Giles, Bohn's Antiquarian Library, 1847, pp. 341, 344. William of Malmesbury was one of a group of writers who began to flourish in the reign of Henry I. Prolific and intelligent, he was an eyewitness of many of the incidents which he described.

Further Reading: R. R. Darlington, *Anglo-Norman Historians*, 1947.

Should anyone be desirous, however, to know the make of his person, he is to understand, that he was well set; his complexion florid, his hair yellow; of open countenance; different-coloured eyes, varying with certain glittering specks; of astonishing strength, though not very tall, and his belly rather projecting; of no eloquence, but remarkable for a hesitation of speech, especially when angry. . . .

The day before the king died, he dreamed that he was let blood by a surgeon; and that the stream, reaching to heaven, clouded the light, and intercepted the day. Calling on St. Mary for protection, he suddenly awoke, commanded a light to be brought, and forbade his attendants to leave him. They then watched with him several hours until daylight. Shortly after, just as the day began to dawn, a certain foreign monk told Robert Fitz Hamon, one of the principal nobility, that he had that night dreamed a strange and fearful dream about the king: ' That he had come into a certain church, with menacing and insolent gesture, as was his custom, looking contemptuously on the standers by; then violently seizing the crucifix, he gnawed the arms, and almost tore away the legs: that the image endured this for a long time, but at length struck the king with its foot in such a manner that he fell backwards: from his mouth, as he lay prostrate, issued so copious a flame that the volumes of smoke touched the very stars.' Robert, thinking that this dream ought not to be neglected, as he was intimate with him, immediately related it to the king. William, repeatedly laughing, exclaimed, ' He is a monk, and dreams for money like a monk: give him a hundred shillings.' Nevertheless, being greatly moved, he hesitated a long while whether he should go out to hunt, as he had designed: his friends persuading him not to suffer the truth of the dreams to be tried at his personal risk. In consequence, he abstained from the chase before dinner, dispelling the uneasiness of his unregulated mind by serious business. They relate, that, having plentifully regaled that day, he soothed his cares with a more than usual quantity of wine. After dinner he went into the forest, attended by a few persons; of whom the most intimate with him was Walter, surnamed Tirel, who had been induced to come from France by the liberality of the king. This man alone had remained with him, while the others, employed in the chase, were dispersed as chance directed. The sun was now declining, when the king, drawing his bow and letting fly an arrow, slightly wounded a stag which passed before him; and, keenly gazing, followed it still running, a long time with his eyes, holding up his hand to keep off the power of the sun's rays. At this instant Walter conceiving a noble exploit, which was while the king's attention was otherwise occupied to transfix another stag which by chance came near him, unknowingly, and without power to prevent it, Oh, gracious God! pierced his breast with a fatal arrow. On receiving the wound the king uttered not a word; but breaking off the shaft of the weapon where it projected from his body, fell upon the wound, by which he accelerated his death. Walter immediately ran up, but as he found him senseless and speechless, he leapt swiftly upon his horse, and escaped by spurring him to his utmost speed. Indeed there was none to pursue him: some connived at his flight; others pitied him; and all were intent on other matters. Some began to fortify their dwellings; others to plunder; and the rest to look out for a new king.

A few countrymen conveyed the body, placed on a cart, to the cathedral at Winchester; the blood dripping from it all the way. Here it was committed to the ground within the tower, attended by many of the nobility, though lamented by few. Next year [actually 1107], the tower fell; though I forbear to mention the different opinions on this subject, lest I should seem to assent too readily to unsupported trifles, more especially as the building might have fallen, through imperfect construction, even though he had never been buried there.

He died in the year of our Lord's incarnation 1100, of his reign the thirteenth, on the fourth of the nones of August, aged above forty years. . . . He was a man much to be pitied by the clergy, for throwing away a soul which they could not save; to be beloved by stipendiary soldiers, for the multitude of his gifts; but not to be lamented by the people, because he suffered their substance to be plundered.

HENRY I AND ANSELM AGREE ABOUT INVESTITURES AT BEC, 1107

Henry I established his authority but the independence of the church meant his authority was not total. Was the king or the archbishop to appoint the bishops? The archbishop and no layman was to consecrate them, but the king's men might still be bishops, for a bishop elect might do homage to the king and the king would still have a hold over ecclesiastics as barons holding lay baronies. This agreement between Church and State was made at Bec.

Source: Florence of Worcester. This is the only account of the settlement between Henry I and Anselm. Nothing is known of Florence of Worcester, except that he died on 7 July 1118. His *Chronicle* is valuable for its use of a lost version of the Anglo-Saxon Chronicle and has been translated by T. Forester in Bohn's Antiquarian Library, 1847, and by J. Stevenson in *Church Historians*, vol. ii, pt. i, 1852.

Further Reading: R. W. Church, *Anselm*, 1888.

The King assented and decreed that from henceforth no man should be invested with any bishopric or abbacy by the King or any lay hand in England by the gift of the pastoral staff and ring. Anselm in turn conceded that no man elected to the prelacy should be deprived of that honour on account of homage done to the King.

THE CISTERCIANS

The first English Cistercian house was Waverley, Surrey, founded in 1118, but the most famous Cistercian abbeys were in Yorkshire where Rievaulx was founded in 1132, for the devastation wrought by the Conqueror meant that there was vacant land there. Sixty-eight foundations were made by 1216. Cistercians were great sheep farmers, and famous for austerity.

Source: William of Malmesbury, *Chronicle of the Kings of the English*, translated by J. A. Giles, Bohn's Antiquarian Library, 1847, p. 347.

Further Reading: N. Hadcock and M. D. Knowles, *Medieval Religious Houses*, 1953. Ordnance Survey, *Map of Monastic Britain*, 2nd ed. 1955.

In his time began the Cistercian order, which is now both believed and asserted to be the surest road to heaven. To speak of this does not seem irrelevant to the work I have undertaken, since it redounds to the glory of England to have produced the distinguished man who was the author and promoter of that rule. To us he belonged, and in our schools passed the earlier part of his life. . . . He was named Harding, and born in England of no very illustrious parents. From his early years, he was a monk at Sherborne; but when secular desires had captivated his youth, he grew disgusted with the monastic garb, and went first to Scotland, and afterwards to France. . . . He went to Rome. . . . Returning into Burgundy, he was shorn at Molesmes, a new and magnificent monastery. . . [Harding and others came to desire stricter rules.]

Eighteen only, among whom was Harding, otherwise called Stephen, persevering in their holy determination, together with their abbot, left the monastery, declaring that the purity of the institution could not be preserved in a place where riches and gluttony warred against even the heart that was well inclined. They came therefore to Citeaux; a situation formerly covered with woods, but now so conspicuous from the abundant piety of its monks, that it is not undeservedly esteemed conscious of the Divinity himself. . . .

Certainly many of their regulations seem severe, and more particularly these: they wear nothing made with furs or linen, nor even that finely spun linen garment, which we call Staminium; neither breeches, unless when sent on a journey, which at their return they wash and restore. They have two tunics with cowls, but no additional garment in winter, though, if they think fit, in summer they may lighten their garb. They sleep clad and girded, and never after matins return to their beds: but they so order the time of matins that it shall be light ere the lauds begin; so intent are they on their rule, that they think no jot or tittle of it should be disregarded. Directly after these hymns they sing the prime, after which they go out to work for stated hours. They complete whatever labour of service they have to perform by day without any other light. No one is ever absent from the daily services, or from complines, except the sick. The cellarer and hospitaller, after complines, wait upon the guests, yet observing the strictest silence. The abbot allows himself no indulgence beyond the others—everywhere present—everywhere attending to his flock; except that he does not eat with the rest, because his table is with the strangers and the poor. Nevertheless, be he where he may, he is equally sparing of food and of speech; for never more than two dishes are served either to him or to his company; lard and meat never but to the sick. From the Ides of September till Easter, through regard for whatever festival, they do not take more than one meal a day, except on Sunday. They never leave the cloister but for the purpose of labour, nor do they ever speak, either there or elsewhere, save only to the abbot or prior. They pay unwearied attention to the canonical services, making no addition to them except the vigil for the defunct. They use in their divine service the Ambrosian chants and hymns, as far as they were able to learn them at Milan. While they bestow care on the stranger and the sick, they inflict intolerable mortifications on their own bodies, for the health of their souls. . . .

GODRIC THE MERCHANT, Twelfth Century

Source: *Life of St. Godric*, Surtees Soc., 1847. Written before St. Godric died in 1170, by Reginald, monk of Durham, translated by G. G. Coulton, *Social Life in Britain from the Conquest to the Reformation*, C.U.P., 1918 reprinted 1938.

Further Reading: E. Lipson, *The Economic History of England*, 1929.

This holy man's father was named Ailward, and his mother Edwenna; both of slender rank and wealth, but abundant in righteousness and virtue. They were born in Norfolk, and had long lived in the township called Walpole. . . . Aspiring to the merchant's trade, he began to follow the chapman's way of life, first learning how to gain in small bargains and things of insignificant price; and thence, while yet a youth, his mind advanced little by little to buy and sell and gain from things of greater expense. For, in his beginnings, he was wont to wander with small wares around the villages and farmsteads of his own neighbourhood; but in process of time, he gradually associated himself by compact with city merchants. Hence, within a brief space of time, the youth who had trudged for many weary hours from village to village, from farm to farm, did so profit by his increase of age and wisdom as to travel with associates of his own age through towns and boroughs, fortresses and cities, to fairs and to all the various booths of the market-place, in pursuit of his public chaffer. . . . At first, he lived as a chapman for four years in Lincolnshire, going on foot and carrying the smallest wares; then he travelled abroad, first to St. Andrews in Scotland

and then for thé first time to Rome. On his return, having
formed a familiar friendship with certain young men who were
eager for merchandise, he began to launch upon bolder courses,
and to coast frequently by sea to the foreign lands that lay
around him. Thus, sailing often to and fro . . . he traded
in many divers wares and, amid these occupations, learned much
worldly wisdom. . . . For he laboured not only as a merchant
but also as a shipman . . . to Denmark and Flanders and Scotland;
in all which he found certain rare, and therefore more precious,
wares . . . for he sold dear in one place the wares which he had
bought elsewhere at a small price.

Then he purchased the half of a merchant-ship with certain
of his partners in the trade; and again by his prudence he bought
the fourth part of another ship. At length, by his skill in navi-
gation, wherein he excelled all his fellows, he earned promotion
to the post of steersman. . . .

For he was vigorous and strenuous in mind, whole of limb
and strong in body. He was of middle stature, broad-shouldered
and deep-chested, with a long face, grey eyes most clear and
piercing, bushy brows, a broad forehead, long and open nostrils,
a nose of comely curve, and a pointed chin. His beard was thick,
and longer than the ordinary, his mouth well-shaped, with lips
of moderate thickness; in youth his hair was black, in age as
white as snow; his neck was short and thick, knotted with veins
and sinews; his legs were somewhat slender, his instep high, his
knees hardened and horny with frequent kneeling; his whole
skin rough beyond the ordinary, until all this roughness was
softened by old age. . . . In labour he was strenuous, assiduous
above all men; and, when by chance his bodily strength proved
insufficient, he compassed his ends with great ease by the skill
which his daily labours had given, and by a prudence born of
long experience. . . . He knew, from the aspect of sea and stars,
how to foretell fair or foul weather. In his various voyages he
visited many saints' shrines, to whose protection he was wont
most devoutly to commend himself; more especially the church
of St. Andrew in Scotland, where he most frequently made and
paid his vows. On the way thither, he often-times touched at the
island of Lindisfarne, wherein St. Cuthbert had been bishop, and

at the isle of Farne, where the Saint had lived as an anchoret, and where St. Godric (as he himself would tell afterwards) would meditate on the Saint's life with abundant tears. Thence he began to yearn for solitude, and to hold his merchandise in less esteem than heretofore. . . .

[This true picture of a merchant is two centuries earlier than Chaucer's description of a ' Marchant with a forked berd '. But Chaucer describes the others in the company that went to visit the shrine of St. Thomas of Canterbury.]

LOSS OF THE WHITE SHIP, 25 November, 1120

In the White Ship perished Henry I's beloved son and heir William ' educated and destined to the succession, with the fondest hope and surpassing care.'

Source: William of Malmesbury, *Chronicle of the Kings of the English* translated by J. A. Giles, Bohn's Classical Library, 1847, p. 455.

Further Reading: R. L. Poole, *Chronicles and Annals*, 1926.

. . . Nevertheless, the calm of this brilliant, and carefully concerted peace, this anxious, universal hope, was destroyed in an instant by the vicissitudes of human estate. For, giving orders for returning to England, the king set sail from Barfleur just before twilight on the seventh day before the kalends of December; and the breeze which filled his sails conducted him safely to his own kingdom and extensive fortunes. But the young man, who was now somewhat more than seventeen years of age, and, by his father's indulgence, possessed everything but the name of king, commanded another vessel to be prepared for himself; almost all the young nobility flocking around him, from similarity of youthful pursuits. The sailors, too, immoderately filled with wine, with that seaman's hilarity which their cups excited, exclaimed, that those who were now ahead must soon be left astern; for the ship was of the best construction, and recently fitted with new materials. When, therefore, it was now dark night, these imprudent youths, over-whelmed with liquor, launched the vessel from the shore. She flies swifter than the winged arrow, sweeping the rippling surface of the deep: but the carelessness of the intoxicated crew drove her on a rock, which rose above the waves not far from shore. In the greatest consternation, they immediately ran on deck, and with loud outcry got ready their boat-hooks, endeavouring, for a considerable time, to force the vessel off: but fortune resisted and frustrated every exertion. The oars, too, dashing, horribly crashed against the rock, and her battered prow hung immoveably fixed. Now, too, the water washed some of the crew overboard, and, entering the chinks, drowned others; when the boat having been launched, the young prince was received into it, and might certainly have been saved by reaching the shore, had not his illegitimate sister, the Countess of Perche, now struggling with death in the larger vessel, implored her brother's assistance; shrieking out that he should not abandon her so barbarously. Touched with pity, he ordered the boat to return to the ship, that he might rescue his sister; and thus the unhappy youth met his death through excess of affection: for the skiff, overcharged by the multitudes who leaped into her, sank, and buried all indiscriminately in the deep. One rustic alone escaped; who, floating all night upon the mast, related in the morning, the dismal catastrophe of the tragedy. No ship was ever productive of so much misery to England; none ever so widely celebrated throughout the world. . . .

ANARCHY, 1137

Source: *The Anglo-Saxon Chronicle*, translated by the Rev. J. A. Giles, Bohn's Antiquarian Library, 1881.

Further Reading: R. A. Brown, *English Medieval Castles*, Batsford, 1954.

1137. This year King Stephen went over sea to Normandy, and he was received there because it was expected that he would be altogether like his uncle, and because he had gotten possession of his treasure, but this he distributed and scattered foolishly. King Henry had gathered together much gold and silver, yet did he no good for his soul's sake with the same. When King Stephen came to England, he held an assembly at Oxford; and there he seized Roger Bishop of Salisbury, and Alexander Bishop of Lincoln, and Roger the Chancellor, his nephew, and he kept them all in prison till they gave up their castles. When the traitors perceived that he was a mild man, and soft, and a good, and that he did not enforce justice, they did all wonder. They had done homage to him, and sworn oaths, but they no faith kept; all became forsworn, and broke their allegiance, for every rich man built his castles, and defended them against him, and they filled the land full of castles. They greatly oppressed the wretched people by making them work at these castles, and when the castles were finished they filled them with devils and evil men. Then they took those whom they suspected to have any goods, by night and by day, seizing both men and women, and they put them in prison for their gold and silver, and tortured them with pains unspeakable, for never were any martyrs tormented as these were They hung some up by their feet, and smoked them with foul smoke; some by their thumbs, or by the head, and they hung burning things on their feet. They put a knotted string about their heads, and twisted it till it went into the brain. They put them into dungeons wherein were adders and snakes and toads, and thus wore them out. Some they put into a crucet-house [torture-chamber], that is, into a chest that was short and narrow and not deep, and they put sharp stones in it, and crushed the man therein so that they broke all his limbs. There were hateful and grim things called Sachenteges [noose-and-traps] in many of the castles, and which two or three men had enough to do to carry. The Sachentege was made thus: it was fastened to a beam, having a sharp iron to go round a man's throat and neck, so that he might no ways sit, nor lie, nor sleep, but that he must bear all the iron. Many thousands they exhausted with hunger. I cannot and I may not tell of all the wounds, and all the tortures that they inflicted upon the wretched men of this land; and this state of things lasted the nineteen years that Stephen was king, and ever grew worse and worse. They were continually levying an exaction from the towns, which they called Tenserie [protection money], and when the miserable inhabitants had no more to give, then plundered they, and burnt all the towns, so that well mightest thou walk a whole day's journey nor ever shouldest thou find a man seated in a town, or its lands tilled.

Then was corn dear, and flesh, and cheese, and butter, for

there was none in the land—wretched men starved with hunger
—some lived on alms who had been erewhile rich: some fled
the country—never was there more misery, and never acted
heathens worse than these. At length they spared neither church
nor churchyard, but they took all that was valuable therein,
and then burned the church and all together. Neither did they
spare the lands of bishops, nor of abbots, nor of priests; but
they robbed the monks and the clergy, and every man plundered
his neighbour as much as he could. If two or three men came
riding to a town, all the township fled before them, and thought
that they were robbers. The bishops and clergy were ever
cursing them, but this to them was nothing, for they were all
accursed, and forsworn, and reprobate. The earth bare no corn;
you might as well have tilled the sea, for the land was all ruined
by such deeds, and it was said openly that Christ and his saints
slept. These things and more than we can say did we suffer
during nineteen years because of our sins.

THE BATTLE OF THE STANDARD, 22 August 1138

King David championed his niece, the Empress Matilda, against
Stephen. He was defeated at the Battle of the Standard, 22 August
1138.

(1) *Source*: *The Deeds of Stephen*, translated by K. R. Potter, Nelson's
Medieval Texts, 1955.
Further Reading: Cosmo Innes, *Scotland in the Middle Ages*, 1860.

In Scotland, which borders on England, with a river fixing
the boundary between the two kingdoms, there was a king of
gentle heart, born of religious parents and equal to them in his
just way of living. . . . At last King Henry's daughter sent him
a letter, stating that she had been disinherited and deprived of
the kingdom promised to her on oath . . . and therefore she
humbly and mournfully besought him to aid her as a relation.
. . . So King David, for that was his name, sent out a decree
through Scotland and summoned all to arms, and giving them
free licence he commanded them to commit against the English,
without pity, the most savage and cruel deeds they could invent.
Scotland, which is also called Albany, is a land hemmed in

by marshy places, well supplied with productive forests, milk and herds, encircled by safe harbours and rich islands, but it has inhabitants that are barbarous and filthy, neither overcome by excess of cold nor enfeebled by severe hunger, putting their trust in swiftness of foot and light equipment; in their own country they care nothing for the awful moment of the bitterness of death ; among foreigners they surpass all in cruelty. From this people then and from the nearer parts of Scotland the king collected a mass of rebels into an incredible army and led it towards England, and after crossing the boundary between the two kingdoms into the region of Northumbria, which was wide and populous and filled with supplies of all things needful, he there encamped.

(2) *Source*: Richard of Hexham's continuation of Simeon of Durham, written from a Northern point of view before 1154 by one who was strongly anti-Scottish.   Translated in D. C. Douglas and G. W. Greenaway, *English Historical Documents* 1042–1189, Eyre and Spottiswoode, 1953, p. 319.

Further Reading: Translation by J. Stevenson in *Church Historians of England*, vol. iv, 1856.

. . . Their archbishop Thurstan, a man of great firmness and worth, animated them [the Northern barons] by his counsel and exhortations . . . he promised them also that the priests of his diocese, bearing crosses, should march with them to battle together with their flocks . . . and although he was himself so greatly reduced by age and infirmity, that he had to be carried on a litter where need was, yet, in order to animate their courage, he would readily have accompanied them to the field of battle. But they compelled him to stay behind . . . and they proceeded to Thirsk, from whence they dispatched Robert ' de Bruce ' and Bernard ' de Baliol ' to the king of the Scots. . . . They very humbly and courteously besought him that he would at least desist from his acts of ferocity. . . . But he, together with his followers, with a hardened heart, spurned their request, and disdainfully taunted them. They therefore returned to their associates; Robert abjured the homage he had rendered to the Scottish king, and Bernard the fealty he had sworn to him on one occasion, when he had been taken prisoner. . . .

While thus awaiting the approach of the Scots, the scouts whom they had sent forward to reconnoitre, returned, bringing the information that the king with his army had already passed the river Tees and was ravaging their province in his wonted manner. They hastened to resist them; and, passing the village of Northallerton, they arrived early in the morning at a plain distant from it by about two miles. Some of them soon erected, in the centre of a frame which they brought, the mast of a ship, to which they gave the name of the Standard; whence those lines of Hugh ' Sotevagina ', archdeacon of York:

> Soldiers, to-day shall fight or fall
> Strong in the Standard's right
> Its holy Sign, confessed by all,
> Shall fortify our might.

On the top of this pole they hung a silver pyx containing the Host, and the banner of St. Peter the apostle, and John of Beverley and Wilfrid of Ripon, confessors and bishops. In doing this, their hope was that our Lord Jesus Christ, by the efficacy of his Body, might be their leader in the contest. They also provided for their men a certain and conspicuous rallying-point, by which they might rejoin their comrades in the event of their being cut off.

Scarcely had they put themselves in battle array when tidings were brought that the king of Scots was close at hand with his whole force, ready and eager for the contest. The greater part of the knights, then dismounting, became foot-soldiers, a chosen body of whom, interspersed with archers, were arranged in the front rank. The others, with the exception of those who were to dispose and rally the forces, mustered with the barons in the centre, near and around the Standard, and they were guarded by the rest of the host, who closed in on all sides. The troop of cavalry and the horses of the knights were stationed at a little distance, lest they should take fright at the shouting and uproar of the Scots. In like manner, on the enemy's side, the king and almost all his followers were on foot, their horses being kept at a distance. In front of the battle were the Picts; in the centre, the king with his knights and English; and the rest of the barbarian host poured roaring around them.

As they advanced in this order of battle, the Standard with its banners became visible at no great distance; and at once the hearts of the king and his followers were overpowered by extreme terror and consternation; yet they persisted in their wickedness, they pressed on to accomplish their evil ends. On the Octave of the Assumption of St. Mary, being Monday, 22 August, between the first and third hours, the struggle of this battle was begun and finished. For numberless Picts being slain immediately on the first attack, the rest, throwing down their arms, disgracefully fled. The plain was strewed with corpses; very many were taken prisoner; the king and all the others took to flight; and at length of that immense army all were either slain, captured, or scattered as sheep without a shepherd. They fled like persons bereft of reason, away from their own country instead of towards it, thus entering the land of their enemies. But wherever they were discovered, they were put to death like sheep for the slaughter; and so, by the righteous judgment of God, those who had cruelly massacred multitudes, and left them unburied, giving them neither their country's nor a foreign rite of burial (leaving them a prey to dogs, birds, and wild beasts), were themselves either dismembered and torn to pieces or left to decay and rot in the open air. The king also . . . fled dishonoured and meanly attended, and barely escaped with his life. . . . Of that army which came out of Scotland alone, more than ten thousand were missing; and in various localities of the Deirans, Bernicians, Northumbrians, and Cumbrians, many more perished in the flight than fell in the battle. The army of the English thus, by God's help, with a small loss, easily obtained the victory, and took possession of the spoil, which was found in great abundance.

ESCAPE OF THE EMPRESS MATILDA FROM OXFORD, Christmas 1142

The central position of Oxford, situated on an important crossing over the Thames and naturally fortified by the presence of water on almost every side, perhaps had combined to attract the Empress Matilda thither in her struggle against Stephen just as it attracted Charles I in the Great Rebellion. Like Charles I the Empress had alienated the sympathies of London. In flying to Wallingford she reached a castle which was also well situated, for there the Icknield Way, one of the great natural routes of England, crosses the Thames.

Source: *The History of the English by Henry, Archdeacon of Huntingdon*, Ed. by T. Arnold, Rolls Series 1879, p. 276.

William of Malmesbury's account ends at this point with the wish that he knew the truth about this story.

The same year the king [Stephen] besieges the Empress at Oxford after the feast of Michaelmas until Advent. At that time not long from Christmas the Empress robed herself in white garments and fled over the frozen Thames. The dazzle of the snow and the protective coloration tricked the eyes of the besiegers. She fled to the castle of Wallingford and thus was Oxford surrendered to the King.

SCORCHED EARTH, 1149

In May 1149 the Scottish King knighted Henry Plantagenet. King Stephen tried to intercept him and plundered land round Salisbury, Marlborough and Devizes.

Source: *The Deeds of Stephen*, translated by K. R. Potter, Nelson's Medieval Texts, 1955, p. 144.

Missing sections of this chronicle were discovered in a manuscript at Valenciennes by Professor Mynors after the text had been already long in type. These give a connected story for years about which other witnesses are silent or less well informed. The writer was a supporter of Stephen. These events are news unknown to previous scholars. This newly discovered section ends with the death of Stephen and the accession of Henry II.

Not long after this the king was much concerned with suppressing the hostilities that were on the increase round

York; sometimes he destroyed castles belonging to the enemy or his own adherents that were burdensome to the city, sometimes he built others in more suitable and advantageous places. After acquiring much treasure in those regions he went back with great glory to London, and there, when some days had passed, he deliberated on the most effective means of shattering his opponents and the easiest way of checking the continual disorder that they fomented in the kingdom. Different people gave advice of different sorts, but at last it seemed to him sound and judicious to attack the enemy everywhere, plunder and destroy all that was in their possession, set fire to the crops and every other means of supporting human life and let nothing remain anywhere, that under this duress, reduced to the extremity of want, they might at last be compelled to yield and surrender. It was indeed evil, he thought, to take away the sustenance of human life that God had vouchsafed, yet far worse for the kingdom to be constantly disturbed by the enemy's raiding and impoverished by daily pillage; it was more endurable to put up for a time with whatever troubles cruel fate might offer than bear so much continually from each one of the enemy. And no wonder, either, if he must rage with such cruelty against the enemy, as many opponents cannot be wiped out without much slaughter. So gathering together a large body of finely equipped knights, his son too with his men and some of the barons massed on the opposite flank, he sets himself to lay waste that fair and delightful district, so full of all good things, round Salisbury; they took and plundered everything they came upon, set fire to houses and churches, and what was a more cruel and brutal sight, fired the crops that had been reaped and stacked all over the fields, consumed and brought to nothing everything edible they found. They raged with this bestial cruelty especially round Marlborough; they showed it also very terribly round Devizes, and they had in mind to do the same to their adversaries all over England. [But Stephen had to go to defend Lincoln from the Earl of Chester.]

THE TOWN BELL, 1154

Knight, husbandman and cleric were the three important kinds of people. But in young growing towns artisans and traders began to thrive in a new way and to win independence of neighbouring lords.

Source : Customs of Hereford, *Archaeological Journal*, xxvii, 466.

Further Reading : C. Gross, *The Gild Merchant*, 1890. Mrs. J. R. Green, *Town Life in the Fifteenth Century*, 1894.

Concerning our bell, we use it in a public place where our chief bailiff may come as well by day as by night, to give warning to all men living within the city and suburbs. And we do not say that it ought to ring unless it be for some terrible fire burning any row of houses within the said city, or for any common contention whereby the city might be terribly moved, or for any enemies drawing near unto the city, or if the city shall be besieged, or any sedition shall be between any, and notice thereof given by any unto the chief bailiff. And in these cases aforesaid, and in all like cases, all manner of men abiding within the city and suburbs and liberties of the city, of what degree soever they be, ought to come at any such ringing, or motion of ringing, with such weapons as fit their degree, etc.

HENRY II, 1154–89

Henry II's grandmother was Henry I's queen, Matilda. Her daughter, the Empress Matilda, took for her second husband Geoffrey, Count of Anjou, ten years her junior. As lord of Anjou, Touraine and Maine, he rivalled the ruler of Normandy and England. In May 1152 Henry added the duchy of Aquitaine to his dominions by marrying Eleanor of Aquitaine, and in November 1153 by the Treaty of Wallingford, he was adopted heir of King Stephen.

Source: Walter Map, *De Nugis Curialium*, translated by M. R. James, Cymmrodorion Record Series, no. ix, 1923, p. 261. Map, a witty courtier of Henry II, became Archdeacon of Oxford when Henry died.

Further Reading: J. E. A. Joliffe, *Angevin Kingship*, 1955.

I saw the beginning of his reign and his subsequent life, which in many respects was commendable. He was taller than the tallest men of middle height, and was blessed with soundness of limb and comeliness of face, one, in fact, whom men flocked to gaze upon, though they had scrutinized him a thousand times already. In agility of limb he was second to none, failing in no feat which anyone else could perform; with no polite accomplishment was he unacquainted; he had skill of letters as far as was fitting or practically useful, and had a knowledge of all the tongues used from the French sea to the Jordan, but spoke only Latin and French. He had discretion in the making of laws and the ordering of all his government, and was a clever deviser of decisions in unusual and dark cases: affable, sober, and modest: tolerant of the discomforts of dust and mud; when oppressed by importunate complaints or provoked by abuse, bearing it all in silence. On the other hand, he was always on the move, travelling in unbearably long stages, like a post, and in this respect merciless beyond measure to the household that accompanied him: a great connoisseur of hounds and hawks, and most greedy of that vain sport; perpetually wakeful and at work. . . . This same King Henry was a man of many and large and fat almsdeeds, but in secret, lest it should be known to his left hand what his right hand gave. . . .

There is a fault which, as I have already said, he contracted from his mother's teaching: he is wasteful of time over the affairs of his people, and so it comes about that many die before they get their matters settled, or leave the court depressed and penniless, driven by hunger. Another fault is that when he makes a stay anywhere (away from home), which rarely occurs, he does not allow himself to be seen as honest men would have him do, but shuts himself up within, and is only accessible to those who seem unworthy of such ready access. There is a third fault, that he is intolerant of quiet and does not in pity refrain from troubling almost half of Christendom. In these three ways he goes wrong: in other respects he is very good, and in all amiable. There does not seem to be anyone beside him possessed of such temper and affability. Whatever way he goes out he is seized upon by the crowds and pulled hither and thither, pushed whither he would not, and surprising to say, listens to each man with patience, and though assaulted by all with shouts and pullings and rough pushings, does not challenge anyone for it, nor show any appearance of anger, and when he is hustled beyond bearing silently retreats to some place of quiet. He does nothing in a proud or overbearing fashion, is sober, modest, pious, trustworthy and careful, generous and successful, and ready to honour the deserving.

Some time ago I crossed the Channel with him with twenty-five ships which had the obligation of carrying him over without payment. But a storm scattered them all and drove them upon rocks and shores unmeet for ships, except his own, which by God's grace was conveyed into harbour. So in the morning he sent, and to each sailor restored the estimated amount of his loss, though he was not obliged to do so; and the whole sum came to a large amount; and perhaps there have been kings who have not paid even their just debts. . . .

A clever workman had taken an impression of the king's seal in pitch, and had made a copper seal so exactly like it that no one could see the difference. When this became known to the king, he ordered the man to be hanged: but he saw a venerable man, good and virtuous, the brother of the criminal, weeping with covered head, and was straightway overcome with pity, and made more account of the goodness of the virtuous man than of the villainy of the culprit, and with tears restored joy to the tearful one. However, when the thief was set free, he ordered him to be confined in a monastery, lest his pity should appear more indulgent than was right.

This lord king was served by a certain clerk, who has written these matters for you, whose surname was Map. He was dear and acceptable to the king, not for his own merits, but for those of his forebears who had been faithful and useful to the king, both before his accession and after it.

NORTHERN GOSSIP ABOUT DEER-HUNTING IN SCOTLAND, 1165

Game formed an important source of food, and consumption by large households was enormous. Much of the countryside was wooded and royal forests were subject to special laws in order to protect the game for royal needs. In the forests might lurk outlaws like Robin Hood.

Source: Reginald, monk of Durham, *Libellus de admirandis Beati Cuthberti virtutibus*, summarized in Surtees Soc., 1834, i, 311. The Surtees Society is a pioneer among local societies which publish for their members' subscriptions volumes of local or particular interest which could not be published commercially. Reginald was encouraged to write by Ethelred Abbot of Rievaulx. His simple faith, condemned by his editor as ' excessive credulity ', enables him to record faithfully the superstitious hearsay of his time and his writing is full of intimate glimpses of everyday life. The edition concludes with ' Historical notices, illustrations of manners, customs, etc. contained in each chapter of Reginald '.

Further Reading: The periodical publications of the local archaeological and record societies. A bibliography of all these is shortly to be published by the Royal Historical Society.

Chapters 86–8. Robert Fitz Philip, a Knight of the Lothian district, a person who had obtained his rank of nobility, not on account of his character for good moral conduct for charity, but on account of his riches alone—goes, in the year 1165, in the month of September, a deer-hunting—Deer then fat and easily taken—Finds a stag (upon the description of which Reginald bestows much pains, and proves that he knew something of venison—The picture which he draws is extremely animated)— The stag, hard pressed, takes refuge in a neighbouring churchyard, where he is suffered by the hunters to remain unhurt. . . . A multitude assembles, it being a festival, to see the stag in his sanctuary—The weather being fine, some began to dance, and leap, and sport, and put the stone, and joke and sing, whilst others were spectators of the amusements—With a few, the stag, reposing in the porch of the church, was the sole object of attraction—At last, an indiscreet lad, instigated by a profane person older than himself, attacks it with a stake—The stag, roused from its resting-place, bounds into the midst of a party of dancers, and, after goring to death the son of the person who had advised the lad to disturb it, bounds over the wall of the churchyard, and on its road to the woods is killed by its original pursuers, who, hearing, however, of the death which it had just occasioned, leave it upon the spot as a homicide, not to be eaten.

Half a year afterward, at the time of summer spring, a maker of combs, draughtsmen, chessmen, dice, spigots, etc., belonging to a neighbouring village, finds the remains of the animal, and attempts to cut off its horns, to be used as materials in his trade—Some curious information respecting the then forest laws . . . Aethelred, abbot of Rievaulx, goes into Lothian, visits Melrose, and hears the particulars of this . . . from Philip, the Knight himself, who had married his niece.

Chapter 90. King Stephen . . . his patience and clemency—England in consequence overrun with thieves—one district invading another—Roger Pavie, constable of Thirsk castle, makes an inroad into the county of Durham—William, surnamed Sergant (surnames then in use), who lived at Hartburne (near Stockton) flees for safety with forty oxen towards the churchyard of Sadberg—Rides a bad horse, and in consequence, falls into the hands of the marauders along with his cattle—Carried prisoner to Thirsk castle along with others, and put into wooden stocks, where they are closely kept, and badly fed—They offer a ransom, but in vain—Sergant had been previously employed about Durham Cathedral.

Chapters 91–2. During the time of Hugh, Bishop of Durham, William, Archbishop of York, visits the Shrine of St. Cuthbert for devotional purposes—The Bishop exhibits to his guest the more precious relics of the church, and among others, the book of St. Cuthbert (produced by Benedict, the Sacrist, arrayed in his alb), which he suspends round his neck by a string—The Archbishop takes the book and opens it, and turns over the pages, and hangs it round the neck of his domestics and friends—Brother John, then the Sacrist, had never seen the book opened before—The duties of the Sacrist—The book kept in three bags, one inclosed within another made of red leather—Alan, then Subprior, takes his nap after dinner—The Monks had a room called the *collocutorium*—Their Infirmary.

Whitsuntide at Durham—The Pontifical benediction—Forty days' indulgence—Great concourse of people—The monks ornament the walls of the church for the occasion. The young men of Durham great adepts in bell-ringing from frequent practice—The great bell tower, its floor, etc., described—The tongue of one of the bells falls through the floor, upon the head of a young man, called Wictred, and fractures his skull.

Chapter 93. A person unknown attacks Rodbert, brother of Osbern, the Sheriff, and cuts a large slice from his head—Ralph Fitz William, one of the nobles of the Palatinate (and ancestor of the Surteeses, of Dinsdale), suspects one of his tenants, William, the miller, of Thorp, near Sedgfield—Seizes him, and brings him in chains to Durham—The feudal system—The miserable state of the accused person whilst confined in prison—Ralph, the town crier, then gaoler.

Chapter 94. A foreigner, in consequence of having shed the blood of a kinsman, wears a girdle round his waist made of the sword with which he had committed the crime—His miserable condition from want of rest, occasioned by the eating of the iron into his body, and the intense pain which it occasioned—Goes to Durham, finds Bishop Pudsey celebrating mass in the Cathedral.

Chapter 95. Christian, the Durham mint-master, rents a mine of the Bishop (perhaps a lead mine from which silver might be obtained by refining for coinage)—Finds a person who was reported to have discovered a treasure which of right belonged to the Bishop, in his capacity of Count Palatine—Commits him to the Bishop's prison within the Castle, and informs the Sheriff and other officers, who, hoping to obtain a share of the wealth which was believed to have been discovered, load the poor man with fetters and chains of more than usual weight, and threaten him with the ' judiciale examen ' (an appeal to personal, or some other mode of feudal purgation). . . .

Chapter 98. A Monk (sent by Hugh Pudsey, the Bishop) and his companions go to Dunfermline on the festival of St. Margaret, Queen of Scotland, who was buried there—In the procession, the relics of St. Cuthbert permitted to precede those of the Queen—The history of her life—Her gift to the Monks of Durham of a copy of the Gospels in letters of silver, a cross sparkling with gems and other precious stones, etc., etc.—The Monk of Durham preaches to the people—An insane person, whose malady is described, gapes like a crow in hot weather—St. Andrews. . . .

Chapters 102 and 111. Farne.—A man belonging to Dunbar, in the Lothian district, whose character for piety, for unlimited charity, and for extreme resignation under a grievous disease, is

vigorously drawn, a tenant of Earl Cospatric, who, out of respect
to him, lets him live rent free, has sons who subscribe, along with
others, to buy a ship at Newcastle—A deputation sent to purchase
the ship—As the sons are engaged at home, the father goes in
their stead—The ship bought, and driven by stress of weather
to Farne, on its way to Dunbar—The Guest House at Farne, and
the large stones of which it was built—It had stood from the time
of Cuthbert. . . . Bartholomew, the Monk there, has a little
tame bird which had dwelt with him for a long time, and which
affords him and those who were with him much amusement. . . .
The bird killed by a hawk during the absence of Bartholomew,
who had been obliged to sail across to one of the adjacent
islands.

BECKET'S EMBASSY TO PARIS, 1158

The embassy was to ask for the hand of the French king's daughter for the son of Henry II. Here is a picture of Becket, as the king's
trusted agent. Later he became archbishop and found a different
loyalty.

Source: William FitzStephen, in *Materials for the History of Becket*.
FitzStephen's claim to be Becket's best biographer is supported by
his words ' I was the fellow citizen of my lord, his chaplain, and of
his household, called by his mouth to be a sharer of his cares. I was
his remembrancer in the chancery, in chapel, when he celebrated I
was sub-deacon; when he sat to hear causes I was the reader of the
letters and documents that were put in, and, at his command, sometimes the advocate of certain causes. I was present with him at the
Council of Northampton, where matters of so great import occurred;
I saw his passion at Canterbury, and many other things which are here
written I saw with my own eyes and heard with my ears; others again
I learnt from those who witnessed them.' Translated by W. H.
Hutton, *S. Thomas from the Contemporary Biographers*, English History
by Contemporary Writers, D. Nutt, 1889, p. 23.

Further Reading: H. W. C. Davis, *England under the Normans and
Angevins* 1062–1272, 1905.

He had above two hundred on horseback, of his own household, knights, clerks, butlers, serving men, esquires, sons of the
nobles trained by him in arms, all in fit order. These and all

their following shone in new holiday attire, each according to his rank. For he had four-and-twenty changes of raiment ' whose texture mocks the purple dyes of Tyre ', many garments entirely of silk—almost all to be given away and left over sea— and every sort of material, griese and furs, of robes also and carpets, such as those with which the chamber and bed of a bishop are wont to be adorned. He had with him hounds, and birds of all kinds, such as kings and nobles keep. He had also in his company eight carriages, each drawn by five horses, in size and strength like destriers, for each one being set apart a strong young man, girt in a new tunic, walking by the carriage; and each carriage had its driver and guard. Two carriages bore nothing but beer, made by a decoction of water from the strength of corn, in iron-hooped barrels—to be given to the Franks who admire that sort of drink, which is wholesome, clear, of the colour of wine, and of a better taste. One carriage was used for the chancellor's chapel furniture, one for his chamber, one his bursary, one his kitchen. Others carried different kinds of meat and drink; some had the hangings, bags with his nightgowns, packs and baggage. He had twelve sumpter-horses, and eight chests containing the chancellor's plate, of gold and silver; vessels, cups, platters, goblets, pitchers, basons, saltcellars, tankards, salvers, dishes. Other coffers and packs contained the chancellor's money—coin enough for daily expenses and presents— his clothes, books, and such-like. One sumpter-horse going before the others bore the sacred vessels of the chapel, the ornaments and books of the altar. Each of the sumpter-horses had its own groom provided as was meet. Each wagon had a dog chained above or below, great, strong and terrible, which seemed able to subdue a bear or a lion. And on the back of each sumpter-horse was a tailed monkey, or ' the ape that mocked the human face.' At this entry of the French villages and castles first came footboys, ' born to eat up the land ' [Horace]—about two hundred and fifty—going six or ten or even more abreast, singing something in their own tongue, after the fashion of their land. There followed at some distance hounds in couples, and greyhounds in leash, with huntsmen and keepers. Then there rattled over the stones of the streets the iron-bound wagons covered with great hides sewn together. Then at a little distance the sumpter-horses, their grooms riding on them, with their knees on the flanks of the horses. Some of the Franks rushing forth from their houses at this great noise asked who this was, and whose the train? They answered that it was the chancellor of the king of the English going on an embassy to the king of the Franks. Then said the Franks, ' Marvellous is the king of the English whose chancellor goeth thus and so grandly.' Then the squires carrying the shields of the knights and leading their destriers; then other squires, of fresh youth, and those who carried hawks on their wrist; after them the butlers, and masters, and servants of the chancellor's house; then the knights and clerks, riding all two and two; last, the chancellor and some of his nearest friends.

HERETICS BEATEN, 1166

St. Germanus of Auxerre visited in Britain in 429 and 447 to fight the heresy of Pelagius, but until the fourteenth century the country was remarkably free from heresy. Foreign heretics were easily discouraged, as here related, by a Great Council at Oxford in 1166, a citizen of Amiens was burnt in London in 1210 and a leader of the Pastoureaux was torn to pieces for trying to convert rustics at Shoreham.

Source: William of Newburgh, *History of England*, one of the best contemporary sources for 1154-70.

William was born at Bridlington, Yorkshire, in 1135 or 1136, and after marrying an heiress with property in Oxfordshire about 1154, left her to become an Augustinian canon at Newburgh in 1180. His impartiality has been admired, though of course it would not be fair to expect such a quality in describing heretics. William's youth, like his old age, was spent at Newburgh, but Dr. Salter has shown that in 1170-3 he was near Thame in south Oxfordshire, where he knew a lay brother, and was probably the same as that William Fitz-Ellis, who gave Waterperry church to Oseney Abbey about 1175-8 before entering Newburgh Priory where his brother was Prior. The point is overlooked in *English Historical Documents* and elsewhere, where it is said that his life was apparently wholly spent in Durham and Yorkshire, but it is interesting as it suggests that vivid touches in his account of the heretics at Oxford may have been due to the presence as an eyewitness in Oxford of the scholarly ancestor of the medieval squires of Waterperry, halfway between Thame and Oxford.

Translated in D. C. Douglas and G. W. Greenaway, *English Historical Documents* 1042–1189, 1953, p. 329.

Further Reading: J. Stevenson's translation of William of Newburgh in *Church Historians of England*, iv, pt. ii, 1856.

There were, however, rather more than thirty persons, both men and women, who, dissimulating their errors, came hither as if in peace for the purpose of propagating their noxious teaching, their leader being a certain Gerard, whom they all looked up to as teacher and master; for he alone among them had a smattering of learning, but the others were ignorant folk, unlettered and wholly uncultivated, peasants of German race and tongue. Sojourning for some time in England they only deceived one wretched woman with their lying whispers, and, so it is said, having bewitched her with certain spells they joined her to their coterie. For they could not long lie hidden but were detected by certain men curious to explore to what strange sect they belonged, then seized and held in public custody. The king, however, being unwilling either to discharge them or to punish them without examination, ordered an episcopal synod to meet at Oxford. Here they were solemnly charged concerning their religion; the one among them who seemed literate, undertaking their common defence and speaking for them all, replied that they were Christians and reverenced the apostolic teaching. Interrogated successively concerning the articles of the Holy Faith, they answered rightly concerning the nature of Christ, the heavenly Physician; but concerning the saving remedies whereby he condescends to heal our human infirmity, that is, the Divine Sacraments, they answered perversely. Holy Baptism, the Eucharist, and Holy Matrimony they abhorred, and the Catholic unity sustained by these divine aids they wickedly dared to disparage When they were pressed by texts taken from Holy Scripture, they answered they believed what they had been taught but were unwilling to dispute about their faith. Admonished that they should do penance and be united to the body of the Church, they spurned all sound advice. They laughed at the threats, with which in all piety they were confronted to induce them to recover their senses through fear; making wrongful use of the Lord's words: ' Blessed are they which are persecuted for righteousness' sake, for theirs is the kingdom of heaven.' Wherefore, lest the poison of heresy should be more widely dispersed, the bishops took the precaution of having the accused publicly proclaimed heretics and handed them over to the king to be subjected to corporal punishment. He commanded that the mark of heretical infamy should be branded upon their foreheads and in the sight of the people they should be beaten with rods and expelled from the city, sternly forbidding anyone to presume to offer them hospitality or supply any comfort. Sentence having been passed, they vere led away rejoicing to suffer just punishment, their master marching in front with rapid strides and chanting, ' Blessed are ye when men shall revile you.' To such an extent did this deceiver mislead the minds of those seduced by him. The woman, however, whom they had perverted in England, deserted them through fear of punishment and on confession of her error obtained pardon and reconciliation. Next this hateful band were branded upon their foreheads and suffered stern justice. To mark his primacy of office their chief endured the shame of being twice branded, first on his forehead and then on his chin. Then with their clothes cut off to the waist they were publicly flogged and with resounding blows driven forth from the city into the intolerable cold, for it was winter-time. None shewed the slightest pity on them and they perished miserably. This pious severity not only purged the realm of England of this pest which had lately crept into it, but also prevented further inroads through the terror stricken into the heretics. . . .

MURDER OF THOMAS BECKET, 29 December, 1170

The organization of the royal court with increasing efficiency in the administration of justice led to a conflict between the Archbishop of Canterbury, Thomas Becket, and King Henry II, for the Church was a highly organized and ancient institution with its own courts. Thomas failed in an attempt to get his predecessor Anselm canonized as a Saint, but his struggle with the King ended in himself winning a martyr's crown.

Source: Edward Grim's eyewitness account in *Materials for the History of Becket*, Rolls Series, 1875–85, translated by the Rev. W. H. Hutton in *S. Thomas from the Contemporary Biographers*, English History by Contemporary Writers, D. Nutt, 1889, p. 240. Grim was the only man present at the murder who tried to prevent it. He was badly wounded, but he heard the saint's last words and wrote his story between five and seven years later.

Further Reading: W. Stubbs, *The Constitutional History of England*, 1883.

. . . When the monks had entered the church, already the four knights followed behind with rapid strides. With them was a certain subdeacon, armed with malice like their own, Hugh, fitly surnamed for his wickedness Mauclerc, who showed no reverence for God or the saint, as the result showed. When the holy archbishop entered the church, the monks stopped vespers which they had begun and ran to him, glorifying God that they saw their father, whom they had heard was dead, alive and safe. They hastened, by bolting the doors of the church, to protect their shepherd from the slaughter. But the champion, turning to them, ordered the church doors to be thrown open, saying, ' It is not meet to make a fortress of the house of prayer, the church of Christ: though it be not shut up it is able to protect its own; and we shall triumph over the enemy rather in suffering than in fighting, for we came to suffer, not to resist.' And straightway they entered the house of prayer and reconciliation with swords sacrilegiously drawn, causing horror to the beholders by their very looks and the clanging of their arms.

All who were present were in tumult and fright, for those who had been singing vespers now ran hither to the dreadful sight.

Inspired by fury the knights called out, ' Where is Thomas Becket, traitor to the king and realm? ' As he answered not, they cried out the more furiously, ' Where is the archbishop? ' At this, intrepid and fearless, as it is written, ' The just, like a bold lion, shall be without fear,' he descended from the stair where he had been dragged by the monks in fear of the knights, and in a clear voice answered ' I am here, no traitor to the king, but a priest. Why do ye seek me? ' And whereas he had already said that he feared them not, he added, ' So I am ready to suffer in

His name, Who redeemed me by His Blood: be it far from me
to flee from your swords, or to depart from justice.' Having thus
said, he turned to the right, under a pillar, having on one side the
altar of the blessed Mother of God and ever Virgin Mary, on
the other that of S. Benedict the Confessor: by whose example
and prayers, having crucified the world with its lusts, he bore all
that the murderers could do with such constancy of soul as if
he had been no longer in the flesh. The murderers followed him;
'Absolve,' they cried, 'and restore to communion those whom
you have excommunicated, and restore their powers to those
whom you have suspended.' He answered: ' There has been no
satisfaction, and I will not absolve them.' ' Then you shall die,'
they cried, ' and receive what you deserve.' ' I am ready,' he
replied, ' to die for my Lord, that in my blood the Church may
obtain liberty and peace. But in the name of Almighty God, I
forbid you to hurt my people whether clerk or lay.' Thus
piously and thoughtfully, did the noble martyr provide that no
one near him should be hurt or the innocent be brought to death,
whereby his glory should be dimmed as he hastened to Christ.
Thus did it become the martyr-knight to follow in the footsteps
of his Captain and Saviour Who when the wicked sought Him
said: ' If ye seek Me, let these go their way.' Then they laid
sacrilegious hands on him, pulling and dragging him that they
might kill him outside the Church, or carry him away a prisoner,
as they afterwards confessed. But when he could not be forced
away from the pillar, one of them pressed on him and clung to
him more closely. Him he pushed off calling him ' pander ',
and saying, ' Touch me not, Reginald; you owe me fealty and
subjection; you and your accomplices act like madmen.' The
knight, fired with terrible rage at this severe repulse, waved his
sword over the sacred head. ' No faith ', he cried, ' nor subjection
do I owe you against my fealty to my lord the king.' Then the
unconquered martyr seeing the hour at hand which should put
an end to this miserable life and give him straightway the crown
of immortality promised by the Lord, inclined his neck as one
who prays and joining his hands he lifted them up, and commended his cause and that of the Church of God, to S. Mary, and
to the blessed martyr Denys. Scarce had he said the words than

the wicked knight fearing lest he should be rescued by the people and escape alive, leapt upon him suddenly and wounded this lamb, who was sacrificed to God, on the head, cutting off the top of the crown which the sacred unction of chrism had dedicated to God; and by the same blow he wounded the arm of him who tells this. For he, when the others, both monks and clerks, fled, stuck close to the sainted archbishop and held him in his arms till the one he interposed was almost severed. . . .

Then he received a second blow on the head but still stood firm. At the third blow he fell on his knees and elbows, offering himself a living victim, and saying in a low voice, ' For the Name of Jesus and the protection of the Church I am ready to embrace death.' Then the third knight inflicted a terrible wound as he lay, by which the sword was broken against the pavement, and the crown which was large was separated from the head; so that the blood white with the brain and the brain red with blood, dyed the surface of the virgin mother Church with the life and death of the confessor and martyr in the colours of the lily and the rose. The fourth knight prevented any from interfering so that the others might freely perpetrate the murder. As to the fifth, no knight but that clerk who had entered with the knights, that a fifth blow might not be wanting to the martyr who was in other things like to Christ, he put his foot on the neck of the holy priest and precious martyr, and, horrible to say, scattered his brains and blood over the pavement, calling out to the others, ' Let us away, knights; he will rise no more.'

ST. THOMAS THE MARTYR, 1170

Becket was martyred significantly as it seemed, on 29 December, the day next that of the Holy Innocents.

Further Reading: E. A. Abbott, *St. Thomas of Canterbury, his Death and Miracles*, 1898.

Source: Benedict of Peterborough, translated in D. C. Douglas and G. W. Greenaway, *English Historical Documents* 1042–1189, Eyre and Spottiswoode 1953, p. 768.

While the body still lay on the pavement, some of them [Canterbury townsfolk] smeared their eyes with blood. Others brought bottles and carried off secretly as much of it as they could. Others cut off shreds of clothing and dipped them in the blood. At a later time no one was thought happy who had not carried off something from the precious treasure of the martyr's body. And indeed with everything in such a state of confusion and tumult, each man could do as he pleased. Some of the blood left over was carefully and cleanly collected and poured into a clean vessel and treasured up in the church. The archbishop's pallium and outer vesture, stained with blood, were with indiscreet piety given to the poor to pray for his soul, and happy would it have been for them, if they had not with inconsiderate haste sold them for a paltry sum of money. . . . [The monks prepare a speedy burial.] They therefore stripped him of his outer garments to put on him his pontifical vestments; in so doing they discovered that the body was covered in a hair-shirt, no less painful from its stiffness than from other causes [i.e. lice, according to Grim] and—a circumstance of which we have neither read nor heard of an example in the case of any other saint—they found the body covered in sackcloth, even from the thighs down to the knees, beneath the cowl and robe of the Cistercian habit. At this sight the monks gazed at one another, astounded at this proof of a hidden piety greater than would have been credited the archbishop. . . .

PENANCE OF HENRY II, 12 July, 1174

Should the King or the Church judge clerks who did wrong?

Henry II and Thomas Becket struggled over the question of ' criminous clerks '. As a martyr Becket became more formidable than in life, and as a symbol of ecclesiastical independence of the State his ghost was to stand in the way of Henry VIII when he claimed to be head of the Church; and Henry VIII was determined to eradicate a cult which had arisen in 1174 and had attracted Chaucer's famous pilgrims to Canterbury. Pious eyewitnesses noted that Henry II's painful humiliation at Canterbury was rewarded in this world on the following day by the defeat and capture at Alnwick of William, King of Scots.

Source: Gervase of Canterbury, *Chronicles*, translated by D. C. Douglas and G. W. Greenaway, *English Historical Documents*, 1042–

1189, Eyre and Spottiswoode 1953, p. 775. Gervase was a monk at Christ Church, Canterbury, from 1163 to 1210 who wrote merely ' for you, brother Thomas, and our humble community.'

Further Reading: Z. N. Brooke, *The English Church and the Papacy*, Cambridge 1931. M. D. Knowles, *Archbishop Thomas Becket: a Character Study*, British Academy, 1949. W. H. Hutton, *Thomas Becket*, 2nd ed., Cambridge 1926.

So then, the king returned to England at the beginning of July [1174]. Taught by good advice he postponed dealing with nearly every matter of State, and immediately on landing set out with a penitent heart to the tomb of St. Thomas of Canterbury. Accordingly on Saturday, 12 July, he left the church of St. Dunstan, which is sited a good distance outside the city, and walked barefoot and clad in a woollen smock all the way to the martyr's tomb. There he lay prostrate for a great while and in devout humility, and of his own free will was scourged by all the bishops and abbots there present and each individual monk of the church of Canterbury. There he remained, constant in prayer before the holy martyr all that day and night. He neither took food nor went out to relieve nature, but, as he had come, so he remained, and would not permit a rug or anything of the kind to be provided for him. After lauds he made a tour of the altars in the choir of the church and the bodies of the saints interred there, and then returned to the tomb of St. Thomas in the crypt. At dawn on Sunday he heard Mass. Last of all he drank of water [from the well] of the holy martyr and was honoured with the gift of a phial [of the martyr's blood?]. So he departed from Canterbury rejoicing, reaching London on the Sunday.

THE EXCHEQUER, 1176—9

Kings needed money and had an office to manage its collection. Modern historians have studied deeply the ways officials worked and need to understand administrative procedure properly in order to get the real meaning of the records which survive from medieval government offices. Among such records the most important sources for studying the twelfth century are the Pipe Rolls which record the work of the Exchequer.

Source: Richard fitz Nigel, *The Course of the Exchequer* edited and translated by C. Johnson, Nelson's Medieval Classics, 1950, p. 6. This description of the Exchequer, in dialogue form, was written before 1179 as a result of a request to the author made ' in the twenty-third year of King Henry II, as I was sitting at a turret window over-looking the Thames '. Richard's father had been Treasurer of Henry I and had restored the office for Henry II after the anarchy. Richard became Treasurer about 1158.

Further Reading: R. L. Poole, *The Exchequer in the Twelfth Century*, Oxford 1912. T. F. Tout, *Chapters in the Administrative History of Medieval England*, Manchester 1920.

Scholar. What is the Exchequer?

Master. The Exchequer [chess-board] is an oblong board measuring about ten feet by five, used as a table by those who sit at it, and with a rim round it about four finger-breadths in height, to prevent anything set on it from falling off. Over the [upper] Exchequer is spread a cloth, bought in Easter term, of a special pattern, black, ruled with lines a foot, or a full span, apart. In the spaces between them are placed the counters, in their ranks, as will be explained in another place. But though such a board is called ' Exchequer ', the name is transferred to the Court in session at it; so that if a litigant wins his case, or a decision on any point is taken by common consent, it is said to have happened ' at the Exchequer ' of such a year. But where we now say ' at the Exchequer ', they used to say ' at the Tallies'.

Scholar. Why is the Court so called?

Master. I can think, for the moment, of no better reason than that it resembles a chess-board.

Scholar. Was its shape the only reason why our wise fore-fathers gave it that name? For they might equally well have called it a draught-board.

Master. I was justified in calling you ' precise '. There is another less obvious reason. For as on the chess-board the men are arranged in ranks, and move or stand by definite rules and restrictions, some pieces in the foremost rank and others in the foremost position; here, too, some [the barons] preside, others assist *ex officio*, and nobody is free to overstep the appointed laws, as will appear later. Again, just as on a chess-board, battle is joined between the kings; here too the struggle takes place, and battle is joined, mainly between two persons, to wit, the Treasurer and the Sheriff who sits at his account, while the rest sit by as judges to see and decide.

BOYHOOD OF GERALD OF WALES

Gerald was born between 1145 and 1147. He wrote eyewitness accounts of his times.

Source: *The Autobiography of Giraldus Cambrensis* edited and translated by H. E. Butler, Jonathan Cape, 1937.

Concerning the birth of Giraldus and the deeds of his boyhood and youth.

Giraldus was born in South Wales on the sea-coast of Dyfed, not far from the chief town of Pembroke, in the Castle of Manorbier. He came of noble lineage; for his mother was Angharad, daughter of Nesta, the famous child of Rhys ap Tewdwr, Prince of South Wales, and his father was her lawful husband, the noble William de Barri. He was the youngest of four brothers ... and when the other three, preluding the pursuits of manhood in their childish play, were tracing or building, in sand or dust, now towns, now palaces, he himself, in like prophetic play, was ever busy with all his might in designing churches or building monasteries. And his father, who often saw him thus engaged, after much pondering, not unmixed with wonder, being moved by this omen, resolved with wise forethought to set him to study letters and the liberal arts, and would oft in approving jest call him ' his Bishop '.

Now it happened that one night, when the country was disturbed by a raid of the enemy, and all the young men of the castle sprang to arms, the boy on seeing this and hearing the tumult burst into tears and, seeking some place of safety, begged that he might be carried to the church, thus with marvellous foreknowledge proclaiming that the peace of the church and the sanctuary of God's house should be the strongest and most secure place of refuge; and in truth all that heard of this thing, as soon as the tumult was abated, when they pondered on this utterance of the child and spoke of it together, called to mind with wonder that he promised greater safety for himself in a lonely church exposed to all the winds and to the strokes of chance than in a town filled with men-at-arms and strongly fortified with walls and towers. Moreover, as often as he heard disputes concerning the law of the land and the law of the Church, the boy would put himself forward with all his might as the advocate and champion of the Church, God inspiring him with the same zeal and increasing His grace day by day and enduring with him all his life even to the end. . . .

AN EISTEDFODD, 1176

Source: *Brut Y Tywysogyon or The Chronicle of the Princes*, translated by Thomas Jones, Board of Celtic Studies, University of Wales History and Law Series, no. xi, 1952, p. 71.

Further Reading: J. E. Lloyd, *History of Wales from the Earliest Times to the Edwardian Conquest*, 2 vols., 1939.

At Christmas in that year the Lord Rhys ap Gruffudd held court in splendour at Cardigan, in the castle. And he set two kinds of contests there: one between bards and poets, another between harpists and crowders and pipers and various classes of music-craft. And he had two chairs set for the victors. And he honoured those with ample gifts. And of the harpists, a young man from Rhys's court won the victory. As between the bards, those of Gwynedd prevailed. Each of the suitors obtained from Rhys that which he sought, so that no one was refused. And that feast, before it was held, was announced for a year through all Wales and England and Scotland and Ireland and the other islands.

THE WELSH, LATE Twelfth CENTURY

Source: *Gerald the Welshman, Description of Wales*, translated by Sir R. C. Hoare, 1806. Gerald told the Pope 'I am sprung from the princes of Wales and from the barons of the Marches, and when I see injustice in either race, I hate it.' But he despised the Saxons. He knew the kings and archbishops of his time and his methods are those of an observant journalist.

Further Reading: W. Ll. Williams, *Making of Modern Wales*, 1919. J. Rhys and D. Brynmor-Jones, *The Welsh People*, 1923.

(1) *Warriors.*

They make use of light arms, which do not impede their agility, small coats of mail, bundles of arrows, and long lances, helmets and shields, and more rarely greaves plated with iron. The higher class go to battle mounted on swift and generous steeds, which their country produces; but the greater part of the people fight on foot, on account of the marshy nature and unevenness of the soil. The horsemen, as their situation or occasion requires, willingly serve as infantry, in attacking or retreating; and they either walk bare-footed, or make use of high shoes, roughly constructed with untanned leather. In time of peace, the young men, by penetrating the deep recesses of the woods, and climbing the tops of mountains, learn by practice to endure fatigue through day and night; and as they meditate on war during peace, they acquire the art of fighting by accustoming themselves to the use of the lance, and by inuring themselves to hard exercise. . . .

Not addicted to gluttony or drunkenness, this people who incur no expense in food or dress, and whose minds are always bent upon the defence of their country, and on the means of plunder, are wholly employed in the care of their horses and furniture. Accustomed to fast from morning till evening, and trusting to the care of Providence, they dedicate the whole day to business, and in the evening partake of a moderate meal; and even if they have none, or only a very scanty one, they patiently wait till the next evening; and, neither deterred by cold nor hunger, they employ the dark and stormy nights in watching the hostile motions of their enemies.

(2) *Genealogists.*

The Welsh esteem noble birth and generous descent above all things, and are, therefore, more desirous of marrying into noble than rich families. Even the common people retain their genealogy, and can not only readily recount the names of their grandfathers and great-grandfathers, but even refer back to the sixth or seventh generation, or beyond them, in this manner; Rhys, son of Gruffyd, son of Rhys, son of Tewdwr, son of Eineon, son of Owen, son of Howel, son of Cadell, son of Roderic Mawr, and so on.

Being particularly attached to family descent, they revenge with vehemence the injuries which may tend to the disgrace of their blood; and being naturally of a vindictive and passionate disposition, they are ever ready to avenge not only recent but ancient affronts; they neither inhabit towns, villages, nor castles, but lead a solitary life in the woods, on the borders of which they do not erect sumptuous palaces, nor lofty stone buildings, but content themselves with small huts made of the boughs of trees twisted together, constructed with little labour and expense, and sufficient to endure throughout the year. They have neither orchards nor gardens, but gladly eat the fruit of both when given to them. The greater part of their land is laid down to pasturage; little is cultivated, a very small quantity is ornamented with flowers, and a still smaller is sown.

(3) Hosts.

No one of this nation ever begs, for the houses of all are common to all; and they consider liberality and hospitality amongst the first virtues. So much does hospitality here rejoice in communication, that it is neither offered nor requested by travellers, who, on entering a house, only deliver up their arms. When water is offered to them, if they suffer their feet to be washed, they are received as guests: for the offer of water to wash the feet is with this nation an hospitable invitation. But if they refuse the proffered service, they only wish for morning refreshment, not lodging. The young men move about in troops and families under the direction of a chosen leader, Attached only to arms and ease, and ever ready to stand forth in defence of their country, they have free admittance into every house as if it were their own.

Those who arrive in the morning are entertained till evening with the conversation of young women, and the music of the harp; for each house has its young women and harps allotted to this purpose. . . . The kitchen does not supply many dishes, nor high-seasoned incitements to eating. The house is not furnished with tables, cloths or napkins. . . . They place dishes before them [guests] all at once upon rushes and fresh grass, in large platters or trenchers. They also make use of a thin and broad cake of bread, baked every day . . . and they sometimes add chopped meat, with broth. . . . While the family is engaged in waiting on the guests, the host and hostess stand up, paying unremitting attention to everything. and take no food till all the company are satisfied; that in case of any deficiency, it may fall upon them. A bed made of rushes, and covered with a coarse kind of cloth manufactured in the country, called *brychan* [blanket] is then placed along the side of the room, and they all in common lie down to sleep; nor is their dress at night different from that by day, for at all seasons they defend themselves from the cold only by a thin cloak and tunic. The fire continues to burn by night as well as by day, at their feet, and they receive much comfort from the natural heat of the persons lying near them; but when the under side begins to be tired with the hardness of the bed, or the upper one to suffer from cold, they immediately leap up, and go to the fire, which soon relieves them from both inconveniences; and then returning to their couch, they expose alternately their sides to the cold, and to the hardness of the bed. . . .

The heads of different families, in order to excite the laughter of their guests, and gain credit by their sayings, make use of great facetiousness in their conversation; at one time uttering their jokes in a light, easy manner, at another time, under the disguise of equivocation, passing the severest censures. . . .

(4) *Patriots.*

If the Welsh were more commonly accustomed to the Gallic mode of arming, and depended more on steady fighting than on their agility; if their princes were unanimous and inseparable in their defence; or rather, if they had only one prince, and that a good one; this nation, situated in so powerful, strong and inaccessible a country, could hardly ever be completely overcome. If, therefore, they would be inseparable, they would become insuperable, being assisted by these three circumstances; a country well defended by nature, a people both contented and accustomed to live upon little, a community whose nobles as well as privates are instructed in the use of arms; and especially as the English fight for power, the Welsh for liberty; the one to procure gain, the other to avoid loss; the English hirelings for money, the Welsh patriots for their country. . . . For the perpetual remembrance of their former greatness, the recollection of their Trojan descent, and the high and continued majesty of the kingdom of Britain, may draw forth many a latent rebellion. Hence during the military expedition which King Henry II made in our days against South Wales, an old Welshman at Pencadair, who had faithfully adhered to him, being desired to give his opinion about the royal army, and whether he thought that of the rebels would make resistance, and what would be the final event of this war, replied, ' This nation, O King, may now, as in former times, be harassed, and in a great measure weakened and destroyed by your and other powers, and it will often prevail by its laudable exertions; but it can never be totally subdued through the wrath of man, unless the wrath of God shall concur. Nor do I think that any other nation than this of Wales, or any other language, whatever may hereafter come to pass, shall, in the day of severe examination before the Supreme Judge, answer for this corner of the earth.'

TRADE IN NORMAN LONDON

Source: *A Description of London*, by William FitzStephen, translated by H. E. Butler with *A map of London under Henry II* by Marjorie B. Honeybourne, Historical Association Leaflets, Nos. 93, 94, 1934. FitzStephen was secretary of St. Thomas Becket and wrote before 1183.

Further Reading: John Stow's *Survey of London* ed. C. L. Kingsford, 2 vols., Oxford, 1908. R. R. Sharpe, *London and the Kingdom*, 3 vols., 1894–5 (national history from London's point of view).

Those that ply their several trades, the vendors of each several thing, the hirers out of their several sorts of labour are found every morning each in their separate quarters and each engaged upon his own peculiar task. Moreover there is in London upon the river's bank, amid the wine that is sold from ships and wine-cellars, a public cook-shop. There daily, according to the season, you may find viands, dishes roast, fried and boiled, fish great and small, the coarser flesh for the poor, the more delicate for the rich, such as venison and birds both big and little. If friends, weary with travel, should of a sudden come to any of the citizens, and it is not their pleasure to wait fasting till fresh food is brought and cooked and ' till servants bring water for hands and bread ' they hasten to the river bank, and there all things desirable are ready to their hand. However great the infinitude of knights or foreigners that enter the city or are about to leave it, at whatever hour of night or day, that the former may not fast too long nor the latter depart without their dinner, they turn aside thither, if it so please them, and refresh themselves each after his own manner. . . .

In the suburb immediately outside one of the gates there is a smooth field, both in fact and in name [Smithfield]. On every sixth day of the week, unless it be a major feast-day on which solemn rites are prescribed, there is a much-frequented show of fine horses for sale. Thither come all the Earls, Barons and Knights who are in the City, and with them many of the citizens, whether to look on or buy. It is a joy to see the ambling palfreys, their skin full of juice, their coats a-glisten, as they pace softly, in alternation raising and putting down the feet on one side together; next to see the horses that best fit Esquires, moving more roughly, yet nimbly, as they raise and set down the opposite feet, fore and hind, first on one side and then on the other; then the younger colts of high breeding, unbroken and ' high-stepping with elastic tread,' and after them the costly destriers of graceful form and goodly stature, ' with quivering ears, high necks and plump buttocks.' As these show their paces, the buyers watch first their gentler gait, then that swifter motion, wherein their fore feet are thrown out and back together, and the hind feet also, as it were, counterwise. When a race between such trampling steeds is about to begin, or perchance between others which are likewise, after their kind, strong to carry, swift to run, a shout is raised, and horses of the baser sort are bidden to turn aside. Three boys riding these fleet-foot steeds, or at times two as may be agreed, prepare themselves for the contest. Skilled to command their horses, they ' curb their untamed mouths with jagged bits ', and their chief anxiety is that their rival shall not gain the lead. The horses likewise after their fashion lift up

their spirits for the race; ' their limbs tremble; impatient of delay,
they cannot stand still.' When the signal is given, they stretch
forth their limbs, they gallop away, they rush on with obstinate
speed. The riders, passionate for renown, hoping for victory,
vie with one another in spurring their swift horses and lashing
them forward with their switches no less than they excite them
by their cries. . . .

In another place apart stand the wares of the country-folk,
instruments of agriculture, long-flanked swine, cows with swollen
udders, and ' woolly flocks and bodies huge of kine.' Mares
stand there, meet for ploughs, sledges and two-horsed carts; the
bellies of some are big with young; round others move their
offspring, new-born, sprightly foals, inseparable followers.

To this city, from every nation that is under heaven, merchants
rejoice to bring their trade in ships.

LONDON SPORTS

Source: *A description of London*, by William FitzStephen translated
by H. E. Butler, Historical Association, 1934.

Further Reading: J. Strutt, *Sports and Pastimes of the People of England*,
1801. The Bodleian Library has postcards showing sports illustrated
in the 14th century ' Romance of Alexander '.

Furthermore let us consider also the sports of the City,
since it is not meet that a city should only be useful and sober,
unless it also be pleasant and merry. . . .

London in place of shows in the theatre and stage-plays
has holier plays, wherein are shown forth the miracles wrought
by Holy Confessors or the sufferings which glorified the constancy of Martyrs.

Moreover, each year upon the day called Carnival—to
begin with the sports of boys (for we were all boys once)—boys
from the schools bring fighting-cocks to their master, and the
whole forenoon is given up to boyish sport; for they have a
holiday in the schools that they may watch their cocks do battle.
After dinner all the youth of the City goes out into the fields in
a much-frequented game of ball. The scholars of each school
have their own ball, and almost all the workers of each trade have

theirs also in their hands. Elder men and fathers and rich citizens come on horseback to watch the contests of their juniors, and after their fashion are young again with the young; and it seems that the motion of their natural heat is kindled by the contemplation of such violent motion and by their partaking in the joys of untrammelled youth.

Every Sunday in Lent after dinner a ' fresh swarm of young gentles ' goes forth on war-horses, ' steeds skilled in the contest,' of which each is ' apt and schooled to wheel in circles round.' From the gates burst forth in throngs the lay sons of citizens, armed with lance and shield, the younger with shafts forked at the end, but with steel point removed. ' They wake war's semblance ' and in mimic contest exercise their skill at arms. Many courtiers come too, when the King is in residence; and from the households of Earls and Barons come young men not yet invested with the belt of knighthood, that they may there contend together. Each one of them is on fire with hope of victory. The fierce horses neigh, ' their limbs tremble; they champ the bit; impatient of delay they cannot stand still.' When at length ' the hoof of trampling steeds careers along,' the youthful riders divide their hosts; some pursue those that fly before, and cannot overtake them; others unhorse their comrades and speed by.

At the feast of Easter they make sport with naval tourneys, as it were. For a shield being strongly bound to a stout pole in mid-stream, a small vessel, swiftly driven on by many an oar and by the river's flow, carries a youth standing at the prow, who is to strike the shield with his lance. If he break the lance by striking the shield and keep his feet unshaken, he has achieved his purpose and fulfilled his desire. If, however, he strike it strongly without splintering his lance, he is thrown into the rushing river, and the boat of its own speed passes him by. But there are on each side of the shield two vessels moored, and in them are many youths to snatch up the striker who has been sucked down by the stream, as soon as he emerges into sight or ' once more bubbles on the topmost wave.' On the bridge and the galleries above the river are spectators of the sport ' ready to laugh their fill.'

On feast-days throughout the summer the youths exercise themselves in leaping, archery and wrestling, putting the stone, and throwing the thonged javelin beyond a mark, and fighting with sword and buckler. ' Cytherea leads the dance of maidens and the earth is smitten with free foot at moonrise.'

In winter on almost every feast-day before dinner either foaming boars and hogs, armed with ' tusks lightning-swift,' themselves soon to be bacon, fight for their lives, or fat bulls with butting horns, or huge bears, do combat to the death against hounds let loose upon them.

When the great marsh that washes the northern walls of the City is frozen, dense throngs of youths go forth to disport themselves upon the ice. Some gathering speed by a run, glide sidelong, with feet set well apart, over a vast space of ice. Others make themselves seats of ice like millstones and are dragged along by a number who run before them holding hands. Sometimes they slip owing to the greatness of their speed and fall, every one of them, upon their faces. Others there are, more skilled to sport upon the ice, who fit to their feet the shin-bones of beasts, lashing them beneath their ankles, and with iron-shod poles in their hands they strike ever and anon against the ice and are borne along swift as a bird in flight or a bolt shot from a mangonel. But sometimes two by agreement run one against the other from a great distance and, raising their poles, strike one another. One or both fall, not without bodily hurt, since on falling they are borne a long way in opposite directions.

. . .

Many of the citizens delight in taking their sport with birds of the air, merlins and falcons and the like, and with dogs that wage warfare in the woods. The citizens have the special privilege of hunting in Middlesex, Hertfordshire and all Chiltern, and in Kent as far as the river Cray.

CORONATION OF RICHARD I, 3 September 1189

The statesmanlike Henry II was succeeded by an absentee knight-errant whose adventures required heavy taxes. A troubadour asked ' What more can kings desire than the right to save themselves from

Hell-flames by puissant deeds of arms? ', and Philip Augustus, King of France, and Richard I, took his advice to make peace with one another and combine to go to the rescue of the Holy Sepulchre on the Third Crusade. Regents were appointed, offices were sold and debtors and Crusaders united in a massacre of the Jews. In 1194–8 the literary Peter of Blois reflected the anti-semitic spirit in his work ' Against the Perfidy of the Jews '. The worst slaughter was at York on 16 March 1190.

Richard I was only in England from 13 August to 12 December 1189 and from 13 March to 12 May 1194.

Source: *Itinerary of Richard I*, translated in *Chronicles of the Crusades*, Bohn's Antiquarian Library 1865, p. 154. The *Itinerary* was translated from the French of an unknown eyewitness into Latin by Richard, Prior of Holy Trinity, Aldgate, London. The writer says he jotted down events while ' warm ' in his memory, in the din of war.

Therefore in the same year, after the death of his father, Richard, Count of Poitou, having arranged his affairs in Normandy, in about two months crossed over to England, and on St. Giles's Day he was received at Westminster, with a ceremonious procession; and three days afterwards, viz., on the 3rd of September, the day of the ordination of St. Gregory the Pope, which was a Sunday, he was solemnly anointed king by the imposition of hands, by Archbishop Baldwin, in virtue of his office, who performed the service, assisted by many of his suffragans. At his coronation were present his brother John, and his mother Eleanor [of Aquitaine], who, after the death of King Henry, had been, by the command of her son Richard, the new king, released from prison, where she had been ten years; and there were also present counts and barons, and an immense crowd of men and soldiers; and the kingdom was confirmed to the hands of King Richard. On the 3rd day of September, in the year of our Lord 1189, Richard was anointed king, on a Sunday, with the dominical letter A., viz., in the year after leap year. Many were the conjectures made, because the day above that was marked unlucky in the calendar; and in truth it was unlucky, and very much so to the Jews in London, who were destroyed that day, and likewise the Jews settled in other parts of England endured many hardships. Having celebrated the occasion by a festival of three days, and entertained his guests in the royal palace of Westminster, King Richard gratified all,

by distributing money, without count or number, to all according
to their ranks, thus manifesting his liberality and his great
excellence. His generosity, and his virtuous endowments, the
ruler of the world should have given to the ancient times; for
in this period of the world, as it waxes old, such feelings rarely
exhibit themselves, and when they do they are subjects of wonder
and astonishment. He had the valour of Hector, the magnanimity
of Achilles, and was equal to Alexander, and not inferior to
Roland in valour; nay, he outshone many illustrious characters
of our own times. The liberality of a Titus was his, and, which
is so rarely found in a soldier, he was gifted with the eloquence
of Nestor and the prudence of Ulysses; and he shewed himself
pre-eminent in the conclusion and transaction of business, as
one whose knowledge was not without active goodwill to aid it,
nor his goodwill wanting in knowledge. Who, if Richard were
accused of presumption, would not readily excuse him, knowing
him for a man who never knew defeat, impatient of an injury,
and impelled irresistibly to vindicate his rights, though all he
did was characterized by innate nobleness of mind? Success
made him better fitted for action; fortune ever favours the bold,
and though she works her pleasure on whom she will, Richard
was never to be overwhelmed with adversity. He was tall of
stature, graceful in figure; his hair between red and auburn; his
limbs were straight and flexible; his arms rather long, and not to
be matched for wielding the sword or for striking with it; and
his long legs suited the rest of his frame; while his appearance
was commanding, and his manners and habits suitable; and he
gained the greatest celebrity, not more from his high birth than
from the virtues that adorned him. But why need we take much
labour in extolling the fame of so great a man? He needs no
superfluous commendation, for he has a sufficient need of praise,
which is the sure companion of great actions. He was far
superior to all others both in moral goodness and in strength,
and memorable for prowess in battles, and his mighty deeds
outshone the most brilliant description we could give of them.
Happy, in truth, might he have been deemed had he been without
rivals who envied his glorious actions, and whose only cause of
enmity was his magnificence, and his being the searcher after
virtue rather than the slave of vice.

RICHARD I, 1189—99

The conflict between East and West had been regarded as the main theme of history by Herodotus, the father of history in the West. By peaceful interchange the West learned much from the Arabs, indeed the very words *Chemistry* and *Algebra* are derived from the Arabs.

Source: Bohadin, a scholar who knew Saladin, and wrote a treatise on the Holy War. Translated by T. A. Archer, *The Crusade of Richard I 1189-92*, English History from Contemporary Writers, D. Nutt, 1888, p. 104.

Further Reading: T. A. Archer, *Crusade of Richard I*, London, 1888.

We must now speak of the king of England. Among our enemies he was a man of great activity, and of high soul, strong-hearted, famous for his many wars and of dauntless courage in battle. He was reckoned somewhat less than the king of the French so far as regards his royal dignity; but as much wealthier as he was more renowned for his warlike valour. . . .

RICHARD I's FLEET, 23 September, 1190

A description of the fleet with which Richard I landed at Messina on his way to the Holy Land on the Third Crusade.

Source: Richard of Devizes, *Chronicle of the Acts of Richard I*, probably written before the King was ransomed from his captivity and returned to England. Translated by T. A. Archer, *The Crusade of Richard I 1189-92*, English History from Contemporary Writers, D. Nutt, 1888, p. 22.

Further Reading: S. L. Poole, *Saladin*, London, 1898.

The ships that King Richard found ready at the sea-coast numbered one hundred together with 14 busses, vessels of vast size, wonderful speed, and great strength. They were arranged and set in order as follows. The first ship had three rudders, thirteen anchors, 30 oars, two sails, and triple ropes of every kind; moreover, it had everything that a ship can want in pairs— saving only the mast and boat. It had one very skilful captain, and fourteen chosen mariners were under his orders. The ship was laden with forty horses of price, all well trained for war, and with all kinds of arms for as many riders, for forty footmen, and fifteen sailors. Moreover it had a full year's food for all these men and horses. All the ships were laden in the same way; but each buss took double cargo and gear. The king's treasure, which was exceedingly great and of inestimable value, was divided amongst the ships and the busses so that if one part was endangered the rest might be saved.

When everything was thus arranged, the king with a small following, and the chief men of the army with their attendants, put off from the shore, preceding the fleet in galleys. Each day they touched at some sea-coast town and, taking up the larger ships and busses of that sea as they went along, reached Messina without disaster.

SIEGE OF ACRE, 1191

Richard I became king in 1189 and at once began preparations for the Third Crusade, selling crown domains and rights to raise additional money.

Source: *Itinerary of Richard I* from *Chronicles of the Crusades being contemporary narratives of the Crusade of Richard Coeur de Lion, by Richard of Devizes and Geoffrey de Vinsauf; and of the Crusade of Saint Louis by Lord John de Joinville*, Bohn's Antiquarian Library, 1865.

Further Reading: C. Oman, *Art of War in the Middle Ages*, 1885.

The king of France first recovered from his sickness, and turned his attention to the construction of machines and petrariae [artillery for throwing stones], suitable for attacks, and which he determined to ply night and day, and he had one of superior quality, to which they gave the name of 'Bad Neighbour'. The Turks also had one they called 'Bad Kinsman', which by its violent casts, often broke 'Bad Neighbour' in pieces; but the king of France rebuilt it, until by constant blows, he broke down part of the principal city wall, and shook the tower Maledictum. On one side, the petraria of the duke of Burgundy plied; on the other, that of the Templars did severe execution; while that of the Hospitallers never ceased to cast terror amongst the Turks. Besides these, there was one petraria, erected at the

common expense, which they were in the habit of calling the
' petraria of God '. Near it, there constantly preached a priest, a
man of great probity, who collected money to restore it at their
joint expense, and to hire persons to bring stones for casting.
By means of this engine, a part of the wall of the tower Maledictum was at length shaken down, for about two poles' length.
The count of Flanders had a very choice petraria of large size,
which after his death, King Richard possessed; besides a smaller
one, equally good. These two were plied incessantly, close by a
gate the Turks used to frequent, until part of the tower was
knocked down. In addition to these two, King Richard had
constructed two others of choice workmanship and material,
which would strike at a place at an incalculable distance. He
had also built one put together very compactly, which the people
called ' Berefred ', with steps to mount it, fitting most tightly
to it; covered with raw hides and ropes, and having layers of
most solid wood, not to be destroyed by any blows, nor open to
injury from the pouring thereon of Greek fire, or any other
material. He also prepared two mangonels, one of which was of
such violence and rapidity, that what it hurled reached the inner
rows of the city market-place. These engines were plied day and
night, and it is well known that a stone sent from one of them
killed twelve men with its blow; the stone was afterwards
carried to Saladin for inspection; and King Richard had brought
it from Messina, which city he had taken. Such stones and flinty
pieces of rock, of the smoothest kind, nothing could withstand;
but they either shattered in pieces the object they struck, or
ground it to powder. The king was confined to his bed by a
severe attack of fever, which discouraged him; for he saw the
Turks constantly challenging our men, and pressing on them
importunately, and he was prevented by sickness from meeting
them, and he was more tormented by the importunate attack of
the Turks than by the severity of the fever that scorched him.

ABBOT SAMSON, 21 Feb. 1182—30 Dec. 1211

Abbot Samson was an efficient abbot, concerned with the practical rule of Bury St. Edmunds Abbey and its property. Fortunately he had a sort of Boswell in Jocelin of Brakelond who wrote a lively biography of him. At the abbey gates grew a town and its history was largely one of a violent struggle for independence from the abbey. At Winchester the story was one of a similar struggle against the bishop. For Westminster and St. Albans see pp. 111 and 171.

Source: *The Chronicle of Jocelin of Brakelond, monk of St. Edmundsbury*, translated by L. C. Jane, The King's Classics, Chatto and Windus 1907, p. 62. The chronicle contains the first real reference to a windmill in England, one which Samson disliked, in 1191.

Further Reading: T. Carlyle, *Past and Present*. M. D. Lobel, *Borough of Bury St. Edmunds*, 1934. For much interesting detail about monasticism, by one who does not idealize it, the works of G. G. Coulton, and, for a more sympathetic view, those of Cardinal Gasquet.

Abbot Samson was below the average height, almost bald; his face was neither round nor oblong; his nose was prominent and his lips thick; his eyes were clear and his glance penetrating; his hearing was excellent; his eyebrows arched, and frequently shaved; and a little cold soon made him hoarse. On the day of his election he was forty-seven, and had been a monk for seventeen years. In his ruddy beard there were a few grey hairs, and still fewer in his black and curling hair. But in the course of the first fourteen years after his election all his hair became white as snow.

He was an exceedingly temperate man; he possessed great energy and a strong constitution, and was fond of riding and walking, until old age prevailed upon him and moderated his ardour in these respects. When he heard the news of the capture of the cross and the fall of Jerusalem, he began to wear undergarments made of horsehair, and a horsehair shirt, and gave up the use of flesh and meat. None the less, he willed that flesh should be placed before him as he sat at table, that the alms might be increased. He ate sweet milk, honey, and similar sweet things, far more readily than any other food.

He hated liars, drunkards, and talkative persons; for virtue ever loves itself and spurns that which is contrary to it. He blamed those who grumbled about their meat and drink, and especially monks who so grumbled, and personally kept to the same manners which he had observed when he was a cloistered monk. Moreover, he had this virtue in himself that he never desired to change the dish which was placed before him. When I was a novice, I wished to prove whether this was really true, and as I happened to serve in the refectory, I thought to place before him food which would have offended any other man, in a very dirty and broken dish. But when he saw this, he was as it were blind to it. Then, as there was some delay, I repented of what I had done and straightway seized the dish, changed the food and dish for better, and carried it to him. He, however, was angry at the change, and disturbed.

He was an eloquent man, speaking both French and Latin, but rather careful of the good sense of that which he had to say than of the style of his words. He could read books written in English very well, and was wont to preach to the people in English, but in the dialect of Norfolk where he was born and bred. It was for this reason that he ordered a pulpit to be placed in the church, for the sake of those who heard him and for purposes of ornament.

The abbot further appeared to prefer the active to the contemplative life, and praised good officials more than good monks. He rarely commended anyone solely on account of his knowledge of letters, unless the man happened to have knowledge of secular affairs, and if he chanced to hear of any prelate who had given up his pastoral work and become a hermit, he did not praise him for it. He would not praise men who were too kindly, saying, ' He who strives to please all men, deserves to please none. . . .'

When news reached London of the capture of King Richard [1193], and of his imprisonment in Germany, and the barons had met to take counsel on the matter, the abbot stood forth in their presence, and said that he was ready to seek his lord the king. He said that he would search for him in disguise or in any other way, until he found him and had certain knowledge of him. And from this speech he gained great praise for himself. . . .

When the abbot had purchased the favour and grace of King Richard with gifts and money, so that he believed that he could carry through all his affairs according to his desire, King Richard died, and the abbot lost his labour and expenditure. But King John after his coronation [1199], laying aside all his other work, at once came to St. Edmunds, being led to do so by his vow and devotion. And we thought that he would have made some great offering, but he offered a silken cloth, which his servants borrowed from our sacristan and have not yet paid for.

He enjoyed the hospitality of St. Edmund, which involved great expenses, and when he left he gave nothing at all honourable or beneficial to the saint, except thirteen pence sterling, which he paid for a mass for himself, on the day on which he departed from us.

ACCESSION OF KING JOHN, 1199

This account of John's investiture with the insignia of the Duchy of Normandy, which he was to lose, omits the history of the previous Sunday, Easter, 18 March 1199. The author of the *Great Life* of St. Hugh, Bishop of Lincoln, says that Hugh refused his offering because of his irreverence, as he three times sent to ask the bishop to finish his sermon because he wanted breakfast, and left the church without communicating—as he did at his coronation.

Source: Roger of Hoveden (of Howden, Yorks.), *Annals*. Roger was a retired clerk of Henry II, and a valuable original source for 1192–1201. He includes various occurrences at Howden, of which he may have been parson, and is especially interested in constitutional and foreign questions. His ready faith in miracles led Bishop Stubbs to discuss how an author's credulity affects his credibility. It contrasts with St. Hugh's refusal to accept the imputation of miracles or to be interested in those of others, but a chronicle concluded at the beginning of John's reign is free from the sin of wisdom after the event. MS. Laud Misc. 582 in the Bodleian library is a fair copy which degenerates into a draft. Sir Henry Savile first edited Hoveden in 1596.

Then the Count [of Mortain, John] came to Rouen on Sunday, after Easter, 25 March, on St. Mark's feast, and was girded with the sword of the Duchy of Normandy in the mother church by the hand of Walter, Archbishop of Rouen; and the archbishop set on the duke's head a golden circlet having around its top golden roses; and the duke swore to guard holy church and its dignities in good faith and without guile and do justice and to destroy bad laws and make good ones. . . .

Then the duke John crossed from Normandy to England and landed at Shoreham on 25 June and on the morrow, the vigil of Ascension Day he came to London, and on the morrow he was to be crowned. . . .

Hubert [Walter], Archbishop of Canterbury, crowned and consecrated John, Duke of Normandy, to be King of England at St. Peter's church, Westminster, on 27 June, Ascension Day. Philip, Bishop of Durham, protested that the coronation should not have been made in the absence of Geoffrey, Archbishop of York, primate of all England. . . .

On that coronation day the king gave the chancery to Hubert, Archbishop of Canterbury. He was glorying in that power and making many boasts about his friendship with the king when Hugh Bardolf remarked, ' Sir, I shall speak saving your peace . . . we have never heard or seen a chancellor being made out of an archbishop, though we have seen an archbishop made out of a chancellor.'

THE GREAT CHARTER, 1215

It has been objected that lords and freemen, not serfs, were those whose liberties were protected from the king by the Great Charter which the barons extracted from King John. But the Charter which he sealed (it is incorrect to say he signed it) has been an inspiration to the champions of freedom in many periods.

Source: Roger of Wendover, *Flowers of History*, translated by J. A. Giles, Bohn's Antiquarian Library, 2 vols., 1849. From 1200 to 1235 this is a contemporary chronicle. Roger was not an eyewitness, but as historiographer at St. Albans he was in a key position, in a great abbey on the Great North Road, to learn the news of the world. He was a fearless critic of his times.

Further Reading: F. Thompson, *Magna Carta*, 1948. W. S. McKechnie, *Magna Carta*, 1914.

The conference between the king and the barons.

King John, when he saw that he was deserted by almost all, so that out of his regal superabundance of followers he scarcely retained seven knights, was much alarmed lest the barons would attack his castles and reduce them without difficulty, as they would find no obstacle to their so doing; and he deceitfully pretended to make peace for a time with the aforesaid barons, and sent William Marshal, Earl of Pembroke, with other trustworthy messengers, to them, and told them that, for the sake of peace, and for the exaltation and honour of the kingdom, he would willingly grant them the laws and liberties they required; he also sent word to the barons by these same messengers, to appoint a fitting day and place to meet and carry all these matters into effect. The king's messengers then came in all haste to London, and without deceit reported to the barons all that had been deceitfully imposed on them; they in their great joy appointed the fifteenth of June for the king to meet them, at a field lying between Staines and Windsor. Accordingly, at the time and place pre-agreed on, the king and nobles came to the appointed conference, and, when each party had stationed themselves apart from the other, they began a long discussion about terms of peace and the aforesaid liberties. There were present on behalf of the king, the archbishops, Stephen of Canterbury and H. of Dublin; the bishops W. of London, P. of Winchester, H. of Lincoln, J. of Bath, Walter of Worcester, W. of Coventry, and Benedict of Rochester; master Pandulph, familiar of our lord the Pope, and brother Almeric the master of the Knights Templars in England; the nobles, William Marshal Earl of Pembroke, the Earl of Salisbury, Earl of Warrenne, the Earl of Arundel, Alan de Galway, W. Fitz-Gerald, Peter Fitz-Herbert, Alan Basset, Matthew Fitz-Herbert, Thomas Basset, Hugh de Neville, Hubert de Burgh seneschal of Poictou, Robert de Ropeley, John Marshal, and Philip d'Aubeny. Those who were on behalf of the barons it is not necessary to enumerate, since the whole nobility of England were now assembled together in numbers not to be computed. At length, after various points on both sides had been discussed, King John, seeing that he was inferior in strength to the barons, without raising any difficulty, granted the underwritten laws and liberties, and confirmed them by his charter as follows:

[Then follows the text of the Charter].

How the king of England by letters patent ordered the aforesaid liberties to be observed.

After this King John sent his letters patent throughout all

the English territories, strictly ordering all the sheriffs of the whole kingdom to make the inhabitants in their jurisdictions of every rank swear to observe the above-written laws and liberties, and also, as far as lay in their power, to annoy and harass him, the king, by taking his castles till he fulfilled all the above-mentioned terms, as contained in the Charter. After which, many nobles of the kingdom came to the king asking him for their rights of land and possessions, and the custody of the castles, which as they said, belonged to them by hereditary right; but the king delayed this matter till it was proved on the oath of liege men, what of right was due to each; and, the more fully to effect this, he fixed the 16th of August as a day for them all to come to Westminster. Nevertheless he restored to Stephen Archbishop of Canterbury the castle of Rochester and the Tower of London, which by old right belonged to his custody: and then breaking up the conference, the barons returned with the above-named charter to London.

How king John retired clandestinely to the Isle of Wight and laid plans against the barons.

After the barons, as has been stated, had gone from the conference, the king was left with scarcely seven knights out of his proper body of attendants. Whilst lying sleepless that night in Windsor Castle, his thoughts alarmed him much, and before daylight he fled by stealth to the Isle of Wight, and there in great agony of mind devised plans to be revenged on the barons. At length, after divers meditations, he determined, with the assistance of the apostle Peter, to seek revenge on his enemies with two swords, the spiritual and temporal, so that if he could not succeed with the one, he might for certain accomplish his purpose with the other. To strike at them with the spiritual sword, he sent Pandulph the Pope's subdeacon with other messengers to the court of Rome, to counteract, by the apostolic authority, the intentions of the barons. He also sent . . . with his own seal, to all the transmarine territories to procure supplies of troops in those parts, promising them lands, ample possessions, and no small sum of money. . . .

KING JOHN'S FURY, 1215

After sealing Magna Carta, King John planned a counter-revolution with French help. Professor Galbraith has shown that Roger of Wendover drew a savage portrait of King John which has transmitted to later historians a legend of wickedness which circulated among the clerical enemies of the king. Matthew Paris added corroborative details to make a vivid picture which is historically ' not merely worthless but very misleading', as a portrait of John, but at least he gives a true reflexion of political prejudice equal to anything which future historians will find in modern journalism.

Source: Matthew Paris, *Chronica Majora* (Rolls Series 1874), ii, 611. Matthew Paris thought this account worth including in Wendover's account. He was not an eyewitness but the story is either based on a first-hand account or else witnesses to the inventiveness of John's enemies. It is left out of the translations of Wendover and of Matthew Paris's continuation of Wendover in Bohn's Antiquarian Library.

Further Reading: Kate Norgate, *John Lackland*, 1902. S. Painter, *Reign of King John*, 1949. V. H. Galbraith, *Roger Wendover and Matthew Paris*, 1944.

His mental state underwent a transformation and he tended to welcome the worst suggestions. For it is easy to unbalance an unstable person and to precipitate into crime one already inclined to evil. Then the king heaved deep sighs, began to feel the utmost irritation, started to turn in upon himself and languish. He kept moaning and groaning ' Why did my mother bear me to misery and shame . . . ?' He started to gnash his teeth and roll his staring eyes in fury. Then he would pick up sticks and straws and gnaw them like a lunatic and sometimes he would cast them away half-chewed. His uncontrolled gestures gave indications of the melancholy, or rather of the madness, that was upon him.

LONDONERS RIOT AGAINST WESTMINSTER ABBEY, 1223

Struggles between citizens and their monastic neighbours occurred in many places, such as Abingdon, as well as London, at various dates.

Source: Translated from *Annals of Dunstable*, passage printed in R. F. Glover and R. W. Harris, *Latin for Historians*, 1956, p. 32. The situation of Dunstable at the junction of Watling Street and the Icknield Way, two of the chief cross-country routes of England, enabled its Prior, Richard de Morins, to hear what was going on between 1202 and 1242. Once he was sent by King John to the Pope and in 1223 he was a commissioner inquiring into the independence of Westminster Abbey from the Bishop of London.

Further Reading: W. H. Godfrey, *A History of Architecture in London*, 1911.

In the year of Our Lord 1223 there was strife at London between the Abbot of Westminster's household and some young London citizens; but their laughter was turned to tears. The abbot's household might triumph by night and many were hurt on both sides, but next morning the London people chose a new mayor, publicly hired men-at-arms by proclamation, appointed a captain for themselves and burst into the church of Westminster. They spoiled the abbot's goods, livestock and chattels. After a few days Philip Daubeni, of the royal household, was staying in London and the Abbot of Westminster went to him to complain about the violence which he had suffered. The Londoners learnt this and swarmed round his house like bees, beating his servants and maltreating the soldiers that came with him, and tried to capture the abbot himself. Philip tried in vain to calm the mob while the abbot escaped secretly from the back. He embarked in a small boat on the Thames and thus escaped with difficulty. The justiciar heard of this frenzied outbreak of the citizens and summoned the mayor and chief citizens to inquire who were the ringleaders. Upon concluding this inquiry he arrested Constantine Aloph and his two nephews. They gave a rude reply to his charges and were hung. The citizens murmured at this so the king took sixty hostages from them and sent them in custody to various castles. He deposed the mayor and appointed his own warden in the city. He ordered a great gallows to be prepared and at last after royal threats and many discussions between them and the barons peace was made between them and the king on payment of many thousands of marks.

MARRIAGE OF ELEANOR OF PROVENCE TO HENRY III, 14 January, 1236

Eleanor, daughter of Raymond Berenger, Count of Provence, was the sister of the Queen of France, Marguerite wife of St. Louis. Another sister was wife of Richard Earl of Cornwall, ' King of the Romans '. Despite the pageantry at her wedding Eleanor was disliked in London where all corn and wool cargoes had to be unladen at her quay called Queenhithe as the dues pertained to the queens of England. Her son, Edward I, never forgave the Londoners for pelting her with rotten eggs and sheep bones and trying to sink her barge by throwing stones at it from the bridge, with cries of ' Drown the witch ', when she tried to flee from the Tower to Windsor in 1264. Eleanor was married at Canterbury on 14 January and crowned at Westminster on 20 January when these festivities occurred.

Source: Matthew Paris, *English History*, 1235–73, translated by J. A. Giles, Bohn's Antiquarian Library, 1889, i, 8. The historian of St. Albans is proud of the precedence of his abbot.

Further Reading: A bibliography of the writings of Sir M. Powicke, the authority on the thirteenth century, but only up to his retirement in 1947 is given at the end of *Studies in Medieval History presented to F. M. Powicke*, 1948.

There were assembled at the king's nuptial festivities such a host of nobles of both sexes, such numbers of religious men, such crowds of the populace, and such a variety of actors, that London, with its capacious bosom, could scarcely contain them. The whole city was ornamented with flags and banners, chaplets and hangings, candles and lamps, and with wonderful devices and extraordinary representations, and all the roads were cleansed from mud and dirt, sticks, and everything offensive. The citizens too, went out to meet the king and queen, dressed out in their ornaments, and vied with each other in trying the speed of their horses. On the same day, when they left the city for Westminster, to perform the duties of butler to the king (which office belonged to them by right of old, at the coronation), they proceeded thither dressed in silk garments, with mantles worked in gold, and with costly changes of raiment, mounted on valuable horses, glittering with new bits and saddles, and riding in troops arranged in order. They carried with them three hundred and sixty gold and silver cups, preceded by the king's trumpeters and with horns sounding, so that such a wonderful novelty struck all who beheld it with astonishment. The Archbishop of Canterbury, by the right especially belonging to him, performed the duty of crowning, with the usual solemnities, the Bishop of London assisting him as a dean, the other bishops taking their stations according to their rank. In the same way all the abbots, at the head of whom, as was his right, was the Abbot of St. Albans (for as the Protomartyr of England, B. Alban was the chief of all the martyrs of England, so also was his abbot the chief of all the abbots in rank and dignity), as the authentic privileges of that church set forth. The nobles, too, performed the duties, which, by ancient right and custom, pertained to them at the coronations of kings. In like manner some of the inhabitants of certain cities discharged certain duties which belonged to them by right of their ancestors. The Earl of Chester carried the sword of St. Edward, which was called ' Curtein ', before the king, as a sign that he was earl of the palace, and had by right the power of restraining the king if he should commit an error. The earl was attended by the Constable of Chester, and kept the people away with a wand when they pressed forward in a disorderly way. The grand marshal of England, the Earl of Pembroke, carried a wand before the king and cleared the way before him both in the church and in the banquet-hall, and arranged the banquet and the guests at table. The wardens of the Cinque Ports carried the pall over the king, supported by four spears, but the claim to this duty was not altogether undisputed. The Earl of Leicester supplied the king with water in basins to wash before his meal; the Earl Warenne performed the duty of king's cupbearer, supplying the place of the Earl of Arundel, because the latter was a youth and not as yet made a belted knight. Master Michael Belet was butler *ex officio*, the Earl of Hereford performed the duties of marshal of the king's household, and William Beauchamp held the station of almoner. The justiciary of the forests arranged the drinking cups on the table at the king's right hand, although he met with some opposition, which however fell to the ground. The citizens of London passed the wine about in all directions, in costly cups, and those of Winchester superintended the cooking of the feast; the rest, according to the ancient statutes, filled their separate stations, or made their claims to do so. And in order that the nuptial festivities might not be clouded by any disputes, saving the right of anyone, many things were put up with for the time which they left for decision at a more favourable opportunity. The office of Chancellor of England, and all the offices connected with the king, are ordained and assized in the Exchequer. Therefore the chancellor, the chamberlain, the marshal, and the constable, by right of their office, took their seats there, as also did the barons, according to the date of their creation, in the city of London, whereby they each knew his own place. The ceremony was splendid, with the gay dresses of the clergy and knights who were present. The Abbot of Westminster sprinkled the holy water, and the treasurer, acting the part of sub-dean, carried the paten. Why should I describe all those persons who reverently ministered in the church of God as was their duty? Why describe the abundance of meats and dishes on the table? the quantity of venison, the variety of fish, the joyous sounds of the glee-men, and the gaiety of the waiters? Whatever the world could afford to create pleasure and magnificence was there brought together from every quarter.

FRANCISCANS AND DOMINICANS, 1243

The Dominicans came to England in 1221 and the Franciscans in 1224, having been approved by the pope in 1210 and 1216. By 1350 three hundred friaries had been founded.

The growing influence of the Friars in the thirteenth century with their emphasis on preaching led to wider churches being built to hold people listening to sermons. The convents of Friars were built in towns, often in situations which had been hitherto left open because of being unattractive. The monks, whose monasteries had been built before the Friars came, were rather prejudiced against them, and Matthew Paris, a great historian who happened to be a monk of St. Albans, was no exception.

Source: Matthew Paris, *English History*, 1235–73, translated by J. A. Giles, Bohn's Antiquarian Library 1889.

Further Reading: D. M. Knowles, *The Religious Orders in England*, Cambridge 1948.

Matthew's objections to fine building by Friars is echoed a century later by a detailed and sarcastic description of the house of the London Dominicans of Piers Plowman.

And that the world might not appear to be devoid of increasing troubles on every side, a controversy arose between the Minorite brothers [Franciscans] and Preachers [Dominicans], to the astonishment of many, because they seemed to have chosen perfection's path, viz. that of poverty and patience. On one side the Preachers declared that they were instituted first, and on that account, more worthy; that they were also more decent in their apparel, and had deservedly obtained their name and office from their preaching, and that they were more truly distinguished by the apostolic dignity: on the other side, the Minorites gave answer, that they had embraced, for God, a way of living more rigorous and humble, and so the more worthy, because more holy; and that the brothers could and certainly ought to pass over from the order of Preachers to their order, as from an inferior community to one more rigorous and superior. The Preachers contradicted them to their face, saying, that though the Minorites went barefooted, coarsely clad, and girded with a rope, the privilege of eating flesh or a more delicate article of diet was not denied them even in public, a thing which is forbidden to the community of Preachers, wherefore it could not be allowed that the Preachers could enter the order of Minorites, as one more rigorous and more worthy, but quite the contrary. Therefore, between these, even as between the Templars and Hospitallers, in the Holy Land, through the enemy to the human race sowing the seeds of dissension, a great and scandalous strife arose; and inasmuch as it was between learned men and scholars, it was more dangerous to the Catholic Church, and a sign of a great judgment impending at its threshold. And what is terrible, and a sad presage, for three or four hundred years, or more, the monastic order did not hasten to destruction so quickly as their order, of whom now, the brothers, twenty-four years having scarcely elapsed, had first built, in England, dwellings which rivalled regal palaces in height. These are they who daily expose to view their inestimable treasures, in enlarging their sumptuous edifices, and erecting lofty walls, thereby impudently transgressing the limits of their original poverty, and violating the basis of

their religion, according to the prophecy of the German Hilde-
garde. When noblemen and rich men are at the point of death,
whom they know to be possessed of great riches, they, in their
love of gain, diligently urge them, to the injury and loss of the
ordinary pastors, and extort confessions and hidden wills, lauding
themselves and their own order only, and placing themselves
before all others. So no faithful man now believes he can be
saved, except he is directed by the counsels of the Preachers and
Minorites. Desirous of obtaining privileges in the courts of
kings and potentates, they act the parts of councillors, chamber-
lains, treasurers, bridegrooms, and mediators for marriages; they
are the executors of the papal extortions; in their sermons, they
either are flatterers, or most cutting reprovers, revealers of confessions, or impudent accusers. Despising, also, the authentic
orders which were instituted by the holy fathers, namely, by
St. Benedict and St. Augustine, and also the followers of them
(as the thing clearly appears in the case of the church of Scar-
borough, when the Minorites shamefully retreated), they set
their own community before the rest. They look upon the
Cistercian monks as clownish, harmless, half-bred, or rather
ill-bred, priests; and the monks of the Black order as proud
epicures.

ROBERT GROSSETESTE

In 1235 Grosseteste became Bishop of the vast Diocese of Lincoln
which included the archdeaconries of Lincoln, Leicester, Stowe,
Buckingham, Huntingdon, Northampton, Oxford and Bedford and
in reforming his diocese removed seven abbots and four priors. He
protected the students of Oxford Universitiy, of which he had been
chancellor, from the consequences of attacking Otho, the papal
legate. The titles of his learned works fill twenty-five closely printed
pages, and more significant than the miracles which followed his
death on 9 October 1253, is the frequency with which the learned
writers of succeeding generations quoted his works. Though in-
fluential with Henry III and a friend of Queen Eleanor, he educated
the sons of Simon de Montfort, and though regarded by Benedictines
as an oppressor of monks his career evoked this summary from
Matthew Paris.

Source: Matthew Paris, as translated in the *Dictionary of National
Biography*. Matthew became a monk on 21 January 1217 and succeeded

Roger of Wendover in 1236. An artist, of whom several portraits remain, as well as a writer, he travelled to court and elsewhere. He names twenty people who gave him information and on 13 October 1247 Henry III recognized him and sat him on the steps of the throne asking if he had seen and would remember so as to record how he carried the Sacred Blood from St. Paul's to Westminster. On 5 November 1251 at the dedication of Hayles church, Gloucestershire, Richard Earl of Cornwall told him what it cost, and in March 1257 Henry III saw him much at St. Albans, reciting to him the 250 English baronies. Matthew begged him to uphold Oxford University against the Bishop of Lincoln. Thanks to Matthew, English history in the thirteenth century is seen through Benedictine eyes at St. Albans, and the tradition which he strengthened persisted.

Further Reading: Publications of the Lincolnshire Record and Canterbury and York Societies for editions of episcopal registers.

He was a manifest confuter of the pope and the king, the blamer of prelates, the corrector of monks, the director of priests, the instructor of clerks, the support of scholars, the preacher to the people, the persecutor of the incontinent, the sedulous student of all scripture, the hammer and the despiser of the Romans. At the table of bodily refreshment he was hospitable, eloquent, courteous, pleasant, and affable. At the spiritual table, devout, tearful, and contrite. In his episcopal office he was sedulous, venerable, and indefatigable.

SANCTITY OF ST. EDMUND RICH, ARCHBISHOP OF CANTERBURY

Edmund Rich, a native of Abingdon, was one of the great early teachers in the schools at Oxford, a generation before the first colleges were built there. He became Archbishop of Canterbury in 1234 and his threats led Henry III to dismiss Peter des Roches, a minister hated for defeating Hubert de Burgh's opposition to the encroachments of churchmen from Rome and royal favourites from Poitou. In 1240 Edmund despaired of King and Pope and went into exile in France where he died and was soon credited with miracles.

Source: Matthew Paris, *English History* 1235–1273, translated by J. A. Giles, Bohn's Antiquarian Library 1889, i, 511.

Further Reading: Sir M. Powicke, *Henry III and the Lord Edward*, 1947 and *The Thirteenth Century*, 1216–1307, 1953.

(1244). In this year, too, the miracles worked by St. Edmund, the Archbishop of Canterbury and confessor, became so frequent at Pontigny, that the days of the apostles seemed to be renewed, and by these miracles not only France, but England also, especially at Cateby, the place where the said saint's pall and some painted pictures, which he used to carry, were known to be kept, and many other places, became famous. . . . Of the kind of cloak which this most blessed man used to wear, it is by no means right to be silent, for we believe it to have been a kind untried by the holy men of former times, and entirely unheard of by those of the present day. His cloak then was not made by the weaver's art, of fine threads, but of small ropes plaited together like a very dense net, the joints of which contained knots as innumerable as painful, in thick order; and that knots might be more pressed into the flesh of the wearer, the cloak was not whole in the back part of it, but was open from the top downwards, with small meshes here and there. With these, knotted and tightly woven, he fought with himself, in order that, as the domestic torture overcame the body, he might become a martyr and obtain the victory over himself. Nor was he satisfied thus to crucify the flesh with torment rather than garment; but what he inflicted on himself in addition increased our astonishment more than all else. . . . His hands and the naked parts of his neck, he covered with hair-cloth at night, that thus he might make the whole of his body a burnt-offering of a most sweet savour to the Lord. . . .

BUILDING BY HENRY III, 1249—50

The story of Henry III's reign is largely of renewals of charters of liberty and resistance to his court favourites and to attempts to raise money. Some of the king's money was spent on buildings such as the improvement of Westminster Abbey. This is regarded as the great period of Early English architecture. Some of his buildings have perished such as the royal Manor House at Woodstock and Clarendon Palace. The Duchess of Marlborough destroyed the latter when Blenheim Palace was built in the 18th century. Clarendon Palace has been excavated recently.

Source: Translations from Public Record Office, Liberate Rolls and from the *Calendar of Papal Registers* by L. F. Salzman, *Building in England down to 1540 a Documentary History*, 1952, p. 384.

Further Reading: Historical Monuments Commission, *Westminster Abbey*, 1924. E. S. Prior and A. Gardner, *Medieval Figure Sculpture in England*, 1912. E. W. Tristram, *English Medieval Wall Painting*, 1944, 1950. L. Stone, *Sculpture in Britain: the Middle Ages*, 1955.

1249 *Woodstock*

Orders to crenellate the queen's chamber with freestone, and to raise the chimney of that chamber to the height of 8 feet; to panel the lower chamber and make the privy chamber in the fashion of that chamber where Bartholomew Pecche used to sleep; to build a chamber at the gateway of Evereswell, 40 feet long and 22 feet wide, with a wardrobe, privy chamber, and fireplace. Also to repair Rosamund's chamber, unroofed by the wind; and to make a door to the queen's chamber, and a door to the old larder. Also to repair the bays of both our fish-stews and the causeway of the lower stew near the enclosure; to put 2 windows of white glass in the gable of the hall, and 2 in the chamber of Edward our son, and 2 windows barred with iron in the old larder. To make leaden spouts round the alures [walks] of the same Edward's chamber; to repair all the buildings of each court where necessary; to bar the windows of the porch with iron; to build a house for our napery; and to pull down the rooms of William our chaplain and rebuild them between the hall and the queen's stable, making a garden on the site of the said rooms.

1250 *Westminster Abbey*

Relaxation of one year's enjoined penance to penitents who assist the fabric of the church of wonderful beauty now being built by the King at Westminster.

1250 *Clarendon*

Orders to make a baptistery in the chapel of All Saints there, and to put on the chapel a bell-turret with two bells, and to make a crucifix with two images on each side of wood, and an image of Blessed Mary with her Child. And let the queen's chamber be decently paved. And in the queen's hall let there be made a

window towards the garden, well barred with iron; and two
windows in the queen's chapel, one on each side of the altar,
which are to be divided down in the middle so that they may be
opened and shut when necessary. . . . And make a bench
round our great garden beside the wall, and whitewash the wall
above it. In Alexander's chamber let there be made a wardrobe
with a privy chamber, and roof those buildings well. Make a
garden below our chamber on the north; also a window in our
wardrobe; and lengthen our chandlery by four or five couples.

A POITEVIN FAVOURITE, 1252

Hubert de Burgh, the Justiciar, fell in July 1232 and at Christmas
Henry III gave most of the important posts to foreigners from Poitou
as he could trust them more than Englishmen. Later, when the king
married Eleanor of Provence in 1236, Savoyards and Provençals
joined the throng of unpopular foreigners at Court. One of them,
Boniface of Savoy, was the successor of Edmund Rich as Archbishop
of Canterbury (1245–70).

Source: Matthew Paris, *English History* 1235–73, translated by
J. A. Giles, Bohn's Antiquarian Library, 1893, ii, 522. The historiographer of St. Albans describes what happened there.

Further Reading: H. W. C. Davis, *England under the Normans and
Angevins*, 1905.

The king, however, persisted in his usual extravagances, and
as if in revenge for this opposition of the prelates, continued to
distribute the vacant escheats and revenues amongst unknown,
scurrilous, and undeserving foreigners, in order to inflict an
irreparable wound upon the heads of his natural subjects. Not to
mention others, we think it right to mention in this volume the
following case, as one out of many. In the service of Geoffrey de
Lusignan, the king's brother, was a certain chaplain, who served
as a fool and buffoon to the king, the said Geoffrey his master,
and all the court, and whose sayings, like those of a silly jester
and club-bearer, contributed to their amusement, and excited
their laughter; and on this man the king bestowed the rich
church of Preston, which had formerly belonged to William
Haverhull, the lately-deceased treasurer of the king, the yearly

proceeds of which church amounted to more than a hundred pounds. This same chaplain, a Poitevin by birth, utterly ignorant alike in manners and learning, we have seen pelting the king, his brother Geoffrey, and other nobles, whilst walking in the orchard of St. Albans, with turf, stones, and green apples, and pressing the juice of unripe grapes in their eyes, like one devoid of sense. Despicable alike in his gesture, mode of speech, and habits, as well as in size and personal appearance, this man might be considered a stage actor rather than a priest as he was, to the great disgrace of the priestly order. Such are the persons to whom the King of England intrusts the care and guardianship of many thousands of souls, rejecting such a vast number of learned, prudent, and proper men as England has given birth to, who know the language of the natives, and how to instruct the ignorant. . . . This digression from the subject of our narrative is elicited by our sorrow for the causes of it.

DEATH OF SIMON DE MONTFORT, 5 August, 1265

Henry III had foreign favourites who aroused strong opposition. Its leader was Simon de Montfort, although he was himself a foreigner and brother-in-law both of Henry III and the King of France. The Friars supported him, and Robert Grosseteste and Adam de Marsh, leading Franciscan teachers at Oxford, were his friends. He defeated Henry III at Lewes on 14 May 1264. In 1264 he summoned knights of the shire to Parliament and in 1265 summoned two burghers from certain towns. Henry's son, Lord Edward, later Edward I, slew him at Evesham, but adopted his programme. His Parliament marks an important step forward in the growth of the principle of representation, and therefore de Montfort plays an important part in histories of the constitution. His importance, however, does not only lie in the minds of those tracing the birth of democracy but to his own generation Earl Simon the Righteous became a hero of popular songs, for he seemed a sort of John the Baptist defying Herod:

' For they that keep the King from sin serve him the best of all
Making him free that else would be to sin a wretched thrall.'

Like Edmund Rich, Simon seems almost a saint to Matthew Paris, a well informed and honest historian, but as much a partisan as the liberal-minded modern historians who inherited the Whig tradition of Lord Macaulay. Parliament and Westminster Abbey stand as monuments to Simon de Montfort and Henry III, like symbols on opposite sides of the road.

Source: Matthew Paris, *English History*, translated by J. A. Giles, Bohn's Antiquarian Library, 1889.

Further Reading: C. Bémont, *Simon de Montfort*, 1884. H. S. Morrison, *Government and Parliament*, 1954.

On the following day he [Henry III's son Edward I then prince] drew near the town of Evesham on one side, and the Earl of Gloucester and Roger Mortimer came up with their respective forces in two other directions; and thus the Earl of Leicester was hemmed in on all sides, and was under the necessity either of voluntarily surrendering, or of giving them battle. On the 5th of August, which fell on the third day of the week, both armies met in a large plain outside the town, where a most severe conflict ensued, till the partisans of the earl began to give way, and the whole weight of the battle falling upon him, he was slain on the field of battle. At the time of his death, a storm of thunder and lightning occurred, and darkness prevailed to such an extent, that all were struck with amazement. Besides the earl, there fell, in that battle, twelve knights bannerets; namely, Henry, his son; Peter de Montfort; Hugh Despenser, justiciary of England . . . and a great many others of inferior rank, such as esquires and foot-soldiers; the greatest loss being amongst the Welsh.

Thus ended the labours of that noble man Earl Simon, who gave up not only his property, but also his person, to defend the poor from oppression, and for the maintenance of justice and the rights of the kingdom. He was distinguished for his learning; to him an assiduous attention to divine duties was a pleasure; he was moderate and frugal; and it was a usual practice of his to watch by night, in preference to sleeping. He was bold in speech, and of a severe aspect; he put great confidence in the prayers of religious men, and always paid great respect to ecclesiastics. He endeavoured to adhere to the counsels of St. Robert, surnamed Grosstête, bishop of Lincoln, and intrusted his children to him to be brought up, when very young. On that prelate's counsel he relied when arranging matters of difficulty, when attempting dubious enterprises, and in finishing what he had begun, especially in those matters by which he hoped to increase his merits. It was reported that the same bishop had enjoined on him, in order to obtain remission of his sins, to take up this cause, for which he fought even to the death; declaring that the peace of the church of England could not be firmly established except by the sword, and positively assuring him that all who died for it would be crowned with martyrdom. Some persons, moreover, stated, that on one occasion, the bishop placed his hand on the head of the earl's eldest son, and said to him, ' My well-beloved child, both thou and thy father shall die on one day, and by one kind of death; but it will be in the cause of justice and truth.' Report goes, that Simon, after his death, was distinguished by the working of many miracles, which, however, were not made publicly known, for fear of kings.

' FEODARY OF THE LORDSHIPS OF HOLKHAM AND OF THEIR TENANTS,' 1272—3

The results of a detailed inquiry, similar to Domesday book, but fuller, are embodied in the *Hundred Rolls* which have been printed so far as they survive by the Record Commission and give a much clearer picture of how land was held in many places in the second half of the thirteenth century than one gets before or after. A similar survey of Holkham shows how complicated the situation could be in a single parish in which there were nine ' fees ', holdings held under different tenants of the king either directly or through intermediate lords. Naturally some of the inhabitants held land under different conditions in each of these separate lordships. Parts are translated as a specimen.

Source: Translated, by permission of the Earl of Leicester, from documents in the Holkham Estate Office. At Holkham are enormous accumulations of medieval estate documents such as are seldom found outside the muniment rooms of ancient colleges.

Geoffrey Lesyney who is a ward of John Harcurt holds of the lord king in chief 6 socmen [freemen] who hold of Geoffrey 8 acres with their houses by the baser [i.e. villein] tenure belonging to the manor of Wython and views of frankpledge with their liberties and wreck of the sea and toll of the harbour of Holkham.

Ralph Noioun of Salle holds in Holkham of the lord Geoffrey Lesyney as a fee in chief of the lord king 23 socmen who hold in

villeinage 132 acres with their houses and 3 cottagers who hold
in villeinage 4 acres with their cottages. And the said Ralph
holds the same by service of half a knight from Geoffrey Leseny
[*or* for 19½d.] John Goldwyne holds of said Ralph of the same
fee 1 messuage, 40 acres, 1 sheep run and pays him 5s. 4d.

John Selk holds of same Ralph 3 acres and 1 rod and pays
him 6d. yearly.

Thomas Dakeney holds in Holkham of John de Dakeney and
pays him one silver cage for one sparrowhawk and John de
Dakeney holds of Ralph Tony and Ralph of the king in chief
1 house, 14 acres, 1 kiln and 1 mill. The said Thomas has 36
socmen holding in villeinage 130 acres with houses of the said
fee. Thomas too has 3 cottagers who hold 3 acres with their
cottages in villeinage.

The Prior of Peterston has of the same fee 40 acres and 1
sheep run and pays Thomas 4 s. 10½ d. That prior also has 2
cottagers holding 2 acres in villeinage with their cottages as
appears by the agreement.

The Abbot of Creyk holds of Thomas of the same fee in
Holkham 40 acres of land and 1 sheep run. He pays yearly
10s. 6d., 4½ bushels of grain. That abbot holds 8 acres with
socmen in villeinage with houses and 2 cottagers who hold of
said fee 1½ acres with cottages for the same services.

Robert le Heyre holds of said fee of Thomas Dakeney in
Holkham 1 house and 40 acres and pays him yearly 15s. 10d.
and ½ quarter of grain. John Silk holds of Robert le Heyre of
same fee 4 acres 1 rod for 2 s. per year.

Henry Bulman holds of Robert 14 acres for 21 d. and 1 lb. of
cumin.

John Sylk holds of Ralph Hakun 24 acres and 1 sheep run
with the marsh of the same fee for 13 d. and 1 lb. cumin. John
Sylk holds of same fee of Geoffrey Bret of Holkham 3 acres for
4 d. per year and same Geoffrey holds of the Abbot of Creyk
2 acres for 1 d. per year.

The lady Dionisia de Monte Canisio holds in Holkham 1
house, 120 acres arable, 120 acres marsh, 8 acres meadow, 1
sheep run, the leet [court] and view of frankpledge with its
liberties by service of ½ knight's fee of Robert de Tatyssale of

the fee of Arundell and said Robert of the king in chief. The said lady holds of the said Robert of that fee 212 acres which villeins hold of same in villeinage with houses. She holds of Robert of same fee 3 acres which cotters hold of same with their cottages. . . .

VILLEIN SERVICES, 1272—3

Villeins were by no means slaves, and as the services which they had to render became fixed and eventually commuted for money payments it was possible for them to thrive. At Holkham in Norfolk a wealthier villein might have servants in his house. Boon-works (see p. 36), were widespread, but the obligation to carry writs or letters for the king and ' wardsea ' were local peculiarities.

Source: ' Roll of the holding held by the lord Warin de Monte Canisio with both free and servile rents and customs at Holcham '. Extracts translated with the permission of the Earl of Leicester from Holkham Deed 4 in the Holkham Estate Office. This gives details of the duties of each of 78 holdings mostly held by single tenants but some held by partnerships. Holkham deed 4a records changes which had occurred a few decades later.

Further Reading: F. Seebohm, *English Village Community*, ed. 1915.

Hervey de Monte holds 18 acres for 22 d. rent at 4 times of payment and 4 hens worth 4 d. and does 3 half days weeding worth ½ d. and 3 boon-works in Autumn at the lord's board worth 6 d. and does 1 boon-work with a plough, if he has a horse, worth 6 d. at the lord's board and gives 2 d. for Wodelode and carries the writ of the king twice a year worth 4 d. and if the lord come to the vill he lends him a horse if he has one to carry bread for 12 leagues and goes twice to the lord's mill pond worth 1 d. twice a year and pays ½ d. for Wardese[a] and carries the lord's corn in Autumn for one day worth 2 d. if he has a horse. Total 4 s. 1 d. . . .

Roger Raven and Hervey Carpenter hold 32 acres for 26 d. and fold service 9 d. and 2 quarters of oats worth 2 s. and make 2 quarters of malt at the lord's board worth 3 d. and will carry half a measure of dung worth 4½ d. and 16 works in Autumn and 3 boon-works in Autumn worth 19 d. and will thrash for 32 days worth 16 d. and 2 boon-works with a plough worth 12 d. if they have horses at the lord's board and will weed for 3 half days worth 1½ d. and will do a carrying duty worth 3 d. and will go to the pond 4 times worth 2 d. and pay 4 hens worth 4 d. and will carry in Autumn if they have a horse at the lord's board worth 6d. Total 10 s. 10 d. . . . .

Total of rents and customs in Holkham £13 4s. 1¾d.

Total plough-works 100 whereof 46 are whether there is a horse or not.

443 works in Autumn.

240 boon-works in Autumn.

Total of carrying services £ 10.

Total of fold-services 9 s. 6d.

Total of carryings of dung 15½ and two thirds of a carrying.

Total of spreadings of dung, 10 measures worth ½ d. each.

Total of weedings 141 customary works worth ½ d. each.

ARABLE AND PASTURE

The conversion of arable to pasture for the profit brought by wool led to many villages being deserted two centuries later.

Source: *Fleta*, a tract written in Latin about 1289, which combines material in *Walter of Henley* and *Seneschaucie* on farming. Extracts translated in F. H. Cripps-Day, *The Manor Farm*, Bernard Quaritch 1931, p. 76.

Further Reading: M. Beresford, *The Lost Villages of England*, 1954.

CONCERNING PLOUGHMEN

The art of the ploughmen consists in knowing how to draw a straight furrow with yoked oxen without striking, pricking or ill-treating them.

Ploughmen ought not to be melancholy, or irritable, but gay, full of song and joyous, so that they may in a sort of way encourage the oxen at their toil with melody and song; they must take them their forage and fodder, and they ought to be attached to them, and sleep in their stable at night, and make much of them, curry and rub them down, look after them well in every way taking care that their forage and fodder is not stolen; the allowance of hay or litter should not be given out for two or three nights at once, but as much as is required for a day's feed should be given to them every day, nor should they be permitted to have a candle unless, as the saying is, it is 'held' [i.e. a lantern].

Other people's beasts found in the ploughmen's pasture ought to be impounded. It is the duty of the ploughmen and husbandmen when the tillage season is over, to ditch, thresh, dig, fence, repair the watercourses in the fields, and to do other such small and useful tasks.

CONCERNING SHEPHERDS

Shepherds should be intelligent, watchful, and kind men who will not harry the sheep by their bad temper, but let them graze peacefully and without disturbing them.

Let each provide himself with a good barking dog and sleep out every night with his flock. Let him prepare his folds and sheepcotes and provide good hurdles covered with pelts and thick rushes for warmth; and he must be careful that the sheep in his charge are not stolen or changed, nor allowed to graze in wet or marshy places, in thickets, or on low-lying bottoms, or on unhealthy pastures, lest, for want of good care, they go sick and die, otherwise he will be held liable for the penalty of the account.

But let there be three folds for the sheep and their lambs, viz. one for the muttons and wethers another for the two-tooth ewes and a third for hogs of one year and under, if the flock is large enough, three shepherds must then be put in charge.

All the sheep must be marked with the same mark. The ewes should not be allowed to be suckled or milked beyond the feast of the Nativity of the Blessed Mary [8 Sept.]; those which it is not expedient to keep should be drafted out between Easter and Whitsuntide, sheared earlier, marked differently from the others, and be sent at once into the wood pastures where they should be kept, or in some other pasture in which they will fatten and improve more rapidly; they may be sold at the feast of the Nativity of St. John the Baptist [24 June].

Those that are sickly can be recognized by the teeth dropping out and by the sign of old age; the wool of these may be sold with the pelts of those dying of murrain; and hence much may be saved on these by shrewdness, for some careful people have the flesh of those dying of murrain put into water for the period between the hour of nine and vespers, and afterwards hung up so that the water drains off; the flesh is afterwards salted and dried and they are made worth something and can be distributed among the workpeople and the household; and to prevent loss in the account an allowance in the daily expenses according to a fixed price can be made for the flesh so used. . . .

OXEN VERSUS HORSES

The Belgae even before 55 B.C. had begun a work with heavy ploughs which the Saxons continued, and the demand for land perhaps reached its greatest in the thirteenth century. This gradual increase in the area under cultivation and the corresponding diminution of waste land does not get recorded by the chroniclers.

Source: Walter of Henley chap. 4 from F. H. Cripps-Day, *The Manor Farm to which are added reprint-facsimiles of The Boke of Husbandry an English Translation of the XIIIth century Tract on Husbandry by Walter of Henley Ascribed to Robert Grosseteste and Printed by Wynkyn de Worde*, c. 1510, Bernard Quaritch 1931.

The plough of oxen is better than the plough of hors but yf it be upon stony grounde ye whiche greveth sore the oxen in theyr fete. And ye plough of hors is more costly than ye plough of oxen and yet shal your plough of oxen doo as moche werke in a yere as youre plough of hors though ye dryve your hors faster than ye do your oxen yet in what grounde so ever it be youre plough of oxen yf ye tele your londe wel and evenly they shal do as moche werke one daye with another as your plough of hors and yf the grounde be tough your oxen shall werke where youre hors shall stande styll.

And yf ye wyll knowe how moche the one is costlver than ye other I shal teche you. It is a costume that bestes that go to the plough shall werke from ye feste of Saynt Luke [18 Oct.] unto the fest of saynt Elene in Maye [21 May] that is to saye xxv wekes and yf youre hors sholde be kepte in a good plyght to werke he must have dayly the syxt parte of a busshel of otes pryce ½d. and in gresse in somer season xii d. And every weke that he standeth at drye mete one with another ½d. in straw for lytter.

And in shoynge as often as he is shodde on all foure fete iiii d. at the leest.

The somme of his expenses in the yere is ix s. vi½ d. besyde hay and chafe and other thynges.

And as for the oxe ye maye kepe hym in good plyght dayly to doo his Journey gyvynge hym every weke thre oten sheves pryce i d. because x oten sheves yelde a busshell of otes yf they be made by the extent and in somer season xii d. in gresse.

The somme of his expenses by the yere is iii s. i d. besyde strawe and chafe.

And yf a hors be overset and brought downe with labour it is adventure and ever he recover it. And yf your oxe be oversette and brought doune with labour ye shall for xii d. in somer season have hym so pastured that he shal be stronge ynough to do your werke or elles shall be so fatte that ye may selle hym for as moche moneye as he coste you.

DEATH OF LLYWELYN EIN LLYW OLAF, 1282

After the fall of Llywelyn Edward I secured his hold on Wales by the construction of castles. In 1301 he gave his son Edward, who was a native of Wales, the principality of Wales.

Source: *Peckham's Letters*, Rolls Series, 1882 translated by Mary Salmon. *A Source-book of Welsh History*, O.U.P. 1952, p. 181.

Further Reading: T. Stephens, *Literature of the Kymry*, 1876.

December 17, 1282. To my Lord the King.

To his very dear Lord, Edward, by Grace of God, King of England, etc., Friar John, by the permission of God, Archbishop of Canterbury and Primate of all England, greeting in great reverence.

Sire, know that those who were at the death of Llywelyn found. . . some small things which we have seen. Among these things there was a treasonable letter disguised by false names. And that you may be warned, we send a copy of the letter to the Bishop of Bath, and the letter itself Edmund Mortimer has, with

Llywelyn's privy seal, and these things you may have at your pleasure. And this we send to warn you, and not that anyone should be troubled for it.

Besides this, Sire, know that Lady Maud Longespere prayed us by letter to absolve Llywelyn, that he might be buried in consecrated ground, and we sent word to her that we would do nothing if it could not be proved that he showed signs of true repentance before his death. And Edmund de Mortimer said to me that he had heard from his servants who were at the death that he asked for the priest before his death, but without sure certainty we will do nothing.

Besides this, Sire, know that the very day that he was killed a white monk sang mass to him, and my Lord Roger de Mortimer had the vestments.

Besides this, Sire, we ask you to take pity on clerks, that you will suffer no one to kill them or to do them bodily injury. And know, Sire, God protect you from evil, if you do not prevent it to your power, you fall into the sentence, for to suffer what one can prevent is the same as to consent. And, therefore, Sire, we pray you that it may please you that the clerks which are in Snowdon may go thence and seek better things with their property in France or elsewhere. For because we believe that Snowdon will be yours, if it happen that, in conquering or afterwards, harm is done to clerks, God will accuse you of it, and your good renown will be blemished, and we shall be considered a coward. And of these things, Sire, if it please you, send us your pleasure, for we will give thereto what counsel we can, either by going thither or by some other way. And know, Sire, if you do not fulfil our prayers you will put us in sadness, which we shall never leave in this mortal life. Sire, God keep you and all that belongs to you.

This letter was written at Pembridge, Thursday after St. Lucy's Day.

QUARRYMEN, 1290—1384

Important quarries at Wheatley, Oxfordshire, used from Roman until recent times, provided the raw material for churches, castles, monasteries and Oxford colleges. E. M. Jope has studied actual buildings in which the stone was used and has shown that the carving in the crossing of the chapel of the oldest Oxford college building, Merton, was the work of a Wheatley mason called Thomas Prat. References in various documents tell us about these obscure men who made the glories of the great period of English Gothic architecture possible.

Source: Facsimiles with translations of original documents in W. O. Hassall, *Wheatley Records* 956–1956, Oxfordshire Record Society, xxxvii, 1956.

1. Merton College, Oxford, accounts, 1290.

   Also on wages of 6 carvers 10 s. 5 d.

   Also on wages of 2 masons for a week 3 s. 2 d.

   Also on 1 cart hired for two turns going to Watele 8 d

   Also paid to Thomas Prat of Watele 15 s. 2½ d.

2. Commission to get stone for Windsor Castle, 1362, from P.R.O., Patent Roll.

The king to all and singular sheriffs, mayors, bailiffs, ministers and his other faithfuls to whom etc. health. Know that we have appointed our beloved William Cok of Whatelee to have transported both by land and water stone which we have had provided in quarries at Teynton and Whatele for our works in our castle of Wyndsore to the said castle and to take sufficient carriage for the same stone both within the liberties and without excepting the fee of the church at our costs to be paid by the hand of our beloved William de Mulsho, clerk of our said works, and to take and arrest all those whom he finds refractory in this part or rebellious and to arrest and lead them to our said castle to be delivered to our prison there to remain in the same until we decide otherwise about ordaining their punishment. And therefore we order you strictly commanding that ye be attentive helpers and allies in the aforesaid to the same William Cok as often as and according as you are required by him about this on our part. . . . Witness the king at Westminster 28 April. By the king himself.

3. Windsor Castle accounts, Nov. 1363—13 April, 1365, from P.R.O., Controller's Roll, E. 101/493/17.

And in 5718 ft. of Whatele stone bought from Nicholas Harald for the said works at 2½ d. a foot, £59.11.3 And in 2598 ft. of stone bought from William Eustas for the said works at 2½ d. a foot, £27.1.3.

4. Abingdon Abbey Treasurer's Account, 1383–4, with Abingdon Corporation, printed in Latin by R. E. G. Kirk, *The accounts of the obedientiars of Abingdon Abbey*, Camden Soc., N.S. 51, 1892, pp. 47–9. (The name of the quarry is mentioned in a royal Saxon charter about an estate given to Abingdon when St. Aethelwold was rebuilding it in 956).

	£	s.	d.
For the boatman at Sandford for water carriage from Whatele	1	0	0
On a tunic for ditto	0	5	5
On lead for cloister gargoyles and plumber's work	0	8	8
On 400 ft. of free stone from Taynton at 3 d. a ft. bought	5	0	0
On 62 loads for same giving 2 s. 4 d. a load ..	7	4	8
On expenses of William Stevens to Taynton on occasions	0	1	2
On 232 ft. of great free stone from Whatele at 4 d. a ft.	3	17	4
On 1099 ft. of common free stone from Whatele at 3 d. a ft.	13	14	9
On 260 ft. rag stone there for key-stones at 3 d. a ft.	3	15	0
On 101 ft. of ashlars giving 18 s. at 100 ft. ..	0	18	2½
On 30 ft. of rags for the steps at the dormitory door, at 4 d. a ft.	0	10	0
On 234 loads for all the above stone at 14 d. a cart..	13	13	0
On cement	0	0	10½

THIRTEEN CLAIMANTS TO THE SCOTTISH CROWN ACCEPT EDWARD I AS SOVEREIGN LORD OF SCOTLAND, 5 June, 1291

Edward I offered himself as arbitrator among thirteen claimants to the throne of Alexander III, who died in 1286, and of his heir the Maid of Norway who died on her way to Scotland in 1290. The three strongest candidates were John Balliol, Robert Brus and John Hastings, descended from the three daughters of David, Earl of Huntingdon, the great-uncle of Alexander. The crown was awarded to Balliol as descendant of the eldest daughter, though Brus was nearer by one degree to Earl David, on 17 November 1292. He swore fealty on 20 November 1292 and did homage for the kingdom of Scotland on 26 December 1292.

Other claimants were Robert de Pinkeny, Patrick Galithly, Roger de Mandeville, and Eric II, King of Norway.

Source: *National Manuscripts of Scotland*, translated by W. C. Dickinson, G. Donaldson and I. A. Milne, *A Source Book of Scottish History*, T. Nelson 1952, i, 113.

Further Reading: Sir Archibald Dunbar, *Scottish Kings: A revised Chronology of Scottish History*, 1005–1625, *with Notices of the Principal Events, Tables of Regnal Years, Pedigrees, Calendars, etc.* 2nd ed., Edinburgh, 1906.

. . . To all who shall see or hear these letters, Florence Count of Holland, Robert de Brus Lord of Annandale, John Balliol Lord of Galloway, John de Hastings Lord of Abergavenny, John Comyn Lord of Badenoughe, Patrik de Dumbar Earl of the March, John de Vescy for his father, Nicolas de Soules and William de Ros, greeting in God.

Seeing that we profess to have right to the kingdom of Scotland, and to set forth maintain and declare such right before that person who has most power, jurisdiction and reason to try our right; and the noble Prince, Sir Edward by the grace of God King of England, has shown to us, by good and sufficient reasons, that to him belongs,. and that he ought to have, the sovereign lordship of the said kingdom of Scotland, and the cognizance of hearing, trying and determining our right; We, of our own will, without any manner of force or constraint, will, concede and grant to receive justice before him as sovereign lord of the land; and we are willing, moreover, and promise to

have and hold firm and stable his act, and that he shall have the
realm, to whom right shall give it before him. In witness of
this thing we have put our seals to this writing. Made and given
at Norham, the Tuesday next after the Ascension, the year of
grace one thousand two hundred and ninety-first.

A HOLKHAM RENTAL, c. 1295

Lists of taxpayers for each place at various dates are kept in the
Public Record Office among Subsidy and Poll tax returns in the fourteenth century. These are not complete as very poor people would
not be included. Sometimes the names of the forgotten people are
recorded in lists of rents due from tenants. The one here includes the
Prior of Peterstone because he had land at Holkham, although he
did not live there, and it only includes those who paid rents to one
out of several landholders. It does give the names of a number of
people who lived at Holkham on what was described in the early
eighteenth century as ' a barren waste ' by the Earl of Leicester who
turned it into Holkham Park.

Source: Translated from Holkham Deed 11, in the Holkham Estate
Office by permission of the Earl of Leicester.

Quitrents due from tenants of Geoffrey le Bret of Holkham.
At the feast of Michaelmas.

Reginald Digge	1½ d.	Emma of Field	2 d.
John Silke	4½ d.	Roger Ernald	4 d.
Roger Belneye	6¾ d.	Richard le Norne	6½ d.
William Curstun	1 d.	Thomas Warin	3 d.
Simon Amund	6¾ d.	John Ide	7 d.
Hervey Buleman	1 d.	Adam Dersi	2 d.
Roger Elurich	3½ d.	Avice Rutele	2 d.
Bartholomew de Burgate	½ d.	Richard Olive	1 d.
Prior of Peterston	11½ d.	John Gerard	2½ d.
Adam Carpenter	12 d.	Ralph Runur	3 d.
William Mere	3 d.	Gilbert Payn	1 d.
Ralph Marut 3 d. and 1 capon		Emma le Colt	3½ d.
Richard Wulmer	½ d.	William Craske	1¼ d.
William Duc	1 d.	Robert son of Emma	2½ d.
Simon Schales	½ d.	John Aynild	1 d.
William son of Beta	1½ d.	Roger Spellere	1 d.

Robert Ape	1½d.	Warin de Ranffles	1 d.
Matilda Ernald	1½d.	Roger son of Emma	2 d.
Gilbert Gurle	1½d.	William de Hyndryngham	½ d.
Roger Thurbern	1½d.	Hervey Quytbred	½ d.
Everard Underhill	1½d.	Humphrey Davy	½ d.
Gilbert Daleman	1d.	John le Ward of Dalling	½ d.

BERWICK CASTLE STORES, 22 October, 1298

The invasion of Scotland by Edward I, Hammer of the Scots, fierce border raids and the association of Scotland with England's traditional enemy France is an exciting story which stirs national pride, and when feelings are stirred accurate observation suffers. In an inventory, however, one enters a building room by room and should find everything listed. Inventories throw an intimate light on the contents of shops and private houses as well as of the Libraries of monasteries.

Source: J. Stevenson, *Documents Illustrative of the History of Scotland*, 1870.

Further Reading: W. C. Dickinson, G. Donaldson, I. A. Milne, *A Source Book of Scottish History*, vol. i from Earliest Times to 1424. W. M. Mackenzie, *The Medieval Castle in Scotland*, 1927.

. . . Two light hauberks, without hoods, three hauberks of strong iron without hoods, five pair of covertures of iron and two headpieces of iron, two pairs of shoes of iron, six old targes, one old shield, one targe of boiled leather, one pair of firepans, four boxes, seven crossbows with winches with old cords, and four of them are out of order for want of cords, six crossbows for two feet, one of which wants two cords and one nut, and seven new ' costes ' varnished as it appears, etc., eight crossbows for one foot, all in order excepting four nuts, one ' teller ' with a winch, and one for one foot, four old bands, one coffer, three vices, one quarter of canvas, 189 wings of geese for feathering crossbow-bolts.

In the hall, four great tables, two pairs of trestles, one form, one chess-board.

In the larder, two pitchers of pewter, one basin of pewter.

In the kitchen, one great cauldron, one brass pot of two gallons, one possnet of half a gallon, two little andirons, one gridiron, one oven.

In the bakehouse (there are three in the castle), four leads, one great tub, three frail ones, four pair of handles, one trough, a barrel for boulting.

In the chapel, a new vestment (and an old one whereof is wanting a stole and a fanon), of new cloth of silk, a gilt chalice, a missal, four napkins, a great cross and a small one, an image of our Lady, a great ' crawe ' [=crow-bar?].

In the forge, three troughs and three anvils, six pair of pincers, three pair of bellows, two great hammers, one great anvil and pickaxe, and one little one, four little hammers, one pickaxe, four chisels, two tongs, one barrel for beating iron, twelve pair of forges, one handle, two stones for grinding with, one axle of iron for stones.

In the great tower for the engineer, four tillers without iron, three posts with windlasses and a tiller, a hundred pounds of lead in one lump, and another great piece of brass of ten stone.

In the body of the castle four engines fit for service, one of which has two cords to draw it, and each of the others one cord.

On the walls of the castle are three springalds with all their furniture excepting three cords.

In the little chamber beyond the bakehouse four score and fifty arrows, a chain with forty-eight links, and another chain of twenty-one links, one great iron hammer for the box of an engine, five corner-pieces of iron for the springalds, and seven quarters and a half of sea coals. And four score bolts for crossbows of one foot, and iron for the heads of guards for crossbows of one foot, and five hundred bolts for crossbows of two feet, and three hundred bolts for crossbows with winches, a headpiece of iron, and a green carpet with a border of red, much worn, which belonged to Sir Osbert de Spaldington.

EDWARD OF CARNARVON, PRINCE OF WALES,
1301

Edward II, as king (1307–27) aroused widespread opposition and Thomas of Lancaster, his chief baronial opponent, came to be regarded as a martyr. He shocked contemporaries by a vulgar interest in driving, swimming and rowing and in rural crafts like thatching and smithing. He was the first king after the Conquest to lose his throne and also the first about whose early years we have intimate detail. He became twenty-one on 25 April 1305.

Source: *Letters of Edward Prince of Wales* 1304–1305, edited by Professor Hilda Johnstone for the Roxburghe Club. The original is a roll containing between six and seven hundred entries. A few extracts were quoted by Mrs. M. A. E. Green in *Lives of the Princesses of England*, 6 vols. 1849–55.

Further Reading: J. Conway Davies, *The Baronial Opposition to Edward II*, 1918. Hilda Johnstone, *Edward of Carnarvon*, 1284–1307, 1946.

[To Louis of Evreux, half-brother of King Philip IV of France] We are sending you a big trotting palfrey, which can hardly carry, and stands still when laden; and we send you some misshapen greyhounds from Wales, which can catch a hare well if they find it asleep, and running dogs which can follow at an amble, for well we know how you love the joy of lazy dogs. And, dear cousin, if you would care for anything else from our land of Wales, we will send you some wild men, if you like, who will know well how to give young sprigs of nobility their education.

[Written when disgraced for insulting a royal minister and ' the lord king removed him from his household for wellnigh half a year, because he had uttered coarse and harsh words to a certain minister of his. Nor did he permit his son to come into his sight until he had made satisfaction.']

Edward etc. to the Earl of Lincoln, etc., greeting and dear friendship. Know, sire, that on Sunday the thirteenth of June we came to Midhurst, where we found our lord the king our father; and on Monday following, on account of certain words which were reported to him as having passed between us and the Bishop of Chester, he became so enraged with us, that he has forbidden us to be so bold as to come into his household, we or any of our following, and he has forbidden all the folk of his household and of the Exchequer to give or lend us anything for the upkeep of our household. We have remained at Midhurst to await his goodwill and favour, and we shall follow him all the

time as best we can, ten or twelve leagues away from his household, so that we may recover his good will as we greatly desire.

Wherefore we pray you especially that on your return from
Canterbury you will come to us, for we have great need of your
aid and counsel.

To Sir Walter Reynolds [Keeper of the Prince's Household]
etc. Because our lord the king is so angry with us on account of
the Bishop of Chester that he has forbidden us or any of our
followers to come into his household, and has also forbidden
the people of his household or of the Exchequer to give or lend
us anything for the sustenance of our household; we bid you to
take counsel for sending us money with all speed for the sustenance of our household; and on no account reveal any of our
business to the Bishop of Chester or to anybody at the Exchequer.

To Sir Walter Reynolds Treasurer, etc. greeting. Since
we hear that Queen Marie of France and Monsire Louis her son
will soon be coming to England, and that we shall have to meet
them and keep them company while they are over here; and it is
desirable therefore to be well mounted in respect of palfreys
and well dressed in respect of robes and other matters against
their coming; we bid you to cause to be brought for our use two
fair palfreys suitable for our own riding and two saddles with
reins out of the best we have in the care of Gilbert of Taunton,
and the best and finest cloth that you can find for sale in London
for two or three robes for our use with the fur and loops appur-
tenant; and when you have provided these things, cause them to
come to us wherever we may be as quickly as you can.

Edward etc. to his dear clerk Sir Walter Reynolds, etc.
greeting. We bid you to cause to be paid to Adam le Poleter
[vintner] of Reading, bearer of these letters, the money which
we owe him, as well you know, and which we have already
bidden you to pay on other occasions; so that he may not have
to return to us again for the said payment.

Edward etc. to all to whom these letters shall come, greeting.
As we are sending Ralph atte Strete, yeoman of our Poultry,
bearer of these letters, into divers parts to make purveyance of

the things that appertain to his office for our household, we require you to give him aid and advice in so doing when he shall ask it of you; and so far as in you lies, do not suffer him to be disturbed or hindered in fulfilling his office aforesaid. Given under etc. at Langley on the nineteenth day of January in the thirty-third year etc. These letters to last till Easter next to come.

PLAYGOERS, 1301

From the twelfth century onwards plays were acted just outside the city of London at Clerkenwell not far from the modern Sadler's Wells theatre. In 1411 one play there ' lastyd vij days contynually and there ware the moste parte of the lordes and gentylles of Ynglond '; in 1391 it lasted five days and showed the story of both the Old and the New Testament but on 12 August 1385 the customary play had been banned on the occasion of Richard II making an expedition against Scotland. The same place was famous for wrestling matches for centuries.

Further Reading: Sir E. K. Chambers, *The Medieval Stage*, 1903 and *English Literature at the Close of the Middle Ages*, Oxford History of English Literature 1945.

(1) *Source*: Public Record Office, Ancient Petition no. 4858, in French.

To our Lord the King. The poor Prioress of Clerkenwell prays that he will to provide and order a remedy because the people of London lay waste and destroy her corn and grass by their miracle plays and wrestling matches so that she has no profit of them nor can have any unless the king have pity for they are a savage folk and we cannot stand against them and cannot get justice by any law. So, Sire, for God's sake have pity upon us.

(2) *Source*: British Museum: *Cartulary of St. Mary Clerkenwell*, in Latin. Summaries of similar royal commands are printed in the *Calendars of Close* and *Patent Rolls*.

Edward by the grace of God King of England Lord of Ireland and Duke of Aquitaine to the Mayor and sheriffs of London greeting. Whereas we have learnt by the earnest complaint of the Prioress of Clerkenwell, our beloved in Christ, that men of the said city on horse and on foot in great number come to the fields, meadows and pastures of the said prioress at Clerkenwell with their followers and make wrestlings and other plays there; and flatten the enclosures, hedges and ditches that are around the corn, the meadows and the pastures of the same prioress; and crush and trample the corn and grass in many ways and this is to the great loss of the said prioress and a grievance; We therefore wish to attend to the redress of the said prioress in this matter and do order you with a firm injunction that if it is thus in the said city you do have ordered and proclaimed publicly on our behalf that they do not dare in future exercise such wrestlings and plays in the fields, meadows and pastures of the said prioress whereby she can receive hurt and loss. In this we hold you that no repeated complaint reach us whereby we have to attend to this matter further. Witnessed by me at Fakenham. 8 April in the twenty-ninth year of our reign [1301].

(3) *Source*: Register of the Charterhouse in Sir William St. John Hope, *History of the Charterhouse*, 1925, in Latin.

On another occasion they [disorderly anti-monastic rioters] came to the convent of the nuns of Clerkenwell with a horrible tumult and the din of trumpet and there they applied fire which they had brought with them to the gates with their bars and posts and with the hedges and they destroyed all the enclosure of these nuns. The only reason they alleged for themselves was that they used to have plays and wrestlings there and other suchlike and these same things they repeated there the same day.

(4) There are many pictures of the Creation, Passion etc. as they would have been acted in plays at the beginning of the fourteenth century in the *Holkham Bible Picture Book*. The surviving texts are somewhat later in date.

Source: F. Devon, *Issues of the Exchequer*, 1837.

1391. A royal gift of £10 to the Clerks for the play of the Passion of our Lord and the Creation of the world at Skynners' Well [Clerkenwell].

A SUBURBAN TITHE DISPUTE, 16 August, 1312

The proper payment of tithes seemed so important in clerical eyes that Cain was regarded as an avaricious peasant who did not pay his tithes properly—the reason why God rejected his sacrifice being that there were tares in the wheat as is illustrated in the *Holkham Bible Picture Book* wherein the smoke decends to Hell's mouth.

St. Sepulchre's parish is just outside the walls of London by Newgate. By the end of the fifteenth century it was populous but in 1312 the dispute shows that land was under the plough there. Much land there belonged to the Prioress of Clerkenwell, and to the Prior of St. Bartholomew's.

Source: Translated from De Banco Roll, Trinity 6 Edward II, printed in *Year Books 6 and 7 Edward II*, Selden Soc., pp. 16–18. The De Banco Rolls and other Plea Rolls contain the records of many disputes, but they are so bulky that it has not been possible to index them, though a typescript summary of cases in them relating to Dorset, deposited in Dorchester Museum, shows how much of litigation the Prioress of Clerkenwell had about an outlying estate in Dorset. Cases of legal interest were reported in *Year Books* which run from 1292 to 1534. No other country has anything like them.

Further Reading: Holdsworth, *History of English Law*, 1903–9, vol. ii. W. B. Bolland, *The Year Books*, 1921.

. . . . The same Prioress and others were attached to answer the Prior of St. Bartholomew of Smithfield, London, in a suit why they, with Walter the carter, William the smith, John the cook, Peter Gerard and John Neulyn, with force and arms took and carried off the goods and chattels of the said Prior to the value of 40 s. and otherwise brought him injuries to his great loss. . . . The Prior by his attorney complains that the said Prioress and others etc. on Wednesday next after the Feast of the Assumption of the Blessed Mary in the sixth year of our present king with force and arms to wit with swords, bows and arrows took and carried off goods and chattels, to wit barley, of the Prior to the value of 40 s. . . . The Prioress says that the place where the Prior complains that the said corn was carried off is the soil of the Prioress whereof she is lady. She says she ploughed and sowed the same and in the following autumn reaped the growing corn and bound it, carrying both the tenth part by reason of her church of Clerkenwell whereof she is parson and the other nine parts, not separate from them, as lady. The Prior claimed the tithe and came and wanted to take tithe and carry it off against the will of the Prioress and she resisted him. Alice [of the byre], Rose [Barage] and William [Bodmyn] say they did nothing against the peace but were with the Prioress. . . . The Prior says the corn was tithed in respect of his church of St. Sepulchre outside Newgate whereof he is parson. . . . Jurors chosen by consent of the parties say on oath that the tithes belonged to the Prior and his predecessors from time beyond memory. . .

SCOTTISH LIBERATION

(1) William Wallace, the leader of Scottish resistance, was executed on 23 August 1305.

Source: ' Matthew of Westminster ', *Flowers of History*. This Matthew is an imaginary name for a person who never existed, the *Flowers* being partly compiled and partly composed by various writers at St. Albans and Westminster.

Further Reading: R. L. G. Ritchie, *The Normans in Scotland*, 1954. A. F. Murison, *William Wallace*, 1898.

(We omit horrible details of atrocities attributed to Wallace which include burning boys in schools and churches.)

Wilielmus Waleis, a man void of pity, a robber given to sacrilege, arson and homicide, more hardened in cruelty than Herod, more raging in madness than Nero . . . was condemned to a most cruel but justly deserved death. He was drawn through the streets of London at the tails of horses, until he reached a gallows of unusual height, especially prepared for him; there he was suspended by a halter; but taken down while yet alive, he was mutilated, his bowels torn out and burned in a fire, his head then cut off, his body divided into four, and his quarters transmitted to four principal parts of Scotland. Behold the end of the merciless man, who himself perishes without mercy.

(2) The Scots won a great pitched battle at Bannockburn, with one third of the forces of the English army, thanks to the superior generalship of Robert Bruce, 24 June 1314. Edward II fled and Scotland remained unconquered for ever.

Source: *The Chronicle of Lanercost*, translated with notes by Sir Herbert Maxwell, James Maclehose 1913, p. 207.

Written by a pro-English Franciscan, not connected with Lanercost, and especially useful for the beginning of the Hundred Years War. The writer was a witness of events at Berwick in 1296, 1312 and 1333.

The Scots made a Carmelite friar, called Barton, who had been brought to celebrate the expected English victory, recount the English defeat. Barbour wrote fifty years after the battle but enlarged the story with facts learnt from combatants whom he knew. No medieval battle has been recorded in so much detail.

Further Reading: W. M. Mackenzie, *The Battle of Bannockburn*, 1913. T. Miller, *The Site of the Battle of Bannockburn*, Historical Association Leaflet no. 85, 1931.

On the morrow—an evil, miserable and calamitous day for the English—when both sides had made themselves ready for battle, the English archers were thrown forward before the line, and the Scottish archers engaged them, a few being killed and wounded on either side; but the King of England's archers quickly put the others to flight. Now when the two armies had approached very near each other, all the Scots fell on their knees to repeat *Pater-Noster*, commending themselves to God and seeking help from heaven; after which they advanced boldly against the English. They had so arranged their army that two columns went abreast in advance of the third, so that neither should be in advance of the other; and the third followed, in which was Robert [Bruce: actually three columns went in front and Bruce with a fourth, behind]. Of a truth, when both armies engaged each other, and the great horses of the English charged the pikes of the Scots, as it were into a dense forest, there arose a great and terrible crash of spears broken and of destriers wounded to the death; and so they remained without movement for a while. Now the English in the rear could not reach the Scots because the leading division was in the way, nor could they do anything to help themselves, wherefore there was nothing for it but to take to flight. This account I heard from a trustworthy person who was present as eyewitness.

In the leading division were killed the Earl of Gloucester, Sir John Comyn, Sir Pagan de Typtoft, Sir Edmund de Mauley and many other nobles, besides foot soldiers who fell in great numbers. Another calamity which befell the English was that, whereas they had shortly before crossed a great ditch called Bannockburn, into which the tide flows, and now wanted to recross it in confusion, many nobles and others fell into it with their horses in the crush, while others escaped with much difficulty, and many were never able to extricate themselves from the ditch; thus Bannockburn was spoken about for many years in English throats.

(Here follows a long dirge in Latin hexameters, which will not repay translation.)

THE MANER OF THE SCOTTIS, AND HOWE THEY CAN WARRE, 1327

Intermittent strife as here described between England and Scotland continued throughout the Hundred Years War, punctuated by occasional battles. It fostered national feeling both sides of the Border.

Source: *Lord Berners' Translation of The Chronicle of Syr John Froissart* (1523), Cap xvii. Froissart derived this account from Jehan le Bel who followed John de Hainault to England and fought in Edward III's early Scottish campaigns.

Further Reading: Reprint of *Chronicle of Froissart* in *Tudor Translations* ed. W. E. Henley, D. Nutt 1901.

And whan they hadde soiourned .iii. weeks after thys sayd fray, than they had knoweledge fro the kyng, by the Marshals of the ooste, that ye next weeke every man shuld provyde for cartis and chairettis, tentis and pavylions to lye in the felde, and for all other necessaryes therto belongynge, to the entent to drawe towarde Scotlande. And whan every man was redy aparailed, the kyng and all his barones went out of the cite, and the first nyght they lodged vi myle forwarde. And syr John of Heynault and his company were lodged alwayes as nere the kyng as myght be, to do hym the more honour, and also to thentent that the archers shulde have noo vauntage of hym nor of his companye. And there the kyng aboode .ii. dayes and .ii.

nyghtes, taryeng for all them that were behynd, and to be well advysed that they lacked nothyng. And on the .iii. daye they dislodged, and went forwarde tyll they came to the cite of Durham a dayes journey within the countrey called Northembrelande, the whiche at that tyme was a savage and a wylde countrey, full of desartis and mountaignes, and a ryght pore countrey of every thyng, savyng of beastis: throughe the whiche there ronneth a ryver ful of flynt and great stones, called the water of Tyne. And on this ryver standeth the towne and castell of Carlyel, the whiche sometyme was kyng Arthurs, and helde his courte there often tymes. Also on that ryver is assysed the towne of Newe castell upon Tyne: in the whiche towne was redy the Marchall of Inglande, with a great company of men of armes, to kepe the countrey agaynst the Scottis; and at Carlyel was the lorde of Huford [Hereford] and the lorde Mowbray, who were governours there, to defende the Scottis the passage; for the Scottis coulde nat entre into Inglande, but they must passe this sayd ryver in one place or other. The Inglisshemen coulde here no tydyngis of the Scottis tyll they were come to the entre of the sayd countrey. The Scottis were passed this ryver so prively, that they of Carlyel nor yet of Newe castell knew nothyng thereof, for bitwene the sayd townes it was .xxiiii. Englisshe myle.

These Scottysshe men are right hardy, and sore travelyng in harneys and in warres; for whan they wyll entre into Ingland, within a daye and a nyght, they wyll dryve theyr hole host .xxiiii.myle, for they are all a horsbacke, without it be the traundals and laggers of ye oost, who folow after, a foote. The knyghtis and squiers are well horsed, and the comon people and other, on litell hakeneys and geldyngis—and they carey with them no cartis nor chariettis for the diversities of the mountaignes that they must passe through in the countrey of Northumberlande. They take with them noo purveyaunce of brede nor wyne, for their usage and sobrenes is suche in tyme of warre, that they wyll passe in the journey a great long tyme, with flesshe halfe soden, without brede, and drynke of the ryver water without wyne: and they nother care for pottis nor pannis, for they seeth beastis in their owne skynnes. They are ever sure to fynde plenty of beastis in the countrey that they wyll passe throughe. Therfore they cary with them none other purveyaunce, but on their horse: bitwene the saddyll and the pannell, they trusse a brode plate of metall, and behynde the saddyl they wyll have a lytle sacke of ootemele, to the entent that whan they have eaten of the sodden flesshe, than they ley this plate on the fyre, and tempre a lytle of the ootemele: and whan the plate is hote, they cast of the thyn paste, theron, and so make a lytle cake in maner of a crakenell, or bysket, and that they eate to comfort with all theyr stomakis. Wherfore it is no great merveile, though they make greatter journeys than other people do. And in this maner were the Scottis entred into the sayd countrey, and wasted and brent all about as they went, and toke great nombre of bestis. They were to the nombre of .iiii. M. men of armes, knightis and squiers, mounted on good horses, and other .x. M. men of warre were armed after their gyse right hardy and firse mounted on lytle hakeneys, the whiche were never tyed nor kept at hard meate, but lette go to pasture in the feldis and busshes. They had .ii. good capitayns, for kyng Robert of Scotland, who in his dayes had ben hardy and prudent, was as than of great age, and sore greved with ye great sickenes, but he hadde made one of his capitaynes, a gentle prince, and a valyant in armes, called the erle of Morrell [Moray], beryng in his armes sylver .iii. Creylles [*oreillers*=cushions] gowles [red], and the other was the lorde William [James] Duglas, who was reputed for the most hardy knyght, and greattest adventurer in al the realme of Scotland, and he bare azure a cheffe sylver. These .ii. lordes were renomed as chief in all dedis of armes, and great prowesse in all Scotlande.

SIR JAMES DOUGLAS, 'THE GOOD', KILLED
25 August, 1330

Edward I stripped Sir James Douglas of his inheritance and he became a constant companion of Robert Bruce from the day of his coronation at Scone, 27 March 1306. He thrice defeated the English at his own castle of Douglas and destroyed it himself twice. He surprised Roxburgh castle by night, having dressed his soldiers in black robes so as to become invisible. He was knighted on the battlefield of Bannockburn. His complexion earned him the nickname of 'the Black Douglas'. He is described in Fordun's *Scotichronicon* as having lost thirteen battles but won fifty-seven.

Source: John Barbour, *The Bruce*. The father of Scottish poetry records the memory of those who saw 'the good' Sir James face to face.

Further Reading: Sir Herbert Maxwell, *Bruce and the Struggle for Scottish Independence*, 1897. Agnes Mure Mackenzie, *Robert Bruce*, 1934.

> In visage was he some deal gray,
> And had black hair, as I heard say;
> But then, of limbs he was well made,
> With bones great, and shoulders braid;
> His body well made and lenzie,
> As they that saw him said to me.
> When he was blyth, he was lovely,
> And meek, and sweet in company;
> But who in battle might him see,
> Another countenance had he;
> And in his speech he lispt some deal,
> But that set him right wonder well.

VILLAGE TROUBLES, 1332-3

Court rolls are largely concerned with the routine of admitting to their holdings new tenants and fining those who fail to attend the courts.

Source: Extracts translated by permission of the Earl of Leicester from 'Court of Richard Neel, Henry Burgeys, Gilbert Burgeys and William de Waterden held on Friday after the feasts of SS. Peter and Paul 6 Edward III', Holkham deed 82 in the Holkham Estate Office. This is one of a long series of Holkham court rolls. A central list of surviving court rolls is kept by the Manorial Rolls Committee at the Public Record Office.

[After routine business about cases of debt and trespass seven villeins are admitted to various holdings with their broods and forty villeins are fined 1 d. or 2 d. each for having removed their corn outside the land which was held by villein tenure from the lord of the manor. Various offences are 'presented'.]

Adam Charle junior made default and it was ordered to keep in the lord's hand a white tunic worth 6 d. and a barmscyn

[leather apron] worth 12 d. and to take more until he answer
Simon Burgoyne in a plea of debt. . . . Thomas son of William
drew blood from Bartholomew Coltyng spitefully and is fined
3d. . . .

Bertha atte Drove broke into the house of Alice Digge and
is fined 2 d.

Edmund Haldeyn broke into the house of Roger de Monte.
Fine 3d.

Henry Lode made a rescue of a distress taken for execution
of a debt by Richard Blakeman. Fine 2 d.

Margaret and Alice Otes broke the lord's pound for 4 pigs
taken for a debt of the lord and for execution of the court's
decisions. Fine 6 d.

Alice Otes rescued from the lord's bailiff a veil taken in
execution of a decision of the lord's court. Fine 3 d.

Agnes Bulwere rescued from the lord's bailiff a cow taken
on the complaint of Alice Otes. Fine 3 d.

Mariota of the household of Henry Spellere rescued from
William son of Thomas 2 horses taken for services due to him.
Fine 3d.

John le Wrighte, Andrew Underclynt, Brother Adam of
Derham, Edmund Haldeyn, John Silke, John Speller and Adam
Crask made an illegal path over the land of Andrew Underclynt
at the Clynt [an arm of the sea now the ornamental lake in
Holkham Park]. Fine 1 d. each.

Brother Adam of Derham made an illegal path over the lord's
land at Holkham western town's end. Fine 4 d.

Margaret wife of Richard Marchal made an illegal path over
the land of Margaret Godecok at Crosgate. Fine 1 d.

William of the household of Matilda Charle made an illegal
path over the land of the lord at Walsinghamgate with a cart.
Fine 3d.

William Curzoun made an illegal path over the land of
Richard Blakeman at Algeres.

Hervey Buleman, John Acke, Geoffrey Casche and Bernard
Cappe made an illegal path as above. Fine 1 d. each.

[This roll contains various cases of offences against the
assizes of bread and ale by which their nature and sale were

regulated. There is a list of 42 tenants of the manor, including the
Prior of Peterstone and William the parson of Holkham, from
whom distresses are to be taken because they had not yet sworn
fealty.]

SEA-FIGHT AT SLUYS, 24 June, 1340

In pursuance of his claim to the French throne Edward III assumed
the title of King of France and quartered the lilies of France with the
leopards of England on 26 Jan. 1340. He was at Ipswich at Whitsun
and was advised not to sail as the French fleet was waiting to intercept
him. Avesbury says that he replied ' I will go, and you who are
afraid without cause may stay at home.' He sailed with 200 ships and
was joined by 50 more. He was in the cog ' Thomas '. The French
fleet contained nineteen of the greatest ships that had ever been seen
including the ' Christopher ', which had been taken from the English.
The English manoeuvred to get the advantage of the wind, but the
French could not manoeuvre as their ships were lashed together in
four lines. French naval power was destroyed.

Source: Geoffrey le Baker of Swinbrook, translated from E. M.
Thompson's edition by E. Rickert, *Chaucer's World*, O.U.P. 1948,
p. 308. Baker's accounts of battles are the best and are clearly derived
from eyewitnesses. Miss Rickert also translates his long and graphic
account of the Battle of Poitiers. Careful drawings of the latest vessels
with new-fangled rudders, bowsprits and forecastles occur in the
Holkham Bible Picture Book, drawn about 1330.

Further Reading: R. and R. C. Anderson, *The Sailing-ship*, 1926.
C. W. C. Oman, *England and the Hundred Years War*, 1898.

King Edward [III] kept his Whitsuntide at Ipswich, because
he intended from thence to make his passage into Flanders; but,
being informed that the French King had sent a great navy of
Spanish ships and also the whole fleet of France to stop his
passage, he caused his ships of the Cinque Ports and others to be
assembled, so that he had in his fleet, great and small, 260 ships.

Wherefore, on the Thursday before the Nativity of Saint
John the Baptist, having a favourable wind, he began to sail;
and the next day, in the even of the said feast, they descried the
French fleet lying in Swinehaven. Wherefore the King caused
all his fleet to come to anchor.

The next day, being the Feast of Saint John the Baptist,

early in the morning the French fleet divided themselves into three parts, withdrew about a mile, and then approached the King's fleet. When the King saw this, about nine o'clock, having the wind and sun on his back, he set forward and met his enemies as he would have wished; at which the whole fleet gave a terrible shout, and a shower of arrows out of long wooden bows so poured down on the Frenchmen that thousands were slain in that meeting. At length they closed and came to hand blows with pikes, poleaxes, and swords, and some threw stones from the tops of ships, wherewith many were brained. The size and height of the Spanish ships caused many Englishmen to strike many a blow in vain. But, to be short, the first part of the French ships being overcome and all the men spent, the Englishmen entered and took them. The French ships were chained together in such a way that they could not be separated from each other, so that a few Englishmen kept that part of the fleet. They then set upon the second part and with great difficulty made the attack; but when this had been done, the second part was sooner overcome than the first because many of the Frenchmen abandoned their ships and leapt overboard. The Englishmen, having thus overcome the first and second parts of the fleet, and now finding night drawing on, partly for want of light and partly because they were weary, determined to take some rest till the next morning. On this account, during the night thirty ships of the third part fled away, but a large ship called the ' James ' of Dieppe, thinking to have carried away a certain ship of Sandwich belonging to the prior of Canterbury, was stopped, for the sailors so stoutly defended themselves by the help of the Earl of Huntingdon that they saved themselves and their ship from the Frenchmen.

The fight continued all night, and in the morning, the Normans being overcome and taken, there were found in the ship 400 men slain. Moreover, the King understanding that the ships were fled, sent forty well-equipped ships to follow them. . . . In the first group of ships that were taken they found these conquered ships: the ' Denis ', the ' George ', the ' Christopher ' and the ' Blacke Cocke ', all of which had been captured by Frenchmen at Sluys and carried into Normandy. The number of ships of war that were taken was about 230 barges; the number of enemies that were slain and drowned was about 25,000, and of Englishmen about 4,000, among whom were four knights. . . .

MISHANDLING BOOKS

Richard de Bury, appointed Bishop of Durham and Chancellor by Edward III, found time between Scottish raids to write a book in which he complains of ill-treatment of books by people who eat fruit and cheese over them or use straws or flowers for markers.

Source: Richard de Bury, *The Philobiblon*, completed on 24 Jan. 1345 shortly before Richard's death on 14 April, translated by A. Taylor, University of California Press, 1948, p. 95.

Especially, moreover, must we restrain impudent youths from handling books—those youths who, when they have learned to draw the shapes of letters, soon begin, if opportunity be granted them, to be uncouth scribblers on the best volumes and, where they see some larger margin above the text, make a show with monstrous letters; and if any other triviality whatsoever occurs to their imagination, their unchastened pen hastens at once to draw it out . . . a practice which we have seen to be too often injurious to the best of books, both as concerns their usefulness and their price. . . . Let no crying child admire the pictures in the capital letters, lest he defile the parchment with his wet hand, for he touches instantly whatever he sees. Laymen, moreover, who look in the same way at a book lying upside down as when it is open in its natural way, are wholly unworthy the intercourse of books. . . . Again, a becoming cleanness of hands would add much both to books and scholars. . . .

BATTLE OF CRECY, SATURDAY, 26 August, 1346

On the death of Charles IV, King of France, Edward III claimed the French throne as the heir of King Philip IV, through his mother Isabella ' the She-wolf of France '. Philip's army was much larger than Edward's and the French intention was to crush the English in a corner between the Somme and the sea. Edward was able to choose his own ground for fighting and there was bad generalship and indiscipline on the French side. These factors combined with the skill of the bowmen gave the victory to the English. Avesbury says that the French losses were probably about equal to the whole English army. After the victory Edward proceeded to Calais which he took after a siege on 3 August 1347.

Source: Sir John Froissart, *The Chronicles of England, France, Spain etc. etc.* Epitomized edition, Routledge 1891. He describes the whole of the battle at length and should be read by all interested in the action and pageantry of fourteenth-century warfare.

Further Reading: A. H. Burne, *The Crecy War*, 1955. I. G. Sanders, *Feudal Military Service in England*, 1956. The Holkham Bible Picture Book contains a picture of Armageddon which shows in detail the arms and armour of about 1330. It is divided into two panels. In the upper the nobles fight the nobles, many using recent inventions like retractable vizors. In the lower panel the commons fight the commons with cheaper and more old-fashioned weapons.

There is no man, unless he had been present, that can imagine or describe truly the confusion of that day, especially the bad management and disorder of the French, whose troops were out of number. What I know, and shall relate in this book, I have learnt chiefly from the English, and from those attached to Sir John of Hainault, who was always near the person of the King of France. The English, who, as I have said, were drawn up in three divisions, and seated on the ground, on seeing their enemies advance, rose up undauntedly and fell into their ranks. The [Black] prince's battalion, whose archers were formed in the manner of a portcullis, and the men-at-arms in the rear, was the first to do so. The Earls of Northampton and Arundel, who commanded the second division, posted themselves in good order on the prince's wing to assist him if necessary.

You must know that the French troops did not advance in any regular order, and that as soon as their king came in sight of the English his blood began to boil, and he cried out to his marshals, ' Order the Genoese forward and begin the battle in the name of God and St. Denis '. There were about 15,000 Genoese cross-bow men; but they were quite fatigued, having marched on foot that day six leagues, completely armed and carrying their cross-bows, and accordingly they told the constable they were not in a condition to do any great thing in battle. The Earl of Alençon hearing this, said, ' This is what one gets by employing such scoundrels, who fall off when there is any need for them.' During this time a heavy rain fell, accompanied by thunder and a very terrible eclipse of the sun; and, before this rain, a great flight of crows hovered in the air over all the battalions, making a loud noise; shortly afterwards it cleared up, and the sun shone very bright; but the French had it in their faces and the English on their backs. When the Genoese were somewhat in order they approached the English and set up a loud shout, in order to frighten them; but the English remained quite quiet and did not seem to attend to it. They then set up a second shout, and advanced a little forward; the English never moved. Still they hooted a third time, advancing with their cross-bows presented, and began to shoot. The English archers then advanced one step forward, and shot their arrows with such force and quickness, that it seemed as if it snowed. When the Genoese felt these arrows, which pierced through their armour, some of them cut the strings of their cross-bows, others flung them to the ground, and all turned about and retreated quite discomfited.

The French had a large body of men-at-arms on horseback to support the Genoese, and the king, seeing them thus fall back, cried out, ' Kill me those scoundrels, for they stop our road without any reason .' The English continued shooting, and some of their arrows falling among the horsemen, drove them upon the Genoese, so that they were in such confusion, they could never rally again.

In the English army there were some Cornish and Welsh men on foot, who had armed themselves with large knives; these advancing through the ranks of the men-at-arms and archers, who made way for them, came upon the French when they were in this danger, and falling upon earls, barons, knights, and squires, slew many, at which the King of England was exasperated. The valiant King of Bohemia was slain there. . . .

TOURNAMENT, 1347

On the surrender of Calais on 5 August 1347 occurred the famous incident when Queen Philippa interceded with Edward III for the burgesses. She obtained general love for her mercifulness in the incident here told. With her from Hainault came Flemish weavers who helped to make the clothing industry important instead of the mere production of raw wool for export.

Tournaments, legalized by Richard I in 1194, were rough baronial battle-schools disliked by Henry III, but regularized by his son, as Lord Edward, with broadswords for weapons. Edward I's tournament at Windsor was for knighting Edward of Carnarvon in 1306. With Edward III pageantry increased and tournaments were associated with the foundation of the Order of the Garter. But the 15th-century tournaments were safer and more picturesque with barriers to separate the heavily armoured knights who ' could only poke at each other from an angle '.

Further Reading: Sir Guy Laking, *European Arms and Armour*, 1920. N. Denholm-Young, ' The Tournament in the Thirteenth Century ' in *Studies in Medieval History presented to F. M. Powicke*, Oxford 1948.

Source: G. Le Baker, *Chronicon*, ed. E. M. Thompson, Clarendon Press, 1889, p. 48.

And a little before the feast of St. Michael at London in Chepe there were very beautiful lists. Here the lady Queen Philippa with a great party of her ladies fell to the ground from the pavilions which had been newly built so that they could watch the knightly deeds; but they were not hurt. That most pious queen would not allow the carpenters to be punished for this, but she assuaged the anger of the king and his courtiers with prayers on bended knee. This merciful act of the queen aroused the love of all towards her when they considered her piety.

THE BLACK DEATH, 1348-9

The Black Death was a kind of bubonic plague which reached southern Europe from China in early 1348. By the autumn it reached southern England. The young and strong were especially liable to attack and after the sudden appearance of small black pustules death followed in a few days, sometimes in a few hours. It devastated Wales and Scotland in 1350. This plague resulted in a shortage of labour and the Statutes of Labourers were introduced in an attempt to stop wages rising.

Source: Henry Knighton, *Chronicle* translated by W. J. Ashley, *Edward III and his Wars*, 1327–1360, English History by Contemporary Writers, D. Nutt 1887, p. 122. Knighton was a canon of St. Mary's Abbey, Leicester and here he speaks of what he knew, though much of his work is taken from Higden (which he acknowledges) and much from Walter of Hemingburgh (unacknowledged). The initial letters of his first sixteen chapters spell ' Henricus Cnitthon '. His own work stops abruptly in 1366 and is continued by another canon from 1377 to 1395. Twysden edited him in 1652.

Further Reading: F. A. Gasquet, *The Black Death*, 2nd ed., 1908. Bertha Putnam, *Enforcement of the Statutes of Labourers*, 1349, Columbia University, Studies in History, vol. xxxii, 1908.

Then the grievous plague penetrated the seacoasts from Southampton, and came to Bristol, and there almost the whole strength of the town died, struck as it were by sudden death; for there were few who kept their beds more than three days, or two days, or half a day; and after this the fell death broke forth on every side with the course of the sun. There died at Leicester in the small parish of S. Leonard more than 380; in the parish of Holy Cross more than 400; in the parish of S. Margaret of Leicester more than 700; and so in each parish a great number. Then the Bishop of Lincoln sent through the whole bishopric, and gave general power to all and every priest, both regular and secular, to hear confessions, and absolve with entire and full episcopal authority except in matters of debt, in which case the dying man, if he could, should pay the debt while he lived, or others should certainly fulfil that duty from his property after his death. Likewise, the pope granted full remission of all sins to whoever was absolved in peril of death, and granted that this power should last till next Easter, and everyone could choose a confessor at his will. . . .

Meanwhile the king sent proclamation into all the counties that reapers and other labourers should not take more than they had been accustomed to take, under the penalty appointed by statute. But the labourers were so lifted up and obstinate that they would not listen to the king's command, but if anyone wished to have them he had to give them what they wanted, and either lose his fruit and crops, or satisfy the lofty and covetous wishes of the workmen. And when it was known to the king that they had not observed his command, and had given greater wages to the labourers, he levied heavy fines upon abbots, priors, knights, greater and lesser, and other great folk and small folk of the realm, of some 100s., of some 40s., of some 20s., from each according to what he could give.

THE FLAGELLANTS COME TO LONDON, MICHAELMAS, 1349

The Dominicans and Franciscans underwent voluntary whipping, as recommended by St. Peter Damian. In 1349 the Brotherhood of Flagellants was encouraged by fear of the Black Death to start public flagellation.

Source: Robert of Avesbury, *On the Acts of Edward III*, edited by T. Hearne, 1720, and in the Rolls Series, 1889, and reprinted in R. A. Browne, *British Latin Selections* A.D. 500–1400, Blackwell 1954, p. 127. Robert was registrar of the Archbishop of Canterbury's court but is mostly interested in expeditions and treaties (1339–56). The account of the Flagellants follows his account of the Black Death. This records the burial of 200 bodies in the new burial ground in Smithfield, i.e. ground bought by the chivalrous Sir Walter Manny on the site where he founded the Charterhouse in 1371. Manny said the number buried was 50,000, a figure popularized by John Stow.

Further Reading: *Encyclopaedia of Religion and Ethics*, article on Flagellants.

About Michaelmas 1349 over six hundred men came to London from Flanders, mostly of Zeeland and Holland origin. Sometimes at St. Paul's and sometimes at other points in the city they made two daily public appearances wearing cloths from the thighs to the ankles, but otherwise stripped bare. Each wore a cap marked with a red cross in front and behind. Each had in his right hand a scourge with three tails. Each tail had a knot and through the middle of it there were sometimes sharp nails fixed. They marched naked in a file one behind the other and whipped themselves with these scourges on their naked and bleeding bodies. Four of them would chant in their native tongue and another four would chant in response like a litany.

Thrice they would all cast themselves on the ground in this sort
of procession, stretching out their hands like the arms of a cross.
The singing would go on and, the one who was in the rear of
those thus prostrate acting first, each of them in turn would step
over the others and give one stroke with his scourge to the man
lying under him. This went on from the first to the last until
each of them had observed the ritual to the full tale of those on the
ground. Then each put on his customary garments and always
wearing their caps and carrying their whips in their hands they
retired to their lodgings. It is said that every night they performed
the same penance.

BAILIFF'S MANORIAL ACCOUNTS, 1349-50

In some places the effects of the Black Death were not sensational
but nevertheless added to the general shortage of labour.

Source: Translated by permission of the Earl of Leicester from
document in the Holkham Estate Office, Holkham deed 45. Many
bailiffs' accounts are in the series of ' Ministers' Accounts ' in the
Public Record Office, having passed into royal custody when the king
took lands, as at the Dissolution of the Monasteries by Henry VIII.

Holkham Hillhall. Account of Thomas Clerk, reaper there,
from Michaelmas to Michaelmas 23–4 Edward III.

Quitrents. He answers for 70 s. 2 d. free and villein quitrents
due at St. Andrew's Day, Annunciation Day and the Nativity
of St. John the Baptist in equal parts and for 1 d. increase of rent
from William Atteston. Total 70 s. 3 d.

Market perquisites. He answers for 12 d. from market toll
this year. Total 12 d.

Court perquisites. He answers for 79 s. 9 d. from perquisites
of 3 courts held this year whereof the last was held on Monday
next after the feast of St. Wytburga the Virgin [patroness of
Holkham church, July 8]. Total 79 s. 9 d. Grant Total received
£7. 11 s.

Allowances of rents. He reckons in allowances on various
tenements on account of the Plague 3 s. 6¼ d. and half a farthing.
In allowance of rent the Prior of Peterstone because the rent is

disputed in court and it is uncertain if the lord ought to get it or not 5s.

Money delivered. He reckons as delivered to the lord 79 s. 1 d. for one tally.

Grand Total of allowances and liveries £4. 7 s. ¼ d. and half a farthing.

[In 1350-1 allowance of quitrent because of the Plague was 3 s. 7¾ d. There was 5 s. fine for the marriage of Alice Mayn, and Hervey Pope owed 12 d. for having the wardship of his daughter Alice until she came of age. The toll of the market dropped first to 3 d., then to nothing in 1355 and allowance for tenements in decay in the lord's hand rose to 5 s. 9½ d.]

ROTHERFIELD PEPPARD MANOR, 1351

The result of the Black Death was that villeins ran away from their lords to get good wages or cheap holdings elsewhere where hands were short. This is reflected in the businesslike but undramatic records of the manor courts, entered on rolls which the peasants came to hate and which they often destroyed in the course of Wat Tyler's rebellion. Those for Rotherfield Peppard, however, still survive.

Source: Translated extracts from an unpublished series of Rotherfield Peppard Court Rolls, 1351-1467. These were unknown to the editor of the famous *Stonor Papers* published for the Camden Society, for he only used Stonor papers in the Public Record Office and did not use those preserved at Stonor Park, in the house in which the Stonor family have lived since before 1300. Court Rolls contain the sole references to many lesser folk before the parish registers begin in 1538. Printed by kind permission of Major the Hon. S. Stonor.

Further Reading: F. A. Gasquet, *The Black Death*, 2nd ed., 1908.

Court held on Friday next after the feast of St. Margaret the Virgin 25 King Edward III [15 July 1351]. . .

It is ordered that there remain in the lord's hand half a virgate [i.e. a peasant's holding] of villein land once occupied by Gilbert Bolle, one virgate of villein land called Kelette and half a virgate once occupied by Robert Fairmere called Hunteslond and Cosyneslond because there are no tenants. The reeve is ordered to answer for the profits. . . .

Court held there on Thursday after the feast of St. Lucy the Virgin 25 King Edward III [15 Dec. 1351] . . .

The jury present that William Seman, villein of the lady of the manor, living at Rotherfield Greys [the next parish] and Gilbert Bolle living at Chesham, Bucks., are natives [villeins] of the lady but live outside her lordship. So their nearest relations are ordered to make them come and live within the lordship by the time of the next court. . . .

[Court of 29 October 1352]

At the last court it was ordered to attach William Seman, William Bolle and Thomas Reyner, villeins remaining outside the lordship without licence. The reeve has not done so, so he is ' in mercy '. . . .

[Court of 8 May 1355]

It is ordered to attach William Seman, Gilbert Bolle, Thomas Reyner and Alice his sister, Robert Reyner and his son, Ralph Reyner, fugitive villeins of the lord, and to take distraint on their nearest relations that they come to the next court. . . .

[Court of 30 Sept., 1356]

Robert Bille, John Baker, Robert Cobat, John Balet and William atte Grene, villeins, in mercy because they refused to elect a reeve as they had been bidden.

John Baker, Robert Cobat and John Balet, villeins, refused the post of reeve. So all their goods and chattels are to be siezed.

John Coksete, the reeve, is removed from office and William atte Grene is appointed in his place and took the oath. . . .

[Court of 11 March, 1360]

The homage present that Thomas Reyner and Robert his brother, villeins of the lady, long remained outside the lordship. It presents too that Cecilia Bulle, villein of the lady, was long outside the lordship but he knows not her place of dwelling— she is dead. . . .

THE SCOTTISH COUNTRYSIDE, 1363-84

Continual hostility between England and Scotland, punctuated by occasional truces or battles, made the countryside each side of the Border familiar to warriors from the other side.

Source: John Fordun, *Chronicles of the People of Scotland*, translated by F. J. H. Skene, *Historians of Scotland*, iv, Edmonston and Douglas 1872, p. 37. Fordun was a chantry priest at Aberdeen Cathedral, but an unlearned man whose historical compilations are of much less value than his remarks about the world in which he lived himself. According to the preface of one manuscript John wandered round ' like a curious bee ' with his manuscript in his breast, visiting England and Ireland, to repair the loss of Scottish historical information caused by the robbery or burning by Edward ' langschankes ' the tyrant of the national records of Scotland.

Further Reading: Ian C. Hannah, *Story of Scotland in Stone*, 1934. J. S. Coltart, *Scottish Church Architecture*, 1936. *County Histories of Scotland*, 1896–1900. F. H. Groome, *Ordnance Gazetteer of Scotland*, 1901.

Scotia, also, has tracts of land bordering on the sea, pretty level and rich, with green meadows, and fertile and productive fields of corn and barley, and well adapted for growing beans, pease and all other produce; destitute, however, of wine and oil, though by no means so of honey and wax. But in the upland districts, and along the highlands, the fields are less productive, except only in oats and barley. The country is, there, very hideous, interspersed with moors and marshy fields, muddy and dirty; it is, however, full of pasturage grass for cattle, and comely with verdure in the glens, along the water-courses. This region abounds in wool-bearing sheep, and in horses, and its soil is grassy feeds cattle and wild beasts, is rich in milk and wool, and manifold in its wealth of fish, in sea, river and lake. . . .

PRICES, 1366

Much of the produce of the Abbot of Dereham's grange at Holkham was sold, and many of its needs were bought, unlike those of the manor of Burghall there which was producing for the lord's household. To understand a price exactly one would need to know the quality and weight of objects priced.

Source: Extracts translated from the bailiff's account for the Abbot of Dereham by permission of the Earl of Leicester deed 53 in the Estate Office at Holkham.

Further Reading: J. E. T. Rogers, *History of Agriculture and Prices*, 1259–1793, 1866–1902.

Issues of the manor.

3000 sheaves of barley straw sold at 6 d. a hundred 15 s.

7000 do. at same price a hundred 35 s.

A quantity of pea straw sold 10 s.

100 sheaves of wheat straw 13 d.

100 sheaves of rye straw 13 d.

Garden produce 12 s.

6 acres ploughed for the chief lord for seed corn 8 s. . .

Profit of 1 pig killed for fat 6 d.

9 quarters 6 bushels wheat sold at 6 s. 8 d. a quarter 65 s.

2 quarters 2½ bushels peas at 4 s. a quarter 9 s. 3 d.

Barley sold in February at 4 s. 3 d. a quarter £8.10.

83 quarters 7 bushels barley as above £17. 16 s. 5½ d.

18 quarters oats at 3 s. 4 d. a quarter 60 s.

40 quarters of barley at 4 s. 4d. £8. 13 s. 4 d.

4 quarters of malt at 5 s. 4 d. a quarter 21 s. 4 d.

2 store cows sold 30 s.

2 store pigs sold 16 s.

[Expenses include:]

1 new plough bought 13 d. [Various parts were extra].

200 bindings for roofing houses 4 d.

2 stots [horses or steers] for the lord's house at the staithe [wharf] 6 d.

50 keys 3 d.

50 sheaves of thatch for roofing 12 d.

200 bindings 4 d.

150 gross of rods for binding the roof 6 d.

18 hurdles for the lord's fold at 1½ d. each 2 s. 3 d.

18 do. at 1¾d. each plus ½ d. extra 2 s. 8 d.

12 hurdles do. plus 1 d. extra 22 d.

1 iron stake 14 d.

4 bushels beans 2 s.

1 cow 10 s. 6 d.

Another cow 9 s.

2 quarters 4 bushels salt 13 s. 4 d.

2000 spits 24 s.

Fish. 14 chelyngs [keelings=codlings], 5 cods and 20 eels in 1½ gallons of butter 21 d.

8½ pairs of cheese 8 s. 6 d.

7 lb. candles at 2½ d. a pound 17½ d.

12 scythes 4 s. 4 d.

13 pairs of gloves 2 s.

1 last of fresh herrings at 6 d. a hundred 52 s. 6 d.

1480 herrings at same price 7 s.

390 herrings 4 s.

2 chelynggis and 1 coddlyngs 2 s.

2 lenges [lings] and 6 chelyngis 7 s. 8 d.

31 playces 10 d.

3 chelynggis, 1 halybut and 1 thornebak [skate] 5 s.

133 chelyngis at 8 d. each plus 3 s. 105 s.

2 chelyngis 2 s.

5 lengis 6 s. 4 d.

51 chelyngs at 10 d. each 41 s. 8 d. with one thrown in.

WAGES, 1366

The Black Death hastened the development of a system of cash payments for agricultural work instead of the exaction of labour services. In contemporary eyes wages were high, to ours they look low. To medieval eyes our wages would seem fantastically high with prices also correspondingly high.

Source: Extracts translated from the bailiff's account for the Abbot of Dereham by permission of the Earl of Leicester from Holkham deed 53 in the Estate Office at Holkham. Totals of medieval accounts sometimes add up wrong.

Further Reading: Bertha Putnam, *Enforcement of the Statutes of Labourers* 1349–59 Columbia University, Studies in History, etc. vol. xxxii, 1908.

For the smith's wage for maintaining the iron parts of ploughs this year 20 s. besides 3 bushels of wheat as extra. . . .

For wage of one man mending collars and gear of a cart for 2 days 10 d. . . .

For 1 carpenter hired to mend carts for 7½ days at 5 d. a day 3 s. 1½ d. . . .

For wage for 1 man making collars and mending harness of cart after 1 August for 2¼ days 7½ d. . . .

Paid to 1 roofer for roofing the Peyntidechaumber, chapel, hall and le Chaffons at 4 d. per day for 7 days 2 s. 4 d. . . .

For wage of 1 carpenter mending the door, mending the cart and helping make the kiln for 3 days 15 d.

For wage of 1 carpenter mending the house at the staithe at 5 d. a day for 18 days 7 s. 6 d. . . .

For wage of 1 roofer roofing the grange, kitchen and the house at the staithe at 4 d. a day for 9 days 3 s. . . .

In costs of washing and shearing the lord's sheep as seen by the auditor by the details examined 2 s. 11 d.

For 1 man hired at 3 d. a day for 4½ days to wash and hang herrings 13½ d.

For 3 men hired for 1 day for same 12 d. . . .

For thrashing at 3 d. a quarter 60 quarters and 2 bushels of wheat, 4 bushels of rye and 5 quarters of peas.

For 275 quarters 4 bushels of barley and 27 quarters of oats thrashed at 2¼ d. a quarter 63 s. ¼ d.

For winnowing said corn nothing, as it was done by the manor house maid. . . .

For weeding the lord's corn this year 18 d. . . .

For mowing and binding ½ acre of wheat 7d.

For mowing and binding 5½ acres of rye at 15 d. each plus 1½ d. in all 7 s.

For reaping and binding 2 acres of rye 2 s.

For reaping 14 acres 3 rods of barley at 12 d. an acre 14s. 9d.

For reaping 2 acres 3 rods of barley 24 d. . . .

Wage for 1 hired reaper as above at the lord's board for 7 weeks 11 s.

Wage for 2 men reaping, binding and sometimes carting for 5½ weeks at the lord's board 18 s.

Wage of 1 other reaper and binder for all autumn 9 s.

Wages of 4 gleaners, reapers and binders at same time at lord's board each taking 7 s. for hire 28 s.

Wage of 1 reaper and binder at the lord's board for all autumn 8 s.

Wage of 1 reaper and binder for 12 days at the lord's board 3 s.

In 20 hirelings as above at lord's board, at 3 d. a day each, 5 s. . . .

Fees of servants for whole year less 7 weeks in autumn at 12 d. a week each 45 s.

For their shoes and robes 20 s.

Wage of William Emueth carter and ploughman for whole year 13 s. 4 d.

For wage of one to follow the plough 9 s.

Wage of 1 harrower and marsh servant for whole year 9 s.

Wage for 1 maid at the hall for whole year 9 s.

Wage for 1 shepherd for whole year 10 s. . . .

For carrying 39 quarters of wheat and 10 quarters of rye by water to Dereham 12 s. 3 d.

For taking 45 quarters 4 bushels of barley there by water 12 s. 3 d. . . .

Paid to the lord's carter sent to Dereham twice with cart 4 d.

Paid to same for going with cart to Massyngham six times 12 d.

To a man sent to Dereham for the lord's business there 2 d. . . .

[But the same year in the same parish in Holkham deed 54 the collector of the manor of Burghall accounts for various payments in kind, and so far from hiring labour, labour services due to that manor from villeins were being sold.]

AN UNSYMPATHETIC VIEW OF THE POOR, c. 1375

Source: J. Gower, *Mirour de l'Omme*, translated by G. G. Coulton, *Social Life in Britain from the Conquest to the Reformation*, C.U.P., 1938, p. 353.

John Gower Esq., was a country gentleman who dedicated the *Confessio Amantis* first to Richard II and then to Henry IV. He retired to live in St. Mary Overy's Priory and his tomb remains there (in the present Southwark Cathedral) showing in effigy his head resting on his *Speculum Meditantis*, *Vox Clamantis* and *Confessio Amantis*. It has lost an accompanying tablet granting 1500 days' pardon to all who prayed for the poet's soul. The *Vox Clamantis* is an allegory of the Peasants' Revolt in Gower's neighbourhood in Kent, and is dedicated to Archbishop Arundel. The best manuscript is at All Souls College, Oxford. Gower was a friend of Chaucer.

Further Reading: *Oxford History of English Literature*, ed. by F. P. Wilson and Bonamy Dobrée.

The world goeth fast from bad to worse, when shepherd and cowherd for their part demand more for their labour than the master-bailiff was wont to take in days gone by. Labour is now at so high a price that he who will order his business aright must pay five or six shillings now for what cost two in former times. Labourers of old were not wont to eat of wheaten bread; their meat was of beans or coarser corn, and their drink of water alone. Cheese and milk were a feast to them, and rarely ate they of other dainties; their dress was of hodden grey; then was the world ordered aright for folk of this sort. . . .

Three things, all of the same sort, are merciless when they get the upper hand; a water-flood, a wasting fire, and the common multitude of small folk. For these will never be checked by reason or discipline; and therefore, to speak in brief, the present world is so troubled by them that it is well to set a remedy thereunto. Ha! age of ours, whither turnest thou? for the poor and small folk, who should cleave to their labour, demand to be better fed than their masters. Moreover, they bedeck themselves in fine colours and fine attire, whereas (were it not for their pride and their privy conspiracies) they would be clad in sackcloth as of old.

JOHN BALL, 1381

John Ball was a priest of York who moved to Essex, where he was forbidden to preach in 1366. He followed Wycliffe in asserting that it was lawful to refuse payment of tithes to unworthy priests and even advocated the equality of bondsmen and gentry. Knighton and Walsingham have preserved copies of curious revolutionary messages

in rhyme which he used to circulate. He preached a seditious sermon
at Blackheath on the text:

> ' When Adam dalf, and Eve span,
> Wo was thanne a gentilman? '

thereby converting, in the eyes of his hearers, into subversive posters
the numerous pictures, on the walls of churches in stained glass and
elsewhere, of the Toil of Adam and Eve. After the suppression of
Wat Tyler's rebellion, in the course of which he was rescued from
Maidstone gaol by his friends, he hid himself in an old ruin at Coventry.
He was brought before Richard II at St. Albans and was hanged,
drawn and quartered in the royal presence there and then on 15 July
1381. His four quarters were sent to four different towns for public
exhibition.

Source: Sir John Froissart, *The Chronicles of England, France, Spain
etc. etc.* Epitomized edition, Routledge 1891.

Further Reading: G. R. Owst, *Preaching in Medieval England*, 1250–
1450, 1926. G. R. Owst, *Literature and Pulpit in Medieval England*,
1933. The relevant passage in Walsingham is printed in R. A. Browne,
British Latin Selections A.D. 500–1400, Blackwell 1954, p. 136.

There happened great commotions among the lower orders in
England, by which that country was nearly ruined. In order that
this disastrous rebellion may serve as an example to mankind,
I will speak of all that was done from the information I had at the
time. It is customary in England, as well as in several other
countries, for the nobility to have great privileges over the
commonalty; that is to say, the lower orders are bound by law
to plough the lands of the gentry, to harvest their grain, to carry
it home to the barn, to thrash and winnow it; they are also bound
to harvest and carry home the hay. All these services the prelates
and gentlemen exact of their inferiors; and in the counties of
Kent, Essex, and Bedford, these services are more oppressive
than in other parts of the kingdom. In consequence of this the
evil disposed in these districts began to murmur, saying, that
in the beginning of the world there were no slaves, and that no
one ought to be treated as such, unless he had committed treason
against his lord, as Lucifer had done against God; but they had
done no such thing, for they were neither angels nor spirits,
but men formed after the same likeness as these lords who treated
them as beasts. This they would bear no longer; they were
determined to be free, and if they laboured or did any work,

they would be paid for it. A crazy priest in the county of Kent, called John Ball, who for his absurd preaching had thrice been confined in prison by the Archbishop of Canterbury, was greatly instrumental in exciting these rebellious ideas. Every Sunday after mass, as the people were coming out of church, this John Ball was accustomed to assemble a crowd around him in the market-place and preach to them. On such occasions he would say, ' My good friends, matters cannot go on well in England until all things shall be in common; when there shall be neither vassals nor lords; when the lords shall be no more masters than ourselves. How ill they behave to us! for what reason do they hold us thus in bondage? Are we not all descended from the same parents, Adam and Eve? And what can they show, or what reason can they give, why they should be more masters than ourselves? They are clothed in velvet and rich stuffs, ornamented with ermine and other furs, while we are forced to wear poor clothing. They have wines, spices and fine bread, while we have only rye and the refuse of the straw; and when we drink it must be water. They have handsome seats and manors, while we must brave the wind and rain in our labours in the field; and it is by our labour they have wherewith to support their pomp. We are called slaves, and if we do not perform our service we are beaten, and we have no sovereign to whom we can complain or who would be willing to hear us. Let us go to the king and remonstrate with him; he is young, and from him we may obtain a favourable answer, and if not we must ourselves seek to amend our condition.' With such language as this did John Ball harangue the people in his village every Sunday after mass. The archbishop, on being informed of it, had him arrested and imprisoned for two or three months by way of punishment; but the moment he was out of prison, he returned to his former course. Many in the city of London, envious of the rich and noble, having heard John Ball's preaching, said among themselves that the country was badly governed, and that the nobility had seized upon all the gold and silver. These wicked Londoners, therefore, began to assemble in parties, and to show signs of rebellion; they also invited all those who held like opinions in the adjoining counties to come to London; telling them that they would find the town open to them and the commonalty of the same way of thinking as themselves, and that they would so press the king, that there would no longer be a slave in England.

By this means the men of Kent, Essex, Sussex, Bedford, and the adjoining counties, in number about 60,000, were brought to London, under command of Wat Tyler, Jack Straw, and John Ball. This Wat Tyler, who was chief of the three, had been a tiler of houses—a bad man and a great enemy to the nobility.

DEATH OF WAT TYLER, 1381

This account differs somewhat from the familiar picture of Richard II heroically facing the rebels at Smithfield and promising them ' I will be your captain. Come with me into the fields and you shall have all you ask ', when their leader was slain. That picture was the creation of Froissart who wished to flatter the king to whom he presented a copy of his chronicles.

Richard's bones were examined in 1871 and found to be those of a man nearly six feet high, though the Monk of Evesham says he was of the common height. Thick curly hair fell either side of a round, feminine face, normally white but often flushed. Two small tufts on his chin represented the fashionable double-pointed beard of the period. Small moustaches grew from the corners of his mouth and accentuated a look of weariness which increased in the latter half of his reign. His skull was distorted behind and under average capacity. The Wilton diptich, the portrait in Westminster Abbey, his effigy (made in 1395 from the life) and an illumination made by 1402 in Creton's Metrical History in British Museum, Harleian MS. 1319, are a consistent series of representations.

The dagger with which Sir William Walworth traditionally slew Wat Tyler was preserved at Fishmongers' Hall and the Sword of St. Paul in the City arms came to be misinterpreted as that dagger.

Source: City Letter Book, in H. T. Riley, *Memorials of London*, 1868, This gives the view of the wealthier citizens.

Further Reading: Sir C. Oman, *Great Revolt of* 1381, 1906.

' Whitewellebeche ', otherwise called St. John's Meadow, lay to the east of the Hospital of St. John of Jerusalem between the modern St. John Street and Goswell Road. Its exact position is shown on a map of the waterpipes leading to the Charterhouse on the south, made in the fifteenth century, and in a sketch-map based on this and other evidence in the *Transactions of the London and Middlesex Archaeological Society*, New Series, vol. viii, facing p. 234.

Among the most wondrous and hitherto unheard-of prodigies that ever happened in the City of London, that which took place there on the Feast of Corpus Christi, the 13th day of June, in the 4th year of the reign of King Richard the Second, seems deserving to be committed to writing, that it may not be unknown to those to come.

For on that day, while the King was holding his Council in the Tower of London, countless companies of the commoners and persons of the lowest grade from Kent and Essex suddenly approached the said City, the one body coming to the town of Southwark, and the other to the place called 'Mileende', without Algate. By the aid also of perfidious commoners within the City, of their own condition, who rose in countless numbers there, they suddenly entered the City together, and, passing, straight through it, went to the mansion of Sir John [of Gaunt], Duke of Lancaster, called 'le Savoye', and completely levelled the same with the ground, and burned it. From thence they turned to the Church of the Hospital of St. John of Jerusalem, without Smethefeld, and burnt and levelled nearly all the houses there, the church excepted.

On the next morning, all the men from Kent and Essex met at the said place called 'Mileende', together with some of perfidious persons of the City aforesaid; whose numbers in all were past reckoning. And there the King came to them from the Tower, accompanied by many knights and esquires, and citizens on horseback, the lady his mother following him also in a chariot. Where, at the prayer of the infuriated rout, our Lord the King granted that they might take those who were traitors against him, and slay them, wheresoever they might be found. And from then the King rode to his Wardrobe, which is situate near to Castle Baynard; while the whole of the infuriated rout took its way towards the Tower of London; entering which by force, they dragged forth from it Sir Simon [of Sudbury], Archbishop of Canterbury, Chancellor of our Lord the King, and Brother Robert Hales, Prior of the said Hospital of St. John of Jerusalem, the King's Treasurer; and, together with them, Brother William Appeltone, of the Order of Friars Minors, and John Leg, Serjeant-at-arms to the King, and also, one Richard Somenour, of the Parish of Stebenhuthe [Stepney]; all of whom they beheaded in the place called ' Tourhille ', without the said Tower; and then carrying their heads through the City upon lances, they set them up on London Bridge, fixing them there on stakes.

Upon the same day there was also no little slaughter within the City, as well of natives as of aliens. Richard Lions, citizen and vintner of the said City, and many others, were beheaded in Chepe. In the Vintry also, there was a very great massacre of Flemings, and in one heap there were lying about forty headless bodies of persons who had been dragged forth from the churches and their houses; and hardly was there a street in the City in which there were not bodies lying of those who had been slain. Some of the houses also in the said City were pulled down, and others in the suburbs destroyed, and some too, burnt.

Such tribulation as this, greater and more horrible than could be believed by those who had not seen it, lasted down to the hour of Vespers on the following day, which was Saturday, the 15th of June; on which day God sent remedy for the same, and His own gracious aid, by the hand of the most renowned man, Sir William Walworthe, the then Mayor; who in Smethe-felde, in presence of our Lord the King and those standing by him, lords, knights, esquires, and citizens on horseback, on the one side, and the whole of this infuriated rout on the other, most manfully, by himself, rushed upon the captain of the said multitude, ' Walter Tylere ' by name, and, as he was altercating with the King and the nobles, first wounded him in the neck with his sword, and then hurled him from his horse, mortally pierced in the breast; and further, by favour of the divine grace, so defended himself from those who had come with him, both on foot and horseback, that he departed from thence unhurt, and rode on with our Lord the King and his people, towards a field near to the spring that is called ' Whitewellebeche ' [in Clerkenwell]; in which place, while the whole of the infuriated multitude in warlike manner was making ready against our Lord the King and his people, refusing to treat of peace except on condition that they should first have the head of the said Mayor, the Mayor himself, who had gone into the City at the instance of our Lord the King, in the space of half an hour sent and led forth therefrom so great a force of citizen warriors in aid of our Lord the King, that the whole multitude of madmen was surrounded and hemmed in; and not one of them would have escaped, if our Lord the King had not commended them to be gone.

Therefore our Lord the King returned into the City of London with the greatest of glory and honour, and the whole of this profane multitude in confusion fled forthwith for concealment, in their affright.

For this same deed our Lord the King, beneath his standard, in the field, with his own hands decorated with the order of knighthood the said Mayor, and Sir Nicholas Brembre, and Sir John Phelipot, who had already been Mayors of the said City; as also, Sir Robert Launde.

WILLIAM GRYNDECOBBE, 1381

' Overlong it were in this booke to set downe ye troubles at Saint Albons by the bondmen there against the Abbot ' said John Stow in his *Annales*, for much is known of them, as one of the best contemporary historians was an interested party and an eyewitness.

Source: epitomized translation from Thomas Walsingham, *English History* or *Short History*. The first edition was printed in 1574, twenty years earlier than the first edition mentioned in the *Dictionary of National Biography* article on Walsingham. Walsingham, the best authority on the reigns of Richard II and Henry IV and V, superintended the copying room at St. Albans and knew the terror of 1381 when the peasants burnt many abbey muniments and extorted fresh charters. In his edition Matthew Parker says he must not keep Walsingham's history to himself, as it begins where Matthew Paris, printed three years before, stopped. He wanted early chronicles printed in full without omitting ' fables and portents which nobody now believes '. Walsingham says as much about the period 1378–94 as about the reigns of the first three Edwards. Of 456 pages he devotes 45 to one year, 1381.

Appalling threats forced all to rally regardless of ploughing and sowing . . . some had sticks, others rusty swords, axes, or smoke-stained bows . . . they slew lawyers old and young . . . and decided to burn all court rolls and old muniments. . . . During Matins on Friday [14 June, 1381] hasty messengers from

Barnet to St. Albans said the Commons bade speed to London
with the Barnet and St. Albans men with their best arms, or else
20,000 would burn the vills and coerce them. Informed at once,
the abbot dreaded the damage of such a raid and quickly summoned the servants and villeins of his court to bid them speed to
London to appease and stop them. So they hurried off enthusi-
astically. They found a mob of 2000 yokels burning the valuable
farm of the [hated] Hospitallers at Highbury and busy pulling
down the ruins. The ringleader John [Jack] Straw made them
swear loyalty to 'King Richard and the Commons.' Other mobs
were at Mile End and at Tower Hill where they killed Archbishop
Sudbury, who worked miracles posthumously. Richard II gave
them charters dated 15 June granting freedom to the serfs of
various counties.

On reaching London the Abbey villeins and servants separated.
The former in St. Mary Arches church debated services to the
Abbey and how to achieve ancient underground aspirations, like
new town boundaries, free pastures and fisheries, revival of lost
sporting rights, freedom to establish hand mills, the exclusion
of the liberty's bailiff from the town limits, and the return of
bonds made by their sires to the late abbot Richard of Wallingford. . . .

They decided both to hurry home with authority from Tyler,
the Kentish vagabond king, making demands with threats of
fire and slaughter, and to extort an order under royal privy seal
to the abbot to restore their rights as in Henry's reign. William
Gryndecobbe, the biggest debtor of the monastery, reared
there, a neighbour and relation of the monks, was so forward
in the business that the mob saw him kneel to the king six times
to get that order, and he was chief spokesman with Walter, the
rustic idol. Walter did not want to leave London or send a
party but Gryndecobbe and other rascals swore loyalty to him
so he promised to come with 20,000 if necessary to shave the
beards of abbot, prior and monks, i.e. to behead them. An abbey
servant got home before them by a dashing ride to say the treasurer and many others were murdered, the Commons were
merciless executioners and the prior would be beheaded and
the other monks imperilled if they stayed. The prior, four monks

and various associates fled on horse and on foot the dangerous trail to Tynemouth. Soon the villeins were back, led by William Gryndecobbe and William Cadyndon, baker, who coveted some obvious success before their comrades arrived, longing to get extra credit so as to seem important afterwards. They reported good progress. They would be masters not slaves, and that very night they would break the abbot's folds in Falcon and other woods and demolish the gates of Eye and other woods with the sub-cellarer's house, opposite the street where fish was sold, as it spoilt the townsman's view and damaged prestige. The fools took rapid action. . . . Thus ended Friday at St. Albans with its train of evil.

On Saturday morning [15 June] the St. Albans men arose to review their crimes. A monster procession marched to Falcon wood, calling out all of military age on pain of death or destruction of their house or goods; threats united the decent and criminal. Our William Gryndecobbe and William Cadyndon led. At the rendezvous the mob plotted its demands, actions and threats. They decided to finish off the folds and coppice gates, and did so. Back in town they awaited peasants from surrounding villages and the home farm. They had summoned with menaces 2000 or more rascals to rally about freedom from St. Albans. They would gain any demands and not let any gentlemen linger at home but bring them as supporters. From Wat Tyler they learnt the trick of executing the hesitant or wrecking their homes.

The sight of the mob they had conjured up raised their spirits, clasping hands and swearing oaths. An arrogant rush to the abbey gates showed Walter's power. The gates were opened and they contemptuously told the porter to open the prison. Some godly villeins had told the abbot and he had told the porter the plan, so he obeyed. They freed the captives in return for unswerving support except for one whom they judged and butchered in the space before the gate, yelling diabolically as they had learnt at the archbishop's murder in London and setting the head on the pillory. Soon allies from Barnet arrived and Richard de Wallingford, a substantial St. Albans villein, briskly rode up from London with the royal letter Gryndecobbe had kept demanding, bearing the banner of St. George like the criminals in London.

They swarmed round as he dismounted and planted his standard where they should stand until he brought the abbot's answer. The leaders entered the church with him and sent word to the abbot's chamber to answer the Commons. The monks convinced the abbot that the death which he would have preferred would not save the abbey's rights so he went down to them like a beaten man. Wallingford showed him the letter extracted from the king by Gryndecobbe dated 15 June about certain charters from King Henry concerning common, pasture and fishing rights. The abbot raised legal objections but Wallingford said the Commons did not expect excuses, would turn on him if kept waiting, and would summon Wat Tyler and 20,000 men. The abbot complained that he had befriended them for 32 years. Admitting this, they said they had hoped to get their demands from his successor. He yielded everything as the lesser evil. They burnt many charters by the market cross and also demanded a certain old charter about the liberties of the villeins 'with gold and blue capital letters'. He had never seen this but would hunt for it. The leaders reported a promise of a new charter, and the rascals went into the cloister with the deeds and ripped up millstones set in the parlour floor to commemorate an old suit between the villeins and the late abbot Richard. Smashing these, they distributed fragments like holy bread in a parish church. Meal time was granted and allowed sad reflections on slaves become masters and life and death in the hands of merciless countrymen. London had lain at their will a day and a night, the archbishop and treasurer were executed, the king was captive, his soldiery powerless. . . .

At the ninth hour the villeins came back for their charters, or else 2000 of them would destroy the gate. The abbot prepared a charter to be read and then sealed, but they sent a squire for clerk with ink and parchment to write at their dictation. They insisted that there was another charter of old liberties which they would have or wreck the abbey. He offered to swear at the morrow's mass that he withheld nothing, but they scorned his oaths, keener to destroy the abbey than get charters. Ale and a great basket of bread were put at the gate for all as a sop, which did not work, until the chief townsmen risked telling them to be quiet. They then left the gate to join another mob sacking houses on Walter's London pattern.

Under the royal colours they dared to set watches round the town against any help and to execute any monks going in or out. On the morrow they invited any with financial claims on the abbey to appear, and one demanded 100 marks damages, threatening to burn St. Peter's Grange and Kyngebury manor, which he had leased until he fled for debt. He had 2000 Commons near to avenge his wrongs and would rather make payment on the prior's body than recover his cash.

The monks had a sleepless night because of the impossible demand of the villeins to produce the unfindable charter, but Sunday [16 June] brought hopeful rumours of Tyler's death and London's rally to the king. A royal messenger enjoined peace, bringing a letter of royal protection for the abbey. Mobs summoned from Luton, Watford, Barnet, Rickmansworth and Tring arrived and the townsmen did not wish to seem disheartened or obedient to the king. Regardless of the future they would get their charters, but with a more conciliatory air. . . . The chief townsmen entered the abbot's chamber, stood over the clerk, inserting their requirements about liberties in the charter, and made the abbot seal a bond in £1000 to produce the non-existent charter, if found. Sir Hugh Segrave, royal steward, and Thomas Percy wrote advising every concession as it would never be held valid, so the abbot gave his bond. They acted as lords, not servants, in the abbot's chamber and chapel, present at the engrossing, dictating words and superintending the sealing. The seal showing St. Alban holding a palm was properly applied to their charter but miraculously it thrice stuck to the wax to show that the martyr did not want them for masters but would keep his lordship over them. They departed gleefully to publish the new charter at the cross with the royal pardon and manumission. They even published the royal charter of protection to show goodwill, but with malice at heart as appears.

On Monday and Tuesday villeins from all the abbey's vills came urgently requiring charters of manumission pursuant to the royal charter. These were made in a standard form. Then the villagers thought themselves gentry of royal blood who need not even pay rent. [Walsingham then surveyed events elsewhere, ' They made grammar school masters swear never to teach boys grammar. . . . They tried to burn all records and killed all who could record past or current events. It was dangerous to be known as a clerk and worse still to be found carrying an inkhorn.']

The abbot sent some villeins to swell the royal army but they claimed to have come on their own authority. Richard Peeres recognized some as ringleaders at St. Albans, imprisoned them and would have executed them—on the vigil of the passion of St. Alban, the eighth day after the Friday. During matins the chief townsmen went to enlist the abbot's help. In distress he despatched a monk to London to see the prisoners released, which he did. . . .

The king proposed to come to do justice at St. Albans, but Sir Walter Atte Lee, a local man, feared the damage done by such a host and persuaded the king to commission him to make peace between villeins and abbot. William Gryndecobbe persuaded them not to bolt but to meet him and if he did not come as a friend to drive him away. They greeted him and he made the people collect in the shape of a rainbow, while he with his armed guard about him explained that he came with a commission to prevent the damage threatened by the proposed arrival of the royal army. He adjured them to give up the ringleaders and make peace with the abbey. Some applauded but the jury said nobody should be indicted. When told to give up the charters they prevaricated, alleging intimidation and ignorance as to who held them. The abbot said he trusted their consciences and mollified the knight by saying he needed no intermediary. The knight called a meeting at Barnet Wood but did little for fear of the villeins there— about 300 stood round with bows, especially Barnet and Berkhamstead men, and if he had tried to do justice they would probably have made a riot and his soldiers have joined them. He secretly told the bailiffs and constables, when the mob dispersed, to compass the capture of William Gryndecobbe, William Cadyndon, John the barber who had removed the millstones from the pavement, with other notorieties. He hastened to Hertford whither he wanted them brought. Richard Peeres, John Chival, Thomas Eydon and William Eccleshale, admirable squires of the abbot, captured the three with the unwilling help of the bailiffs and put them in the gate. Next morning they were taken to Hertford with the chief townsmen of St. Albans and all the abbot's squires and varlets to reinforce the knight in doing justice. On their departure the town seethed with hot air and empty oaths—a hundred would die if one neighbour fell. Mobs gathered in fields and woods outside the town and, with the defenders away, the abbey looked like getting burnt, so the abbot in alarm summoned some local gentry for protection. Hearing his squires were gone executing the prisoners he wrote for them to hurry back to dispel this new danger. The trial was on and they grieved to stop, for otherwise they would have seen them executed, but they hurried home. . . . Two stopped in gaol but William Gryndecobbe was released, on three neighbours going bail for £300 each, to return to prison next Saturday.

The villeins wavered between violence and conciliation, now incited by Gryndecobbe, now depressed by the reported approach of the Earl of Warwick and Thomas Percy, now elated by the diversion of Warwick, now dismayed by the approach of the king himself. The abbot asked Hugh Segrave in London to divert the king because of the damage threatened by the royal entourage to crops, though the villeins alleged that the abbot spent £1,000 to ruin them. They hired an expensive lawyer to compromise with the abbot, repairing damage, replacing as many millstones as were removed, and returning extorted charters. The abbot met the king at the west gate with bells ringing. He had thousands of tenants in chief, soldiers and Robert Tresilian the justiciar. The ringleaders were kept prisoner until Monday while John Ball was brought to St. Albans, tried [14 July] and hanged [15 July]. . . .

The jury refused to indict, but Tresilian produced a list of ringleaders, forcing the jury to indict and getting assent from second and third juries. William Gryndecobbe, William Cadyndon, John the barber and other criminals to the number of 15 were drawn and hanged for riot. Some leading townsmen like

Richard Wallingford, John Garlick, William Berewill and
Thomas the Stink, were imprisoned, with 80 others whom royal
clemency later released. Meanwhile the villeins spitefully
accused the abbot, who had risked royal displeasure by his
intercessions, of forcing them to join the London mob. Such
malice shocked the justiciar who silenced them by asking why the
abbot did so. Other slanders about the abbot's reduction of
freemen to villeinage, compulsion to use his mill instead of
grinding at home, and bribing the king were shaking most of the
abbey's friends, despite penalties for slander, against the abbot, of
hanging for men and burning for women. After 8 days the king
met the obvious perversity of the abbey's dependants by sending a
commission to see that the abbey's dues were rendered—for the
royal chancery was being held in the chapter-house so that the
abbot could manage things better.

On St. Margaret's Day after eating, the king was to go to
Berkhamstead Castle. In the great abbey hall he first took fealty
from the men of Hertfordshire between 15 and 60 years old.
They would prefer death to obedience to agitators, would seize
agitators and render their dues [later]. . . . he was amazed to
hear that the bodies of those hanged at St. Albans had been audaci-
ously taken from the gallows so he sent a writ dated 3 August
to the bailiffs, bidding them be replaced in chains to hang as
long as they lasted. This reduced to a revolting slavery the free-
dom-loving revolutionaries of St. Albans, for none would do
the work for them and with their own hands they had to hang
up their fellow citizens whose decomposing bodies were full of
maggots and stank. It was just for men who usurped the name
' citizens ' to have the disgusting task whereby they earned the
apt name of ' hangmen ' to their lasting shame. . . .

THE PILLORY

Many instances of punishment in the pillory occur in the City
records, often for cheating consumers, for the City regulated even
such trades as galoches (1400), books (1403) and rushes (1416). Into
the pillory went a seller of false bowstrings in 1385 and a shuttle-
maker who pretended to be a hermit in 1412.

Source: London, Letter Books, translated by H. T. Riley, *Memorials of London*, 1868. London lacks a local Record Society but the Corporation publishes a fine series of English summaries of its records, wills, letter books and plea rolls.

For sorcery, 1382.

On the 26th day of March, in the 5th year etc., Henry Pot, a *Duchysman*, was attached to make answer, as well to the Mayor and Commonalty of the City of London, as to Nicholas Freman, and Cristina, his wife, in a plea of deceit and falsehood etc.: as to which, the same Nicholas and Cristina made plaint, that whereas one Simon Gardiner had lately lost a mazer cup, the said Henry came to him, and promised that he would let him know who had stolen the cup, and so cause him to regain it. And hereupon, the same Henry made 32 balls of white clay, and over them did sorcery, or his magic art: which done, he said that the same Cristina had stolen the cup; falsely and maliciously lying therein, and unjustly defaming the said Nicholas and Cristina, to their manifest scandal and disgrace, and to their grievance.

And the same Henry, being questioned how he would acquit himself thereof, of his own accord acknowledged that he could not deny the same, but expressly admitted that he had done in manner aforesaid. And because that he thus acknowledged the same, and confessed that he had many times before practised divers like sorceries, both within the city aforesaid and without, through which various persons had undeservedly suffered injury in their character and good name; and because that sorcery, or the art magic, manifestly redounds against the doctrine of Sacred Writ; it was awarded that the same Henry should be put upon the pillory, there to remain for one hour of the day. And the Sheriffs were ordered to have proclamation made as to the reason for the same.

STUDENT RIOT, 1388–9

This typical clash between two of the ' nations ' at Oxford is less important than the great Town-Gown riot of St. Scholastica's Day, Tuesday 10 Feb. 1355 when cries of ' Slay, Slay, Havoc, Havoc ' resounded in Oxford and the University was able to exact a humiliating revenge on the city authorities which was not abolished until 1825.

Source: *Chronicle of Adam of Usk*, 1377–1421, translated by Sir E. Maunde Thompson, Royal Soc. of Literature, H. Frowde, 1904, p. 147.

Adam was a lawyer who was charged with horse-stealing and left England in 1402 to become chaplain and papal auditor to Popes Boniface IX and Innocent VII. He returned to Wales in 1408 under the pretence of supporting Owen Glendower, was pardoned by the king in 1411 and was buried at his beloved Usk.

Further Reading: Hastings Rashdall, *The Universities of the Middle Ages*, 1895, especially ii, 403–8. C. E. Mallet, *A History of the University of Oxford*, 1924.

In these days there happened at Oxford a grave misfortune. For, during two whole years was there great strife between the men of the south and the men of Wales on the one side and the northerners on the other. Whence arose broils, quarrels, and oft-times loss of life. In the first year the northerners were driven clean away from the university. And they laid their expulsion chiefly to my charge. But in the second year, in an evil hour, coming back to Oxford, they gathered by night, and denying us passage from our quarters by force of arms, for two days they strove sorely against us, breaking and plundering some of the halls of our side, and slaying certain of our men. Howbeit, on the third day our party, bravely strengthened by the help of Merton Hall, forced our adversaries shamefully to fly from the public streets, which for the two days they had held as a camp, and to take refuge in their own quarters. In short, we could not be quieted before many of our number had been indicted for felonious riot; and amongst them I, who am now writing, was indicted, as the chief leader, and abettor of the Welsh, and perhaps not unrighteously. And so indicted we were hardly acquitted, being tried by jury before the king's judge. From that day forth I feared the king, hitherto unknown to me in his power, and his laws, and I put hooks into my jaws.

HENLEY BOROUGH ASSEMBLY BOOK, 1395–1463

Continuous records of the public business of small towns are rare.

Source: Extracts translated from Miss P. Briers' forthcoming edition for the Oxfordshire Record Society. This is largely concerned with elections of officials and admissions to tenements. The Assembly Books give an unbroken panorama of the normal life of a small town, little undisturbed by national troubles.

[3 Nov. 1410]
John Tubbe pays Walter Fyschere 6s. 8d. for mending an instrument called ' Clokke '. . . .

That day were elected the taxers for the clerk of the market, John Kempe, Stephen Webbe, John Cooke, John Gratele. . . .

[2 Oct. 1419].
That day it was agreed by assent of the warden and the whole community that two chaplains called ' chauntery prestys ' of honest conversation and good fame and good singers of plain song should receive yearly from the bridgemen, 9 marks each for his service and adequate rooms. And the said chaplains should keep the choir at the proper times on feast days and their eves. . . .

[21 Dec. 1419]
And if there be any default in payment of that rent at that term, John Warfelde may distrain on the two tenements in which John Kempe and John Tubbe live, which they hold of the community as appears by a charter made to that John Warfelde and sealed under the common seal. . . .

[5 Nov. 1422]. . . .
Also paid William Ludlowe for makyng of ' the comyn belle ' 2 s. 10½ d. . . .
Also paid Walter Carpenter ' for hangyng of the belle at the Cross ', 5 s. . . .

[5 Jan. 1423 or 4 Jan. 1424]
Also paid to William Pycarde for the 'Comune Swan,' 6 d. . . .

[12 Sept. 1449]
That day was elected Richard Tylere *alias* Sovetone to the office called ' Bedeman ' . . . .

[10 Sept. 1451]

That day it was granted by the warden and all the officers and the whole community of the said town that if anyone should play in that town at ball on holidays or feast days in the time of divine service, that then any officer then present might distrain and take 4 d. as often as it happened for the use of the light of the Blessed Mary of Henley aforesaid. Also in the same way for those playing at *tali* except at Christmas time. On the same day William Saare, Richard Malmesbury and Thomas Broune were elected tasters of victuals. . . .

[25 April 1453]

Ordered . . . that no one have any pig loose in the town, penalty 4 d. a pig except the squeelers. Four men are elected to put such pigs in the ' pynfolde ', at 1 d. a pig for their pains and 3 d. to the common chest.

A WORD FROM THE VANQUISHED, 1399

The story of Richard II's defeat by Henry IV is of course written by the winning side, for victors write history after making it. A French squire who had accompanied Richard II to Ireland in 1399 told the tale in French verse.

Source: John Creton, *History of the Deposition of Richard II*, translated by John Webb in *Archaeologia*, vol. xx, 1824.

Further Reading: A. B. Steele, *Richard II*, 1941.

And if I have spoken too freely of them in any way which may displease, I humbly and heartily beg pardon. For I solemnly declare that, according to my ability, I have uttered no evil or slander of them whereof they have not been guilty. Because I beheld their actions for seven whole months, and rode with them in many countries, and parts of Ireland and England. The good Earl of Salisbury also, when he was taken with King Richard, was pleased most earnestly to request, and humbly entreat me, that I would publish the whole of their bad behaviour and disloyal treason. And, certes, I promised it him with free will and loyal heart. For which cause, I have taken the trouble to fulfil the promise that I made him, in the great sorrow and peril in the which I left him. . . .

BOLINGBROKE, DUKE OF LANCASTER, BECOMES HENRY IV, 1399

Henry Bolingbroke returned from exile, seized Richard II, forced him to abdicate and himself became the first king of the House of Lancaster. Circumstances led him to rule 'constitutionally' as one ruling by the will of Parliament.

Source: Sir John Froissart, *The Chronicles of England, France, Spain etc. etc.*, Routledge 1891.

Further Reading: Shakespeare, *King Henry IV*. J. D. G. Davies, *King Henry IV*, 1935.

On Wednesday, the last day of September, 1399, a parliament was holden at Westminster, at which the Duke of Lancaster challenged the crown of England, and claimed it for his own, for three reasons—first, by conquest; second, from being heir to it; and third, from the pure and free resignation which King Richard had made of it. The Parliament then declared, that it was their will he should be king, and the day of coronation was fixed for the feast of Saint Edward, which fell on a Monday, the 13th day of October.

On Saturday before the coronation, the new king went from Westminster to the Tower of London, attended by great numbers, and those squires who were to be knighted watched their arms that night; they amounted to forty-six; each squire had his chamber and bath. The next day after mass the duke created them knights, and presented them with long green coats with straight sleeves lined with minever, after the manner of the prelates. These knights had on their left shoulder a double cord of white silk, with white tufts hanging down.

This Sunday after dinner the duke left the Tower on his return to Westminster; he was bare-headed, and had round his neck the order of the King of France. The Prince of Wales, six dukes, six earls, and eighteen barons accompanied him; and of the nobility there were from 800 to 900 horse in the procession. The duke, after the German fashion, was dressed in a jacket of cloth of gold, and mounted on a white courser, with a blue garter on his left leg. He passed through the streets of London, which were at the time all handsomely decorated with tapestries and other rich hangings; there were nine fountains in Cheapside and other streets through which he passed, and these perpetually ran with white and red wine. He was escorted by prodigious numbers of gentlemen, with their servants in livery and badges; and the different companies of London were led by their wardens, clothed in their proper livery, and with the ensigns of their trade: the whole cavalcade amounted to 6,000 horse. That same night the duke bathed, and on the morrow confessed himself, and according to his custom heard three masses.

The prelates and clergy who had been assembled then came in procession from Westminster Abbey, to conduct the king to the Tower, and back again in the same manner. The dukes, earls, and barons wore long scarlet robes, with mantles trimmed with ermine, and large hoods of the same, the dukes and earls had three bars of ermine on the left arm a quarter of a yard long, or thereabout; the barons had but two; all the knights and squires had uniform cloaks of scarlet lined with minever. In the procession to the church the duke had borne over his head a rich canopy of blue silk, supported on silver staves, with four golden bells at the corners. This canopy was borne by four burgesses of Dover, who claimed it as their right. On each side of the duke were the sword of mercy and the sword of justice; the first being borne by the Prince of Wales, and the other by the Earl of Northumberland, Constable of England; the Earl of Westmorland, the Marshal of England, carried the sceptre. The procession entered the church about nine o'clock. In the middle of the church was erected a scaffold covered with crimson cloth, in the centre of which was the royal throne of cloth of gold. When the duke entered the church, he seated himself on the throne, and was thus in regal state, except having the crown on his head. The Archbishop of Canterbury proclaimed from the four corners of the scaffold how God had given them a man for their lord and sovereign, and then asked the people if they were consenting parties to his being consecrated and crowned king. Upon which the people unanimously shouted ' ay ', and held up their hands, promising fealty and homage.

The duke then descended from the throne and advanced to the altar to be consecrated. Two archbishops and ten bishops performed the ceremony. He was stripped of all his royal state before the altar, naked to his shirt, and was then anointed and consecrated at six places: *i.e.* on the head, the breast, the two shoulders, before and behind; on the back, and hands: a bonnet was then placed on his head, and while this was being done, the clergy chanted the litany, or the service that is performed to hallow a font. The king was now dressed in a churchman's clothes, like a deacon; and they put on him shoes of crimson velvet after the manner of a prelate. Then they added spurs with a point, but no rowel; and the sword of justice was drawn, blessed, and delivered to the king, who put it again into the scabbard, when the Archbishop of Canterbury [Thomas Arundel] girded it about him. The crown of St. Edward, which is arched over like a cross, was next brought, and blessed, and placed by the archbishop on the king's head. When mass was over the king left the church, and returned to the palace, in the same state as before. In the court-yard of the palace there was a fountain that ran constantly with red and white wine. The king went first to his closet, and then returned to the hall to dinner. At the first table sat the king; at the second, five great peers of England; at the third, the principal citizens of London; at the fourth the new created knights; at the fifth, all knights and squires of honour. The king was served by the Prince of Wales who carried the sword of mercy; and on the opposite side, by the constable, who bore the sword of justice. At the bottom of the table was the Earl of Westmorland with the sceptre. At the king's table there were only the two archbishops and seventeen bishops.

When dinner was half over, a knight of the name of Dymock entered the hall completely armed, and mounted on a handsome steed, richly barbed with crimson housings. The knight was armed for wager of battle, and was preceded by another knight bearing his lance. He himself had his drawn sword in one hand, and his naked dagger by his side. The knight presented the king with a written paper, the contents of which were, that if any knight or gentleman should dare to maintain that King Henry was not a lawful sovereign, he was ready to offer him combat in the presence of the king, when and where he should be pleased to appoint.

The king ordered this challenge to be proclaimed by heralds, in six different parts of the town and the hall; and to it no answer was made.

King Henry having dined and partaken of wine and spices in the hall, retired to his private apartments, and all the company separated.

LOLLARDS

John Wycliffe advocated evangelical poverty, criticized ecclesiastical dogmas and endowments and attacked the Papacy and unworthy priests. He had much support both in Oxford University and at court and his learned theological ideas were widely spread by wandering disciples clad in long russet gowns. The followers of Wat Tyler and Wycliffe were not identical, but both attacked monasteries and both were seen as related symptoms of disorder, by an opposition which grew harder. In 1378 the church split in schism between Popes Urban VI and Clement VII at Rome and Avignon, and though this aided theoretical critics of the Papacy it caused Englishmen who disliked French influence over the popes at Avignon to feel less hostile to the Papacy as such; and even supporters of Wycliffe like John of Gaunt, Duke of Lancaster, were shocked when he began to question the doctrine of transubstantiation and thereby strike at the authority of the priesthood. Archbishop Sudbury had a more zealous successor in Courtney, and a suppression of 'dissenters' accompanied the destruction of the ' radicals '.

Wycliffe died in peace on 31 December 1384 and about four years later his English translation of the Bible was finished, of which some 170 MS. copies made before 1450 survive. A Wycliffite rising in 1399 provoked real repression and Adam of Usk says 23,000 Wycliffites were killed. Wycliffe's writings in Oxford were collected and destroyed and under order made on 4 May 1415 by the Council of Constance, Wycliffe's old pupil Richard Fleming, Bishop of Lincoln and founder of Lincoln College, disinterred and burnt his body.

Source: The continuator of Henry Knighton's Compilation of Events in England was, like Knighton, a canon of St. Mary's Abbey, Leicester. He is exceptional among contemporary writers in supporting Lancaster and is instructive on the Peasants' Revolt (considering Tressilian harsh) and Lollardy (which flourished locally). He was edited by Twysden in 1652 and again in the Rolls Series. Summary translation from an account of Lollardy in the reign of Richard II.

Further Reading: G. M. Trevelyan, *England in the Age of Wycliffe*. H. B. Workman, *John Wyclif*, 1926. Margaret Deanesly, *The Lollard Bible*, 1920.

William Smith, so called from his trade, had an insignificant and ugly person. Being crossed in love, he renounced all pleasures, and became a vegetarian and a total abstainer . . . he taught the alphabet and did clerking. Various knights used ot go round protecting him from any harm for his profane teaching, for they had zeal for God but were uninstructed, for they believed what they heard from the false prophets . . . and when one of them would come to the neighbourhood of any of them to preach, they would promptly assemble the local folk with a great ado at some fixed place or church even if people did not want to but did not dare to object. . . . They would attend the sermon with sword and buckler to stop any objections to the blasphemy. . . .

One Richard Waytestathe, priest, and this William Smyth, used to have spells at St. John Baptist's chapel outside Leicester near the leper hospital. Here other sectaries met for their conventicles . . . for there was a hostelry and lodging for that kind of visitor and there they had a school of malignant doctrines and opinions and a clearing-house of heresy. The chapel had been dedicated to God but it now was an asylum for blasphemers who hated Christ's church. Once these two, Richard the priest, and William Smyth, wanted a meal of herbs. They had the herbs but no fire. One peered into a corner of the chapel and saw an old image made in honour of St. Catherine, painted standing up. ' Look, dearly beloved brother,' said he, ' God has given us kindling to cook our meal. This will make a saintly fire.' So axe and flame wrought a new martyrdom, if in the heavenly kingdom the cruelty of modern torturers can make itself felt. This Lollard sect hated images and worked against them calling them idols. . . . If anyone mentioned St. Mary of Lincoln or St. Mary of Walsyngham they would call them names like 'wiche of Lincolle ' [Lincoln], and 'wiche of Walsyngham'. So one took the axe and the other took the image, saying 'Let's test if it's really a saint, for if it bleeds when we knock the head off we'll have to adore it, but if not it can feed our fire and cook our vegetables.' When they came out they could not hide their shame, but gave themselves away to their cost by boasting about it as funny. They were soon after turned out of the inn. . . .

The number of people with such beliefs multiplied fast and filled the kingdom and they became very bold. . . . They were called followers of Wycliffe, Wycliffites or Lollards. . . . At the beginning the leaders of this dreadful sect used to wear russet clothes mostly, to show outwardly an inward simplicity of heart and thus exercise a subtle attraction, like wolves in sheep's clothing, in undyed wool . . . . They gained to their sect half or more than half the people, some genuinely, others intimidated or shamed into it, for they magnified their adherents as praiseworthy. . . . They always claimed to act under ' Goddislawe '. . . . Even the very recently converted strangely acquired a standard way of speaking in accordance with their tenets, and this change of language acted on Doctors and women alike. . . . It divided families and neighbour from neighbour. . . . They were very argumentative with plenty to say. . . .

There was at Leicester a priest called William de Swynderby whom the people called a hermit because he once lived as such. His antecedents are unknown, but it is remarkable how unstable were his life and manners, ever chopping and changing. . . . First he preached against female vanity and dress. Although they behaved well he did not know how to stop, and at last he made the women of the town, good and bad, so cross that they decided to stone him out of town. Seeing his theme unprofitable he turned his sermons against the merchants saying a rich man could not enter the kingdom of God. He doled out this stuff so often that but for God's mercy he would have reduced some worthy men to the sin of desperation. Then he turned hermit, as preaching had not helped him. He lived for a while at a hermitage in the duke's wood, sometimes trotting into the town or country. The pious of Leicester took the trouble to bring him food as usual, but he must needs refuse it saying that what little he had with the duke's help would suffice. He began to run short and to be bored, but shame kept him from moving back to town. He managed to get taken into the abbey there for a time, for the canons put him in a room in the church because they had hopes of his holiness and they supplied him like the other priests. At that time he visited the country churches. . . . He joined up with William Smyth at St. John Baptist's by the leper hospital

and associated there with other Wycliffites. At that time the sect
was growing so much in repute and number that you could
hardly see two people in the street but one was a Wycliffite.
He saw that his usual kinds of sermon were unpopular and did
not attract converts; so he levelled them against the clergy saying
they were bad, and, as the rest of the sect said, parishioners
need not pay tithes to the impure, to non-residents, or those
prevented from teaching and preaching by ignorance or inaudi-
bility, for the other Wycliffites said tithes were a voluntary gift
and payment to evil-livers was connivance. He also preached
that men might ask for payment of debt but not sue or imprison
for it, that excommunication for non-payment of tithes was
extortion and that one who lived contrary to God's law was no
priest though ordained.

Such and other teachings and heresies pleased the people
and won their affection. They said they had never seen or heard
such an exponent of truth and they loved him like another God.

John Bukkyngham, Bishop of Lincoln, had wind of this
and promptly suspended him from all preaching in chapel,
church or graveyard, excommunicating any who should listen
to him and sending notices of this to various churches. William
set himself up a pulpit between two millstones which stood for
sale outside the chapel in the High Street, to preach ' in the
High Street in the bishop's teeth so long as he have the people's
love '. You would have seen crowds from all over the town and
country flocking to hear him more than even before the excommunication. The bishop summoned him to appear in Lincoln
Cathedral. . . . There he was publicly convicted of heresies
and errors and richly deserved to be food for fire. Then his
followers cast their hands and heads in wailing to the walls, for
many Leicester people would have gone to succour him, though
in vain. That day the pious Duke of Lancaster happened to be
at Lincoln and he often protected the Lollards, for their smooth
tongues and faces tricked him and others into thinking them
saints of God. He persuaded the bishop to give William a
different sentence. . . .

HENRY V's CORONATION FEAST, PASSION SUNDAY, 9 April, 1413

Henry V was crowned at Westminster in a violent snowstorm which Walsingham regarded as an omen that the king would put off the winter of his riotous youth. A change in his conduct was remarked by many and in his *Life* Elmham says that on the night of 20 March 1413 when Henry IV was dead the new king made confession to a recluse at Westminster and promised to reform his character. Elmham says that ' he was in his youth a diligent follower of idle practices, much given to instruments of music, and fired with the torches of Venus herself.' His face was oval, with a long straight nose, ruddy complexion, dark smooth hair, and bright eyes, mild as a dove's when unprovoked, but lionlike in wrath. Several portraits survive.

Source: 'A Noble Boke off Cookry', Holkham MS. 674. printed by permission of the Earl of Leicester.

Further Reading: R. B. Mowat, *Henry V*, 1919. J. H. Wylie, *Reign of Henry V*, 1914–29. T. Austin, *Two 15th-century Cookery Books*, Early English Text Soc. vol. 91, 1888.

The Crownacon off Kyng Henry the ffyfte
   The Firste Course
Venyson in brothe Blank de sorre, Potage
Pyk lampry poudrid Gurnard Trout Roche
Fryd Crevet
Tartes
Braun counterfet for lesche withe the ribe therein a gret swan for suttelte sittinge upon a grene stok displaid with a scriptur in his bille
   Regardez Roy
   La droyt voy
And vj signetes growinge out of the sam stok undir hir echon with a scripture:
For the firste Thenez la ley
For the secund Gardez la fey
For the third Hors de court
For the fourthe Soit bannez tort
For the fyfte Eyez pete
For the sexte Det comunalte
Then xxiiij swannys everychon of them a byll in the mouthe Noble Honour and Joy

The secund course

Vyand Ryalle

Gilly with swannys of braun therin for the king and for other estates Congur freche halybut bace melet samon sooles egre elec and lamprous rost place fried lamprey bak flampayne lesche lombard.

Antelopes for suttelte with a scriptur

    Un sauvz plus

    Maynteyn dieux

    The iij cours

Creme frez

Dates in compost

Carpes perche sturgion welks tenche in braissell fflounders porpas rost lamprey roste

Cloves de edewes menewes fried paynpuff dowcettes.

Egilles of gold dissplayde for suttellte withe a scriptur in ye billis

    Dest iour notable

    Est honorable

HENRY V's INVASION OF FRANCE, 1415

After 'the unquiet time of Henry IV', Henry V decided to 'busy restless minds in foreign quarrels', encouraged by Chichele, Archbishop of Canterbury, who felt that war would divert people's minds from schemes to despoil the Church.

Source: Henry V, Speech to the chief Londoners, translated by H. T. Riley, *Memorials of London*, 1868.

Further Reading: E. F. Jacob, *Henry V and the Invasion of France*, 1947. C. L. Kingsford, *English Historical Literature in the 15th Century*, 1913.

Be it remembered, that on the 10th day of March, in the 2nd year of the reign of King Henry the Fifth, the same, our excellent and most gracious Lord the King, commanded Thomas Fauconer, the Mayor, and the Aldermen, and certain of the more substantial Commoners, to come to the Tower of his City of London aforesaid. Who being there assembled, he compendiously disclosed to them the purpose of his excellent intention, in these words.

'Well-beloved. We do desire that it shall not be concealed from the knowledge of your faithfulness, how that, God our rewarder, we do intend with no small army to visit the parts beyond sea, that so we may duly reconquer the lands pertaining to the heirship and crown of our realm, and which have been for long, in the times of our predecessors, by enormous wrong withheld. But, seeing that we cannot speedily attain to everything that is necessary in this behalf for the perfecting of our wishes, in order that we may make provision for borrowing a competent sum of money of all the prelates, nobles, lords, cities, boroughs, and substantial men, of our realm, we, knowing that you will be the more ready to incline to our wishes, the more immediately that the purpose of our intention, as aforesaid, redounds to the manifest advantage of the whole realm, have therefore not long since come to the determination to send certain Lords of our Council unto the City aforesaid, to treat with you as to promoting the business before mentioned.'

AGINCOURT, 25 October, 1415

Source: Jehan de Wavrin, *Collection of Chronicles and Ancient Histories of Great Britain*, translated from the French by William Hardy and E. L. C. P. Hardy, Rolls Series, 1864–91. Jehan was a noble of Artois who fought for the French at Agincourt but later fought the French, serving under the Duke of Burgundy.

Further Reading: Shakespeare, *King Henry V*; Sir Harris Nicolas, *The Battle of Agincourt*, 1833.

Of the mortal battle of Azincourt, in which the King of England discomfited the French.

It is true that the French had arranged their battalions between two small thickets, one lying close to Azincourt, and the other to Tramecourt. The place was narrow, and very advantageous for the English, and, on the contrary, very ruinous for the French, for the said French had been all night on horseback, and it rained, and the pages, grooms, and others, in leading about the horses, had broken up the ground, which was so soft that the horses could with difficulty step out of the soil. And also the said French were so loaded with armour that they could not support themselves or move forward. In the first place they were armed with long coats of steel, reaching to the knees or lower, and very heavy, over the leg harness, and besides plate armour also most of them had hooded helmets; wherefore this weight of armour, with the softness of the wet ground, as has been said, kept them as if immovable, so that they could raise their clubs only with great difficulty, and with all these mischiefs there was this, that most of them were troubled with hunger and want of sleep. There was a marvellous number of banners, and it was ordered that some of them should be furled. Also it was settled among the said French that everyone should shorten his lance, in order that they might be stiffer when it came to fighting at close quarters. They had archers and cross-bowmen enough, but they would not let them shoot, for the plain was so narrow that there was no room except for the men-at-arms.

Now let us return to the English. After the parley between the two armies was finished, as we have said, and the delegates had returned, each to their own people, the King of England, who had appointed a knight called Sir Thomas Erpingham to place his archers in front in two wings, trusted entirely to him, and Sir Thomas, to do his part, exhorted every one to do well in the name of the king, begging them to fight vigorously against the French in order to secure and save their own lives. And thus the knight, who rode with two others only in front of the battalion, seeing that the hour was come, for all things were well arranged, threw up a baton which he held in his hand, saying 'Nestrocq' [?'Now Strike!'], which was the signal for attack; then dismounted and joined the king, who was also on foot in the midst of his men, with his banner before him. Then the English, seeing this signal, began suddenly to march, uttering a very loud cry, which greatly surprised the French. And when the English saw that the French did not approach them, they marched dashingly towards them in very fine order, and again raised a loud cry as they stopped to take breath.

Then the English archers, who, as I have said, were in the

wings, saw that they were near enough, and began to send their arrows on the French with great vigour. The said archers were for the most part in their doublets, without armour, their stockings rolled up to their knees, and having hatchets and battle-axes or great swords hanging at their girdles; some were bare-footed and bare-headed, others had caps of boiled leather, and others of osier, covered with harpoy [skins] or leather.

Then the French, seeing the English come towards them in this fashion, placed themselves in order, every one under his banner, their helmets on their heads. The constable, the marshal, the admirals, and the other princes earnestly exhorted their men to fight the English well and bravely; and when it came to the approach the trumpets and clarions resounded everywhere; but the French began to hold down their heads, especially those who had no bucklers, for the impetuosity of the English arrows, which fell so heavily that no one durst uncover or look up. Thus they went forward a little, then made a little retreat, but before they could come to close quarters, many of the French were disabled and wounded by the arrows; and when they came quite up to the English, they were, as has been said, so closely pressed one against another that none of them could lift their arms to strike against their enemies, except some that were in front, and these fiercely pricked with the lances which they had shortened to be more stiff, and to get nearer their enemies. . . .

BRICKS, 1416–8

Shirburn Castle has a round brick tower at each corner of its square curtain wall and is surrounded by water over which there is a drawbridge which still works. It stands on the spring-line beside the Icknield Way at the foot of the Chilterns where the clay of the vale of Aylesbury meets the chalk. Behind the hills lies another ancient brick dwelling, Stonor. They can be dated to within a year of one another and the date is earlier than that often quoted as the first datable use of brick in later medieval England. Ewelme almshouse and school nearby is of similar fifteenth-century brick.

(1) *Source*: *Calendar of Patent Rolls*, 1374–7, p. 434. This is one of a great series of summaries of original records of the central government prepared under the superintendence of the Deputy Keeper of

the Records and printed by Her Majesty's Stationery Office. The Stationery Office prints a list of such publications.

5 March, 1377.

Licence for Warin de Insula to crenellate his manse at Shirburn, co. Oxford.

(2) Summary of the account of Thomas Stonor's Receiver from Michaelmas 1416 to Michaelmas 1417 now among ' Ministers' Accounts ' in the Public Record Office and printed by C. L. Kingsford, *The Stonor Letters and Papers*, Camden 3rd Series, Royal Historical Society, 1919, i, 30.

Allowances to Michael Warwick in full payment for making 200,000 ' de Brykes ', £40 . . . for carriage of the ' brikes ' from Crokkernende [Nettlebed] to Stonore, £15. . . . [The total of allowances to Thomas Tiler, Thomas Carpenter, lez Flemyngges and Thomas Plomer of Oxford etc. is £77. 12. 4½.]

(3) Extracts translated from Shirburn Manor Court Rolls by permission of the Earl of Macclesfield show that building material was on the spot in 1418.

Shirburn Court held there on Thursday after the feast of the Purification of the Blessed Mary 5 Henry V [3 Feb. 1418].

Bartholomew Colrug, farmer, carried outside the manor to his own home 8 free stones without leave. . . .

[9 June 1418].

Bartholomew Colyngrug, farmer, removed certain stones called plankstones out of the manor without leave. . . . He took and carried away some lead likewise . . . he says he put the lead on the tower for the lord's use with other lead and mended the gutters, and he relies on John Plomere to testify. . . .

[At the next court Plomere says he covered the tower with the lead.]

MARGERY KEMPE SUSPECTED OF BEING A LOLLARD AT LEICESTER, 1417

Margery Kempe's autobiography reveals the life and thoughts of a mystical woman who visited various shrines and undergoes various temptations. She was the daughter of one of the chief citizens of what was one of the chief towns of fifteenth-century England, Lynn in

Norfolk. Her education did not include French or Latin though she knew some Latin phrases from church and discovered that *bon* was a useful word. Piers Plowman testifies that there was little French in 'the farthest end of Norfolk'. She was born about 1373 and died in or after 1438.

Source: *The Book of Margery Kempe a modern Version* by W. Butler-Bowdon, O.U.P. 1954, p. 144.

Afterwards, set she forth to Leicester, and a good man also—Thomas Marchale—of whom is written before; and there she came into a fair church where she beheld a crucifix that was piteously portrayed and lamentable to behold, through beholding which, the Passion of Our Lord entered her mind, so that she began to melt and to relent by tears of pity and compassion. Then the fire of love kindled so eagerly in her heart that she could not keep it secret, for, whether she would or not, it caused her to break out with a loud voice and cry marvellously, and weep and sob so hideously that many a man and woman wondered on her therefor.

When it was overcome and she was going out of the church door, a man took her by the sleeve and said:

' Damsel, why weepest thou so sore? '

' Sir,' she said, ' it is not you to tell.'

So she and the good man, Thomas Marchale, went forth, and took her hostel and there ate their meat. When they had eaten, she prayed Thomas Marchale to write a letter and send it to her husband, that he might fetch her home. And while the letter was in writing, the hosteler came up to her chamber in great haste, and took her scrip and bade her come quickly and speak with the Mayor. And so she did.

Then the Mayor asked her of what country she was, and whose daughter she was.

' Sir,' she said, ' I am of Lynne in Norfolk, a good man's daughter of the same Lynne, who hath been mayor five times of that worshipful borough, and alderman also many years; and I have a good.man, also a burgess of the said town of Lynne, for my husband '

'Ah!' said the Mayor, ' Saint Katherine told what kindred she came of, and yet ye are not like her, for thou art a false

strumpet, a false Lollard, and a false deceiver of the people, and
I shall have thee in prison.'

And she answered: ' I am as ready, sir, to go to prison for
God's love, as ye are ready to go to church.'

When the Mayor had long chidden her and said many evil
and horrible words to her, and she, by the grace of Jesus, had
reasonably answered to all that he could say, he commanded the
jailer's man to lead her to prison.

The jailer's man, having compassion on her with weeping
tears, said to the Mayor:—

' Sir, I have no house to put her in, unless I put her amongst
men.'

Then she was moved with compassion for the man who had
compassion on her. Praying for grace and mercy to that man, as
for her own soul, she said to the Mayor:—

' I pray you, sir, put me not among men.'

Then said the jailer his own self to the Mayor:—

' Sir, I will be under bond to keep this woman in safe ward till
ye will have her back.'

Then was there a man of Boston, who said to the good wife,
where she was at hostel:—

' Forsooth,' he said, ' in Boston this woman is held to be a
holy woman and a blessed woman.'

Then the jailer took her into his ward, and led her home into
his own house, and put her in a fair chamber, shutting the door
with a key, and commending his wife the key to keep.

Nevertheless, he let her go to church when she would, and
let her eat at his own table and made her right good cheer for
Our Lord's sake, thanked be Almighty God thereof.

SIEGE OF ROUEN, 1418-9

Henry V sailed again to invade France on 23 July 1417. He
attacked Rouen on 29 July 1418, it surrendered on 13 January 1419
and he entered in triumph on 19 January 1419. The Treaty of Troyes
was ratified on 19 April 1420 recognizing Henry as regent and heir
of France and on 2 June he married the French princess Catherine.

Source: Continuation of the Chronicle of England called ' the Brut ', in Holkham MS. 670, by permission of the Earl of Leicester. Of many different manuscripts of ' the Brut ', so-called because it begins with legends of Brutus, this resembles that printed by Caxton. It ends with chapter 256, a long account of the siege followed by part of a poem on it by an eyewitness.

Further Reading: *The English Chronicle*, edited by J. S. Davies, Camden Soc. 64, 1856. John Page's poem on the siege in *Collections of a London Citizen*, ed. J. Gairdner, Camden Soc., N.S.17, 1876.

And thoo [then] it drowe nye Cristemasse and by that tyme her vitails scarced sore within the citee for they had nother brede ale nor wyne but water and vineger that was her drinke and flessh nor fissh they had noon but ete horsflessh doggs myce catts and ratts. For a quarter of an hors were he lene were he fatte was tho [then] solde in the cite amonge ye peple for an c s. gode paiement and an horshede for x s. and a dogge for xx s. and a ratte for xl d. and for xiij s. iiij d. they solde a catte and a mows for xx d. And thise wormes were bought and ete so faste that unneth they fonde any for to sell for no money. And tho was a ferthyng lofe bought in ye citee for a franke. And than hem fayled both whete and mele and all other graynes that they myght make of eny brede but of bran and broken ootes and nep [catmint] rotes and lekes was to hem mete of grete value. For a leke was solde for xij d. an ey [egg] for ix d. an apple for x d. Soch merchaunts was there within the citee a grete while. And there was many a carefull creature for their vitaill were all wasted and spent and they myght comme to newe in no maner weye for the siege that lay withoute rounde aboute the citee wold suffre no vitaill com yn to hem nether by water nor by londe. And than bigan the peple within the citee to dei faste both smale and grete for the passyng hungre and enfamyn that was amonge hem, bitwene ij c [two hundred] persones and moo day by day. And there as was first joie and pride and grete boste tho was ther amonge hem weyling sorowe care and wepyng and wringyng of handes. And though a child shold deie the moder wolde give hit no brede ne other fode ne wolde departe no mussell though she myght save the lyf of her oun childe of her body born but wolde save hir self while she myght, for love and hartely kynde- nesse was tho from hem passed. Nor the child wold nat profre

the moder for eche of hem caste hemself to leve, for all kyndenesse and love was tho sette beside for ever. The childe his mete
wold hide fro the moder and fro alle his othere frendes for his
mete they shold nat see for they ete it all in privete. And we may
prove by that peple there that hungre passed kyndenesse and
eke love that made her grete unrightwisnes and her cursed
levyng and pride that regned amonge hem in tho dayes. Wherfor
god sent hem a yerde of chastisement. But yit they that kept the
walles and toures of the citee rounde aboute, bicause the peple
without shold nat knowe ne wete of her grete nede and myschief
that they were in, ever to and to hilde her course and contynaunce
of open werre both with shotte of quarells and gonnes but
amonge there issewed some peple of the citee out and they come
forth and were take of the wacche men without at the siege and
they affrayned hem how it stode with the peple that were left
within the citee. And they answerd and tolde to the englisshe
peple of the grete nede scarste hunger and deth that was every
day newe amonges hem, but our folke wold nat bileve nor trowe
hem bicause that the peple withyn hilde at alle tymes contynaunce lyke day by day in werre as they did before upon the sege
without. Wherfore they hade of hem no trust in no degree.
And than withyn a while after the worthy men that were withyn
the citee gadred alle the pore peple that tho were within the citee
man woman and childe and brought hem to the gates and put
hem oute at every porte by an c persones on a route and badde
hem helpe hemself in her best maner that they myght, for there
they shold no longer abide in no wise with hem. And than they
com forth walkyng to the English sege kneling on her kneis and
wepyng sore both men and women with yonge sowkyng children
in her armes and olde feble men kneling beside hem and makyng
there a dolefull crie for all they cried there at ones ' Have mercy
on us ye good and cristen and worthy englisshmen.' And than
our kyng had rewthe and pitee on hem and gave hem brede and
drynke and made hem turne agen to the citee and there they
kept hem in the diche that they shold nat knowe nor here the
ordynaunce nor counceile of the sege ne of her wacche in no
wise for trayn and treson that myght fall. And whan thise pore
peple shold algates turne agen they made hiegh sorowe and

grete murmeracioun amonge hemself and seid they hade lever be sleyn there then goo agen to the citee and dolefully with hie voice bannyng and cursing her oun nacioun for they that were within the citee wold nat suffre hem comme in agen. Wherfor I trowe they did grete syn and myschief to hemself for many of hem deide there for colde that and they had ben within her lyves myght have be saved and kept.

And tho was comm the tyme of Cristemesse in which our kyng dide the grete mercy and releef to his enemyes at the reverence of that glorious feste of the birth of our lorde Jesu Crist and of his modre our lady seynt Marie that gracious and mercifull Virgyn. For of his pitee mercy and grace and at the reverence of that tyme of the holy fest the kyng of his compassioun that he had in herte and of his worthy and excellent manhode sente oute his herawdes in gode aray both to theym that were withyn the citee as wele as without the citee on the Cristemasse day selfe to theym that lakked vitaill that they sholde comm and have mete and drynke inowe in the worship of the fest and saufe condyte to comm and to goo. And they seid all grauntmercy lightly as they hade no nede therto and sette no price by his sonde and unneth they wolde graunte space unto the pore peple of her oun nacion to be releved that lay in the dyche under the citee walles that they hadde drive and put oute of grete myschief, but ij prests and iiij servaunts to bringe hem vitaill mete and drynke. And yf there comm any moo persones they wold shote hem and slee hem to the deth. And than were all thise pore peple sette arowe and thise ij prestes with her iiij servaunts brought hem plente of mete and drynke of the kyng's almesse. And so they were that tyme made wele at ese and replete of mete and drynke. And as they satte her [their] mete to fonge [take] this talkyng they had amonges them: 'Amighty god,' than thei seide, ' thise englissh men ben of good and tendre herte. Loo how here this excellent prince and kyng that we thought never obey nor never profre ne doon to him homage now hath he on us more pitee and compassioun by a thowsand than hath oure oune nacioun. Therfor our lorde God that art full of myght graunte hym grace to wynne and gete his true right.'

DICK WHITTINGTON, THRICE MAYOR, 1419

Source: London, Letter Book I, translated by H. T. Riley, *Memorials of London*, 1868.

Further Reading: J. Stow, *Survey of London*, ed. C. L. Kingsford, 2 vols., 1908 with *Additional Notes*, 1927.

On Friday, the Feast of St. Edward the King and Confessor [13 October] . . . after the Mass of the Holy Spirit devoutly and becomingly celebrated with solemn music in the Chapel of the Guildhall of the City of London, according to the Ordinance made thereon in the time of John Wodecok . . . in presence of William Sevenok, Mayor [with the Recorder, Aldermen and Sheriffs] and an immense number of the Commonalty of the citizens of the said city, summoned to the Guildhall of London for the election of a Mayor for the ensuing year, by their common assent, consent, and desire, Richard Whitingtone was chosen Mayor for the ensuing year; and on the morrow of the said Feast was presented before the Barons of the Exchequer of our Lord the King, at Westminster, admitted, and accepted as such.

A WOUNDED VETERAN OF AGINCOURT, 1422

Source: An appeal for relief sent to Henry VI in 1422, seven years after the French defeat by Henry V. H. Ellis, *Original Letters*, 2nd ser. vol. 1. 1827.

Further Reading: M. E. Christie, *Henry VI*, 1922.

To the Kyng oure Soverain Lord

Besechith mekely youre poure liegeman and humble horatour Thomas Hostell, that in consideration of his service doon to your noble progenitours of ful blessid memory Kyng Henrj the iiijth, and Kyng Henri the fift, whoos soules God assoille; being at the Siege of Harflewe, there smyten with a springolt [dart] through the hede, lesing his oon ye [eye], and his cheke boon broken; also at the Bataille of Agingcourt, and after at the takyng of the Carrakes on the See, there with a gadde of yren his plates smyten in sondre, and sore hurt, maymed, and wounded; by meane whereof he being sore febeled and debrused, now falle to greet age and poverty; gretly endetted; and may not helpe himself; havyng not wherewith to be susteyned ne releved but of menes gracious almesse; and being for his said service never yit recompensed ne rewarded, it plese your high and excellent Grace, the premises tenderly considered, of your benigne pitee and grace, to releve and refresh your said pouere Oratour, as it shal plese you, with your most gratious Almesse at the reverence of God and in werk of charitee; and he shal devoutly pray for the soules of your said noble Progenitours, and for your moost noble and high estate.

ORLEANS SAVED BY JEANNE D'ARC, 9 May, 1429

The French conquests of the English kings resulted in discontent and brigandage in England and acute misery in France. The war itself was one of unspectacular skirmishes until French patriotism revived under Jeanne d'Arc, a peasant girl who has been variously regarded as a witch, an inspired maniac and a saint sent from God. Her white banner and shining armour caught the imagination of the resistance and after she had relieved Orleans and captured Troyes she had Charles VII triumphantly crowned at Rheims on 17 July 1429.

Source: *Proceedings and Ordinances of the Privy Council* (1386–1542), ed. H. N. Nicolas, Records Commission 1834–7.

Further Reading: Minute details of her life are recorded in depositions of witnesses at her trial and retrial. T. Douglas Murray, *Jeanne D'Arc*, 1902.

There felle by the hand of God, as it semeth, a greet stroke upon youre peuple that was assembled there [Orleans] in greete nombre, caused in greete partye, as I trowe, of lak of sad beleve and of unlieful doubte that thei had of a disciple and leme of the fende called the Pucelle [Maid], that used fals enchantements and sorcerie, the whiche stroke and discomfiture not oonly lessed in greet partie the nombre of youre peuple ther, but as wel withdrawe the courage of the remnant in marvaillous wise, and courage your adverse partie and enemyes.

GODSTOW ABBEY, 29 May, 1445

The Diocese of Lincoln was so large that it included Oxfordshire until the Reformation. William Alnwick, a painstaking bishop (14 Sept. 1436—5 Dec. 1449) has left detailed records of 79 visitations to inquire into the shortcoming of monasteries in his diocese. These inquiries were held by the Bishop in the monastic chapter-houses, generally built on the east side of the cloisters. Visitations may be spoilt as mirrors of truth by tale-bearing or suppression and tend to record what goes wrong, like the records of Quarter Sessions or of a modern police court. It is wonderful however to be able to tune-in to accounts of actual life as opposed to ideal schemes, and such documents show that the charming portrait of the Prioress by Chaucer would have delighted contemporaries by a gentle irony which one only appreciates when conscious that various details of her fashionable and dainty ways were in fact contrary to episcopal policy.

Source: *Visitations of Religious Houses in the Diocese of Lincoln* vol. ii. *Records of Visitations held by William Alnwick Bishop of Lincoln* A.D. 1436 *to* A.D. 1449, pt. i ed. (with translation) by A. Hamilton Thompson, Lincoln Record Society vol. xiv, p. 114.

Further Reading: E. Power, *English Medieval Nunneries*. Many Bishops' Registers have been printed in Latin by the Canterbury and York Society and an English *Calendar of Entries in the Papal Registers relating to Great Britain and Ireland* 1198–1484 was printed in 13 vols. by H.M.S.O. For a selection of English documents see C. J. Offer, *Bishop's Register*, 1929.

Dame Elizabeth Felmersham, the abbess, says . . . that she cannot restrain students from Oxford from having common access in her despite to the monastery and the cloister precincts.

The nuns hold converse with the secular folk that come to visit the monastery, without asking any leave from the abbess.

Dame Alice Lumley, the prioress, says that the nuns have often access to Oxford under colour of visiting their friends. . . .

Dame Juliane Westone prays that the conduit may be speedily repaired, inasmuch as by reason of default in repair they suffer great scarcity of water within the cloister.

Also she prays that the bread and beer be bettered, for that sometimes they are very poor. . . .

Dame Elizabeth Forthey [with others] says that all things are well.

Dame May Hardelle says that dame Katherine Okeley holds too much talk with the strangers that come to the monastery in the church, in the chapter-house [etc.]

PIETY OF HENRY VI

Henry was despised by some as a simpleton and honoured by others as a saint, a sad commentary on the possibility of being a good man and a bad king and on the way that in English, as in Greek, the words 'simple' and 'silly' came to mean 'stupid' though they originally mean 'of good character' or 'holy'. Eton College and King's College Chapel at Cambridge are his legacies to mankind. Like Henry IV and Henry V who began to burn Lollards he resisted heresy.

Source: Master John Blakman, *On the Virtues and Miracles of Henry VI*. Blakman was a priest who knew the king. His wordy production was perhaps written in support of Henry VII's attempt to get Henry VI canonized. Translated from T. Hearne's edition of 1731 by Edith Thompson, *The Wars of York and Lancaster* 1450–1485, English History from Contemporary Writers, D. Nutt, 1892, p. 13.

Further Reading: J. Blacman, *Henry the Sixth*, 1919.

Concerning his humility . . . from his youth up he had been accustomed to wear broad-toed shoes and boots like a countryman. Also he had usually a long gown with a rounded hood after the manner of a burgess, and a tunic falling below the knees, shoes, boots, hose, everything of a dark grey colour—for he would have nothing fanciful.

Moreover, on the principal feasts of the year, but chiefly when by custom he should wear his crown, he would put on next his skin a rough hair-shirt. . . . He was wont to dedicate holy days and Sundays wholly to hearing the divine offices, and to devout offices. . . . But the other less holy days . . . he spent, not less diligently, either in treating of the affairs of the realm with his Council, according as the necessity of the case demanded, or in readings of the Scriptures, or in perusing writings, and chronicles. Concerning which, a certain worthy knight, once a right faithful chamberlain of his, Sir Richard Tunstall, bore verbal and written testimony, saying, 'In the law of the Lord was his delight day and night'. Evidence to the same effect is

afforded by the bitter complaint which the Lord King himself
made to me in his chamber at Eltham, when I was there alone
with him working with him in his holy books, intent upon wholesome admonitions and devout aspirations:—a certain most
powerful Duke of the realm having just then knocked at the
royal door, the King said, ' So do they disturb me, scarce am I
able by snatches, day or night to refresh myself with the reading
of the sacred dogmata, without somebody making a noise.'

It was his wont to use no oaths to confirm the truth of his
sayings, except by uttering these words, ' Forsooth, and forsooth,' that he might make those to whom he spoke certain
of what he said. Wherefore, sometimes by gently advising,
sometimes by severely chiding, he restrained very many, magnates
as well as commons, from great oaths; since every one who
swore was abominable to him. For the King, hearing a certain
great lord, his chamberlain, thoughtlessly break out swearing,
seriously reproved him, saying 'Alas! while you, the master of a
household, thus contrary to God's command, rap out oaths,
you set the worst example to your servants and subjects, for you
incite them to the like.'

PRECEDENCE AT DUKE HUMPHREY'S TABLE, BEFORE 1447

Humphrey Duke of Gloucester (1391–1447), brother of Henry V,
was one of the most powerful men of his day. Though he was
' unprincipled, factious, and blindly selfish ' his gracious and popular
manners and his patronage of learning earned him the title ' Good
Duke Humphrey '. The duke was murdered in 1447, if suspicions
aroused by his sudden death were justified, but some of his friends
like Abbot Whethamstead thought his death a natural one. His
portraits show a man worn and prematurely aged and his health had
been undermined by riotous living. He is commemorated by a great
room in the Bodleian Library which still is called after his name, for
he was a friend of Oxford University and enriched the library.

Source: John Russell, Book of Nurture, written about 1460 by one
who had been usher and marshall of Duke Humphrey. Modernized
by Edith Rickert, The Babees' Book, Medieval Manners for the Young,

Done into Modern English from Dr. Furnivall's Texts, Chatto and Windus 1908, p. 73. Russell is describing ' The Office of Usher and Marshall '.

Further Reading: B. Botfield, *Manners and Household Expenses in England*, 1841.

A marshal must look to the birth of each estate, and arrange officers such as chancellor, steward, chamberlain, treasurer, according to their degree.

He must honour foreign visitors, and strangers to this land, even when they are resident here. A well-trained marshal should think beforehand how to place strangers at the table, for if they show gentle cheer and good manners, he thereby doth honour his lord and bring praise to himself.

If the king send any messenger to your lord, if he be a knight, squire, yeoman of the crown, groom, page or child, receive him honourably as a baron, knight, squire, yeoman or groom (i.e. one degree higher than he actually is), and so forth, from the highest degree to the lowest, for a king's groom may dine with a knight or a marshal.

A commendable marshal must also understand the rank of all the worshipful officers of the commonalty of this land, of shires, cities and boroughs—such must be placed in due order, according to their rank.

The estate of a knight of [good] blood and wealth is not the same as that of a simple and poor knight. Also, the Mayor of Queenborough is not of like dignity with the Mayor of London—nothing like of degree; and they must on no account sit at the same table.

The Abbot of Westminster is the highest in the land, and the Abbot of Tintern the poorest; both are abbots, yet Tintern shall neither sit nor stand with Westminster. Also, the Prior of Dudley may in no wise sit with the Prior of Canterbury. And remember, as a general rule, that a prior who is prelate of a cathedral church, shall sit above any abbot or prior of his own diocese, in church, chapel, chamber or hall.

Reverend doctors of twelve years' standing shall sit above those of nine years', although the latter may spend more largely of fine red gold. Likewise, the younger aldermen shall sit or stand below their elders, and so in every craft, the master first, and then the ex-warden.

RICHARD NEVILLE, EARL OF WARWICK, THE 'KINGMAKER'
AT THE FIRST BATTLE OF ST. ALBANS, 22 May, 1455

William de la Pole became the leading man in England after the deaths of Humphrey Duke of Gloucester and Cardinal Beaufort in 1447. He became Duke of Suffolk in 1448. Military setbacks in France made him very unpopular especially in London, and in 1450 he was murdered. That year Jack Cade rebelled and disorder was rife, for there were local wars between rival barons. A league of barons revolted against the group at court which controlled King Henry VI and this skirmish at St. Albans can be called the first battle of the Wars of the Roses. It is no accident that it occurred only two years after the English were expelled from France and ex-soldiers were unemployed.

Source: An Account of the First Battle of St. Albans, from a contemporary manuscript found among the papers of Sir William Stonor, Steward of the Abbot of St. Albans, ed. by John Bayley in *Archaeologia*, xx, 1824, 519–23.

Further Reading: Sir J. H. Ramsay, *Lancaster and York*, 2 vols. 1892. C. W. C. Oman, *Warwick the Kingmaker*, reprinted 1946.

The Earle of Warrewyk knowyng ther offe, toke and gadered his men to gedere and ferosly brake in by the gardeyne sydes, betuene the signe of the Keye, and the sygne of the Chekkere in Holwell strete; and anoon as they wer wythinne the toon, sodeynly the[y] blew up Trumpettes, and sette a cry with a shout and a grete voyce, ' a Warrewe, a Warrewyk, a Warrewyk!' . . . And at this same tyme were hurt lordes of name; the Kyng our sovereyne lord in the neck with an arowe, the Duke of Buckingham with an arrowe in the vysage, the lord of Dudle with an arowe in the vysage, the lord of Stafford in the hond with an arowe, the lord of Dorsette sore hurt that he myght not go, but he was caryede hom in a cart, and Wenlok knyght, in lyke wyse in a carte sore hurt; and other diverse knyghtes and squyers sore hurt. The Erle of Wyldshyre, Thorp, and many others, fflede and left her harneys behynde hem cowardly; and the substance of the Kyngs partye were dyspoyled of hors and harneys. This don the seyde lordes, that ys to wote the Duke of Yorke, the

Erle of Salesbury, the Erle of Warrewyk, come to the Kyng our sovereyne lord, and on here knees besoughte hym of grace, and for yevenesse of that they hadde doon yn his presence: and besought hym of hys heynesse to take hem as hys true legemen, seyng that they never attendyde hurt to his owne persone and ther fore the kyng oure sovereyne lord toke hem to grace, and so desyred hem to cesse there peple and that there sshulde no more harme be doon; and they obeyde hys commaundement, and lote make a cry on the kyngs name that al maner of pepull shulde cesse and not so hardy to stryke ony stroke more after the proclamacyon of the Crye: and so cessed the seyde Batayle.

SCATTERED ARABLE STRIPS, 1456–7

One must visualize farming ' as they saw it happen '. Except in very hilly and wooded districts farm holdings consisted of strips scattered in a few large fields and divided from each other often by strips belonging to other people. These strips are often still visible in the form of ridge and furrow. The number of fields varied in different places, often three or four. Hedges were few, except round closes near houses, and in open field districts houses were concentrated in villages, so the appearance of an agricultural district differed much from what it is today when farms are often isolated and when most fields are small rectangles.

Source: Translated from the beginning of one of a series of terriers of different holdings at Holkham by permission of the Earl of Leicester. Holkham deed 22a fol. 51, in the Holkham Estate Office. The Prior of Walsingham had 104 acres and 1 rod at Holkham divided into 114 strips. Apart from strips occupied by villeins the Prior of Peterstone had 220 acres, but as some of these were consolidated into blocks of as much as 16 acres the total number of scattered units was only 61. These terriers are preceded by a survey for each of 16 furlongs showing how the Neel family gradually built up an estate at Holkham by a multitude of separate purchases of separate strips during the reigns of Edward II and III with details of each transaction.

Terrier for the lands of the Prior of Walsingham in Holkham renewed by the hands of John Weylond, 35 Henry VI.

5 rods called Walsyngham Grange at Lyndsyde abutting on east and west on the waste and Robert Fuller, between lands of the lord of Burghall [a Holkham manor called after the 'Borough', an earthwork fortification in the marshes].

3 acres at Ede Crosse between the lands lately of John Toral [E.] and Alice Goldale [W.] abutting on the royal road [N.] and the heirs of T. Lucas [S.].

6 rods east of the Grange between lands at south and north of T. Lucas and Pynch *alias* Greve of Wells, abutting on east and west on the waste and Robert Fuller.

7 rods between lands of Robert Fuller [N.] and the lord of Burghall [S.] abutting on the heirs of T. Lucas [E.] and Lambe Hill Hedys [W.]

3 rods between Hugh Tydd [W.] and the common way called Gybbisgate at Tobers [E.] and abutting on Hugh [S.] and Wythunwey [N.]

1 acre and 1 rod at Gybbisgate between Robert Fuller [S.] and Robert Dockyng [N.] and abutting on Lambirhillsti [E.] and Gybbisgate [W.]

1 rod at Lyngsti between bond land of Burghall [E.] and Robert Dockyng [N.] and abutting on Lambirhillsti [W.] and the heirs of T. Lucas [E.]. . . .

BISHOP PEACOCK RECANTS, 4 December, 1457

Reginald Peacock, Bishop of Chichester wrote books against the Lollards. His *Repressor of over-much Blaming of the Clergy* defended the Church in English from the 'lay party' or 'Bible-men' but offended the orthodox by doing so in the light of reason.

Source: Thomas Gascoigne, *Passages from the Book of Truths*, translated from the Latin edition of 1881 by Edith Thompson, *The Wars of York and Lancaster* 1450-1485, English History from Contemporary Writers, D. Nutt 1892, p. 52. He strongly opposed heresy and ecclesiastical abuses alike.

Further Reading: K. B. McFarlane, *John Wycliffe and the Beginnings of English Nonconformity*, 1952.

This Pecock, Bishop of Chichester . . . in the presence of 20,000 men, clad in his episcopal dress, at the feet of the Archbishop of Canterbury Lord Thomas Bourchier, and of Kemp, Bishop of London, and Low, Bishop of Rochester, doctor of divinity of Oxford, and of the Bishop of Durham, there abjured his writings and his written conclusions . . . and three large

erroneous books of his, with eleven others in sheets, he handed
to a certain man who was to commit them to a huge fire there
prepared; and so was it then done in London in Saint Paul's
Churchyard. And also the same Bishop Pecock said publicly,
' My pride and my presumption have brought me into this evil
and disgrace.' After this, the Archbishop of Canterbury sent
him to Maidstone to await judgment.

This Bishop Pecock, sometime a Fellow of Oriel College,
Oxford, in his writings called public preachers ' pulpit-bawlers ';
. . . and when he revoked his erroneous and heretical conclusions
at Saint Paul's Cross, the report went, that if he himself had gone
down to the fire in which his books were burning up, the people
on the spot would have pitched him into that fire.

A BATH, c. 1460

Some of the healing herbs are mentioned as such even in Saxon
times. King John's Household Accounts record when he had baths.

Source: John Russell, *Book of Nurture*, from Edith Rickert, *The
Babees' Book*: *Medieval Manners for the Young*: *Done into Modern English
from Dr. Furnivall's Texts*, Chatto and Windus 1908, p. 68.

If your lord wishes to bathe and wash his body clean, hang
sheets round the roof, every one full of flowers and sweet green
herbs, and have five or six sponges to sit or lean upon, and see
that you have one big sponge to sit upon, and a sheet over so
that he may bathe there for a while, and have a sponge also for
under his feet, if there be any to spare, and always be careful
that the door is shut. Have a basin full of hot fresh herbs and
wash his body with a soft sponge, rinse him with fair rose-water,
and throw it over him; then let him go to bed; but see that the
bed be sweet and nice; and first put on his socks and slippers
that he may go near the fire and stand on his foot-sheet, wipe
him dry with a clean cloth, and take him to bed to cure his
troubles.

The Making of a Medicinable Bath

Boil together hollyhock, mallow, wall pellitory and brown
fennel, danewort, St. John's wort, centaury, ribwort and camo-

mile, heyhove, heyriff, herb-benet, bresewort, smallage, water speedwell, scabious, bugloss[?], and wild flax which is good for aches—boil withy leaves and green oats together with them, and throw them hot into a vessel and put your lord over it and let him endure it for a while as hot as he can, being covered over and closed on every side; and whatever disease, grievance or pain ye be vexed with, this medicine shall surely make you whole, as men say.

TROUBLES OF QUEEN MARGARET OF ANJOU, 1463

After resisting the victorious Edward IV for some time in the North, Margaret of Anjou fled with her son to the Duke of Burgundy. She told his sister her adventures as a fugitive.

Source: George Chastellain, who served the Duke of Burgundy, wrote a *Chronicle* in French edited 1863–66. Translated by Edith Thompson, *Wars of York and Lancaster* 1450–1485, English History from Contemporary Writers, D. Nutt 1892, p. 90.

Further Reading: E. C. Lodge, *English Constitutional Documents*, 1307–1485, 1935.

The Queen related some of her adventures . . . saying that it happened, for the space of five days, that her husband the King, her son, and she had for their three selves only one herring, and not one day's supply of bread; and that on a holy day she found herself at mass without a brass farthing to offer; wherefore, in her beggary and need, she prayed a Scottish archer to lend her something, who, half loth and regretfully drew a Scots groat from his purse and lent it to her. She also related how, at her last unfortunate discomfiture, she was robbed and despoiled of all she had, of her royal jewels and dresses, of her plate and treasures, with which she thought to escape into Scotland; and when all this had been taken from her, she herself was seized upon, villainously reviled, run upon with a drawn sword, caught hold of by her head-gear to have her neck severed, menaced with divers torments and cruelties, while she, on her knees and with clasped hands, wailing and weeping, prayed that, for the sake of divine and human pity, they would have mercy upon her. Withal she perseveringly called upon God's mercy; and Heaven heard her appeal; for speedily there arose such a discord and dissension among her captors about the booty, that furiously slaughtering each other like madmen, they concerned themselves no more about the dolorous Queen their princess. . . . When the poor Queen saw this, she piteously addressed an esquire who was by, and prayed him that, for the sake of Our Saviour's passion, he would help her to escape. Then the esquire looked at her, and God caused him to conceive a pity for her, so that he said, 'Madam, mount behind me, and my lord the Prince before, and I will save you or die, although death seems to me more likely than not.' So the Queen and her son mounted . . . [and went into a forest where a brigand approached them but listened to reason and promised to amend his life. The Queen left the prince in his charge.]

The Duchess felt great pity for her, and said that certainly, short of having passed through the anguish of death, never had so high a princess a harder fortune, and that therefore, if God did not raise her up again, she ought to be put in the book of unhappy women, as having surpassed them all.

WARWICK v. WOODVILLE, 1469

(1) Richard Nevill (1428–71) became Earl of Warwick in right of Anne Beauchamp and with her vast estates overshadowed his father, the Earl of Salisbury. At first he was neutral in the struggle between his uncle and cousin, the Dukes of Somerset and York, but jealousy of the Lancastrian Percies caused him to start his varying career as a Yorkist in the Wars of the Roses, for he typified his class in pursuing personal and family power exclusively. He has been called the ' Last of the Barons ', the long line of overmighty opponents of the crown. After many triumphs his corpse was exposed ' open and naked ' for two days at St. Paul's, in a London whose richer citizens hated him because they were the creditors of Edward IV. On 20 April 1456 he became governor of Calais which long served as his base. Here, in 1469, he was too busy to keep a promise to supply historical materials to Jean de Wavrin and no details of his personal appearance are recorded.

Source: *The Great Chronicle of London*, ed. A. H. Thomas and I. D.

Thornley, City Corporation 1938, p. 207. The anonymous chronicler was Robert Fabian, who was ' apprentyze and abowth the age of xvii or xviii yeres ' in 1468 when his master met trouble for not selling at her own price to the Duchess of Bedford a valuable piece of arras wrought in gold of the story of the siege of Jerusalem.

1469 . . . many murmurous talys Ran in the Cite atwene therle of warwyk & the Quenys blood, The which Erle was evyr hadd In grete ffavour of the comonys of thys land, by Reson of the excedyng howsold whych he dayly kepid In alle Cuntrees where evyr he sojournyd or laye, and when he cam to london he held such an howse that vj Oxyn were etyn at a Brekeffast, and every tavern was ffull of his mete, ffor whoo that had any acqueyntaunce In that hows, he shuld have hadd as much sodyn & Rost as he myght cary upon a long daggar which those dayes were much usid as now they use murderers.

(2) Richard Woodville (d. 1469) rose by two secret marriages. Jacquetta of Luxembourg, widowed Duchess of Bedford, was fined on 23 March 1437 for marrying him without royal consent and his daughter Elizabeth married Edward IV on 1 May 1464. Numerous noble Woodville marriages estranged ' great lords of blood ' from Edward IV. This ' murmurous ' tale was doubtless suggested by the history of the Duchess's sister-in-law, the witch Duchess of Gloucester.

Source: Copy of exemplification of royal inspeximus of a letter from Edward IV to the Bishop of Bath and Wells, his chancellor, about a meeting of ' our great Councell . . . in the chambre of the great Counsail called the parlement chambre ' concerning a petition from ' the highe and noble princesse, Jaquett duchesse of Bedford ' held on 10 February 9 Edward IV. Holkham MS. 677, fol. 475, printed by permission of the Earl of Leicester. The Duchess complains of being accused of witchcraft, and encloses confessions from her accusers. The three documents are recited and entered in the official records.

To the kinge our Soveraigne Lorde sheweth and lamentably complayneth unto your highnes your humble, and true leige-woman Jaquett Duchesse of Bedford late ye wife of your true and faithfull knight and leigeman Richard [Woodville] late Earl of Rivers that wheare shee at all time hath and yett doth trulie beleeve on God accordinge to the faith of holie churche as a true Christen woman ought to doe yett Thomas Wake squire contrarie to the lawe of God, lawe of this land, and all reason and good

conscience in the time of the late truble and riotous season of his
malicious disposicion towardes your said oritrice of longe time
contynued entendynge not only to hurt and appaire her good
name and fame, but also purposed the finall distruccion of her
person and to that effect caused her to be brought in a comon
noyse and disclaunder of wichecraft threuout a great part of this
your reame surmitting that shee should have used wichecraft and
sorcerie. In so much as the said Wake caused to be brought to
Warwick at your last beinge there soveraigne lord to divers of
the lordes then beinge there present a image of lead made like
a man of armes conteyninge the lengthe of a man's finger and
broken in the middes and made fast with a wire sayinge that it
was made by your said oratrice to use with the said wichcraft
and sorcerye where shee ne none for her ne be her ever sawe it
God knoweth, and over this the said Wake for the performinge of
his malicious entent abovesaid entreted one John Daunger
parishe clerk of Stoke Brewerne in ye Countie of Northampton
to have said that there were twoe other images made by your
said oratrice, one for your soveraigne lord and another for our
soveraigne ladie the queene whereunto the said John Daunger
neyther could ne would be intreted to say whereupon it like
your highnes of your noble grace at humble sute made unto your
highnes by your said oratrice for her declaracion in the premisses
to send for the said Wake, and the said John Daunger, comandinge
them to attend upon the reverend fader in God the bishopp of
Carlill the honorable Lord the Earle of Northumberland and the
worshipfull Lordes, Lord Hastinges and Mountjoy, and maister
Roger Radcliffe to be examined by them of such as they coud
allege and saie against your said oratrice in this behalf, thexamin-
acions afore them had apperith in writinge hereunto annexed
whereof one bill conteyninge the sayinges of Wake and writt with
his owne hand, and another shewinge the sayinges of the said
Daunger and writt in the presence of the said Lordes which
seene by your highnes and many other Lordes in this your great
counsell the xixth daie of Januarie last passed then being there
present, your said oratrice was by your grace and them takin and
clered and declared of the said noyses and disclaunders which
as yett remaine not enacted for soe much as divers your lordes

were then absent, wherfore please it your highnes of your abundant grace and great rightwisenes tenderlie to consider the premisses and the declaracion of your said oratrice had in this behalf as is afore shewed to comand the same to be enacted in this your said grete councell so as the same her declaracion may allway remaine there of record and that shee maie have it exemplified under your great seale, and shee shall contynuallie praie to God for the preservacion of your most ryall estate. . . .

John Daunger of Spetellanger sworne and examined saith . . . that he herd never noe wichcraft of my Lady of Bedford. . . .

EDWARD IV SUDDENLY EXPELLED BY WARWICK, THE KINGMAKER, 26 September, 1470

The Earl of Warwick, the Duke of Clarence, Queen Margaret of Anjou and her son, Prince Edward, were enemies of each other; but Louis XI managed to bring them together at Angers to unite in opposition to their common enemy, Edward IV. Warwick's brother, Montague, had been loyal to Edward IV but he suddenly changed sides with six thousand men when he had advanced as if to help Edward IV within five or six miles of him.

Source: Philip de Comines, *Memoirs of His Own Times*, translated by Thomas Danett, 1614. These are the memoirs of an observant diplomat who served both Charles the Bold, Duke of Burgundy, and Louis XI. He had a good knowledge of history and modern languages but regretted his lack of early training in Latin. He enjoyed the confidence of the great and was an excellent historian, remarkably free from anti-English prejudices.

Further Reading: C. L. Kingsford, *Prejudice and Promise in 15th Century England*, 1925.

Five or sixe daies after the Earles arrival his power was so great, that he encamped within three leagues of King Edward. Notwithstanding the Kings force was greater then his, if all his men had been faithfull and true, and lay also in campe to fight with him. Further you shall understand that the King lodged (as himselfe told me) in a strong village—at the least a strong house into the which no man could enter but by a draw bridge, which was a happy chance for him: the rest of his army lay in other villages round about. But as hee sat at dinner, suddenly

one came running in, and brought newes that the Marques of
Montague the Earles brother and certaine other were mounted
on horsebacke, and had caused all their men to crie, God save
King Henry. Which message at the first the King beleeved not,
but in all hast sent other messengers forth, and armed himselfe,
and set men also at the barriers of his lodging to defend it. He
was accompanied with the Lord Hastings Lord Chamberlain of
England, a wise Knight and of the greatest authoritie about him,
who was maried to the Earle of Warwickes sister, yet notwithstanding was true and faithfull to his Master, and had three
thousand horse under his charge in the Kings armie as himselfe
told me. With the King was also the Lord Scales the Queene of
Englands brother, and divers other valiant Knights and Esquiers,
who all perceived that this busines went not well: for the messengers brought word that the report was true, and that the
enimies assembled to assault the King.

But God so provided for the King that he lodged hard by
the sea side, neere to a place where a little ship laden with victuals
that followed his armie, and two hulks of Holland fraughted
with merchandise lay at anchor: he had no other shift but to
run to save himselfe in one of them. The Lord Chamberlaine
staied a while behind him, and talked with the lieutenant of his
band and divers other particular men in the Kings armie, willing
them to go to the enemies, and to beare true and faithfull hearts
to the King and him which talke ended: he went aboord to the
rest being ready to depart. Now you shall understand that the
custome in England is, after the victory obtained, neither to kill
nor ransome any man, especially of the vulgar sort: knowing all
men then to be readie to obey them, because of their good
successe. Wherefore these soldiers after the Kings departure
received no harme. Notwithstanding King Edward himselfe
told me, that in all battels that he wan, so soone as he had
obtained victorie he used to mount on horsebacke, and crie to
Save the people and kil the nobles: for of them few or none
escaped. Thus fled King Edward the yeere 1470 with two hulkes
and a little bote of his owne countrie, accompanied with seven or
eight hundred persons, having none other apparell than that
they ware in the wars, utterly unfurnished of money, and hardly

knowing whether they went. Strange it was to see this poore King (for so might he now well be called) to flie after this sort pursued by his owne servants, and the rather, for that he had by the space of twelve or thirteene yeeres lived in greater pleasures and delicacies than any Prince in his time: for he had wholy given himselfe to dames, hunting, hawking, and banketting, in such sort that he used when he went hunting in the sommer season, to cause many pavilions to be pitched to solace himselfe there with the Ladies. And to say the truth his personage served aswel to make court as any mans that ever I knew: for he was yonge, and as goodly a gentleman as lived in our age, I meane in this time of his adversitie: for afterward he grew marvellous grosse. But behold now how he fell into the troubles and misfortunes of the world. He sailed straight towards Holland, and at that time the Easterlings were enemies both to the English men and the French, and had many ships of war upon the sea, wherefore they were much feared of the English men, and not without cause. . . . The King had not one peny about him, but gave the Master of the ship for his passage a goodly gown furred with martins, promising one day to do him a good turne: and as touching his traine never so poore a company was seene. But the Lord of Gruteuse dealt very honorably with them: for he gave much apparrell among them, and defraied the King to La Hay in Holland whither himself also waited upon him. Afterward he advertised the Duke of Burgundie of this adventure, who was marvellously abashed at the newes, and had much rather have heard of the Kings death: for he feared the Earle of Warwicke, who was his mortall enemy, and bare now the sway in England. The sayd Earle soone after he was landed, found infinite numbers to take his part. For the army that King Edward left behind him, what for love, what for feare yeelded to him, in such sort that every day his forces encreased. And in this estate went hee to London, where a great number of Knights and Esquiers (who afterward did King Edward good service), tooke sanctuary, as also did the Queene his wife, who was there delivered of a sonne in very poore estate.

DEATH OF HENRY VI, Tuesday, 21 May, 1471

Henry VI was killed because the death of his son and heir at the battle of Tewkesbury removed the last motive for keeping him alive. He perished on the night of Edward IV's triumphal entry into London. Warkworth's *Chronicle* records that he died ' on a Tuesday night, 21 May, betwixt xi and xii of the clock, the Duke of Gloucester being then at the Tower and many others '; next day his body was exposed at St. Paul's ' and his face was open that every man might see him, and in his lying be bled.' He was decently buried in Chertsey Abbey, and in Yorkshire Henry was revered as Saint and Martyr. Many miracles attested to his holiness, and prayers were composed to him.

Source: Historie of the arrival of Edward IV in England and the final recoverye of his kingdomes from Henry VI, A.D. 1471, ed. John Bruce, Camden Soc. vol. i, 1838.

An authorized relation put forth by the Yorkists, an accurate but partisan account by ' a servant of the King that presently saw in effect a great part of his exploits.

Here it is remembred, that, from the tyme of Tewkesbery fielde, where Edward, called Prince, was slayne, thanne, and sonne aftar, wer taken, and slayne, at the Kyngs wylle, all the noblemen that came from beyond the see with the sayde Edward, called Prince, and othar also theyr parte-takers as many as were of eny might or puisaunce. Qwene Margaret, hirselfe, taken, and browght to the Kynge; and, in every party of England, where any commotion was begonne for Kynge Henry's party, anone they were rebuked, so that it appered to every mann at eye the sayde partie was extincte and repressed for evar, without any mannar hope of agayne quikkening; utterly despaired of any maner of hoope or releve. The certaintie of all whiche came to the knowledge of the sayd Henry, late called Kyng, being in the Tower of London; not havynge, afore that, knowledge of the saide matars, he toke it so great dispite, ire, and indingnation, that, of pure displeasure, and melencoly, he dyed the xxiij. day of the monithe of May. Whom the Kynge dyd to be browght to the friers prechars at London, and there, his funerall service donne, to be caried, by watar, to an Abbey upon Thamys syd, xvj myles from London, called Chartsey, and there honorably enteryd.

ENGLAND AND FRANCE

Sir John Fortescue boasted that in England wealth was widely spread and the Commons had a stake in the kingdom. The king existed for the sake of the kingdom, not the kingdom for the sake of the king.

(1) *Source*: Sir John Fortescue, ' The Comodytes of Englond ', written before 1451, edited by Lord Clermont for private distribution in *The Works of Sir John Fortescue*, 1869. Edward IV captured Fortescue on 4 May 1471 at the battle of Tewkesbury, but pardoned him and made him a member of his Council after he had disavowed his writings on behalf of the Lancastrians.

. . . the comune peple of thys londe are the beste fedde, and also the best cledde of any natyon crystyn or hethen. . . .

As towchynge the worshyppe of thys londe, the which appendyn to Holy Chyrche, be the two Unyversyteys at Oxforde and Cambryge, the wiche ther ys noo man that travaylythe that knowthe two so goode Universytes in oo lande, where doctors of dyvynyte with all other clergy scyence, that beyn so well red and tawght as they are in thys londe, and Goddes servyes so worthyly, devynly, and devotly seyd, and chastyte in lyvynge passynge ony other londe; and the Worthynes and Ryches of oure Arsbyshoppys and Bysshoppys; and grete Abbeys are indowyd here in thys londe, and every preyst syngynge with chaleys of sylver, and with noo lede nor tyn as they do in other places.

And all the Holy Martyrs, confessors, and vyrgyns that are in thys londe scrynys and odyr Images, as oure Lady Seyntt Mary, they are more rycher of golde, pressyous stonys, and jewells than ony other londe. . . .

(2) *Source*: Sir John Fortescue, *In Praise of the Laws of England*, written in France between 1464 and 1470, chapters 22 and 35.

. . . the laws of France, in capital cases, do not think it enough to convict the accused by evidence . . . but they choose rather to put the accused themselves to the rack, till they confess their guilt. . . . Some are extended on the rack till their very sinews crack, and the veins gush out in streams of blood: others have weights hung to their feet, till their limbs are almost torn asunder, and the whole body dislocated: some have their mouths

gagged to such a wideness for a long time, whereat such quantities of water are poured in that their bellies swell to a prodigious
degree, and then being pierced with a faucet, spigot, or other
instrument for the purpose, the water spouts out in great abundance, like the whale. . . . To describe the inhumanity of such
exquisite tortures affects me with too real a concern, and the
varieties of them are not to be recounted in a large volume. . . .

. . . The peasants live in great hardship and misery. Their
constant drink is water, neither do they taste, throughout the
year, any other liquor; unless upon some extraordinary times, or
festival days. Their clothing consists of frocks, or little short
jerkins made of canvass no better than common sackcloth; they
do not wear any trowse, but from the knees upward; their legs
being exposed and naked. The women go barefoot, except on
holidays: they do not eat flesh, unless it be the fat of bacon, and
that in very small quantities, with which they make a soup; of
other sorts, either boiled or roasted, they do not so much as
taste, unless it be of the inwards and offals of sheep and bullocks,
and the like, which are killed for the use of the better sort of
people, and the merchants: for whom also quails, partridges,
hares, and the like, are reserved, under paid of the gallies: as for
their poultry, the soldiers consume them, so that scarce the eggs,
slight as they are, are indulged them by way of a dainty. And if it
happen that a man is observed to thrive in the world, and become
rich, he is presently assessed to the king's tax, proportionably
more than his poorer neighbours, whereby he is soon reduced to
a level with the rest. This, or I am very much mistaken, is the
present state and condition of the peasantry of France.

(3) Sir John Fortescue, *On the Monarchy of England*, chapter 13,
written not earlier than 1471. Chapter 3 contains a passage very like
the last, adding ' thay eate Apples, with Bred right brown made of
Rye . . . their nature is much wastid, and the Kynd of them brought
to nowght. Thay gone crokyd, and ar feble, not able to fyght, nor
to defend the Realme; nor they have wepon, nor monye to buy them
wepon withal'.

It hath ben often seen in Englond that three or four Thefes,
for Povertie hath sett upon seven or eight true Men, and robbyd
them al. But it hath not ben seen in Fraunce, that seven or

eight Thefes, have ben hardy to robbe three or four true Men. Wherfor it is right seld, that French Men be hangyd for Robberye, for they have no Hertys to do so terryble an Acte. There be therfor mo Men hangyd in Englond, in a Yere, for Robberye, and Manslaughter, than ther be hangid in Fraunce, for such Cause of Crime in seven Yers. There is no Man hangyd in Scot-land, in seven Yers together, for Robberye; and yet thay be often tymes hangyd for Lacenye, and Stelyng of Goods in the Absence of the Owner thereof: But their Harts serve them not to take a Mannys Goods, while he is present, and will defend it; which maner of takyng is callid Robberye. But the Englisch Men be of another Corage; for if he be poer, and see another Man havyng Rychesse, which may be takyn from him by Might, he wol not spare to do so, but if, that poer Man be right true. Wherfor, it is not Povertie, but it is lacke of Harte and Cowardise, that kepyth the French Men from rysyng.

EDWARD IV AND LOUIS XI, 1474–5.

Edward IV proposed to invade France in concert with the Duke of Burgundy and taxes for this purpose were levied. They were heavy but insufficient and Edward IV supplemented them by ' voluntary ' gifts called benevolences. The continuator of the Croyland Chronicle says ' everyone was to give exactly what he pleased, or rather what he did not lease, as a benevolence '. Louis XI and Edward IV were typical princes of the Renaissance, sensible and practical, with no exaggerated ideas of chivalry, and as there was no real advantage to be gained from the war they came to terms, and Edward IV kept his money—with an additional grant from Louis XI.

Source: Philip de Comines, *Memoirs*, translated by T. Danett, 1614.

Further Reading: L. Stratford, *Life and Reign of Edward IV*, 1928.

There is no nation to ignorant and rude as the Englishmen at their first landing in Fraunce, but in very short space they become excellent good soldiers, hardie and wise. . . . King Edward was above three weekes in passing betweene Calice and Dover, yet are they but seven leagues distant: whereby you may perceive with how great difficultie a King of England invadeth Fraunce. And if the King our Master had been as well acquainetd with the wars by Sea as by land: King Edward had never passed

over, at the least not that Sommer. But the King understood
them not, and those that had charge of them much lesse. . . .
Before King Edward embarked, he sent from Dover to the King
one Herault alone called Garter a Norman borne, who brought
a letter of defiance from the King of England in very good
language, and so excellently well penned, that I am verily perswaded it was never of English man's doing. . . . The King
read the letter softly to himselfe, and afterward all alone withdrew
himself into a Wardrob, and commanded the Herault to be
brought to his presence . . . and gave him with his owne hands
three hundred crownes, promising him a thousand more if
peace were concluded: further, openly he gave him for a present
a goodly peece of crimson velvet of thirty ells. . . . When he
had made an end, he called me to him, bidding me continually
to entertaine the Herault, till some were appointed to beare him
companie, to the end no man might commune with him. . . .
Now you shall understand that King Edward and his men were
nothing acquainted with our affaires, but went bluntly to worke,
so that they could not as yet smell out the cunning used heere
on this side the Sea: for naturally, the Englishmen that never
travelled abroad are very cholericke, as also are all people of cold
countries. . . .

Then the King went to dinner debating with himselfe
whether he should send to the English men or not. And before
he sat downe talked three or fower words thereof with mee.
For you know that oftentimes hee communed very familiarly
with those that were neere about him, as I was then, and others
after, and loved to talke in a means eare: hee called then to mind
the herault of Englands advise, which was, that he should not
faile to send to the King of England so soone as he was landed,
to demand a safe conduct for certaine ambassadors hee would
send to him. . . . Hee bad me in mine ears to arise and dine in
my chamber, and send for a certaine servant of the Lord of
Halles, sonne to Merichon of Rochell, and to commune with
him, to know whether hee durst adventure to goe to the King of
Englands campe in a Heraults cote. . . . When the King perceived
this good fellow to be well perswaded to go: hee sent . . . to
fetch a trumpet banner, thereof to make this counterfet herault

a cote armour: for the King because he was not pompous as
other Princes are, had neither herault nor trumpeter with him. ...
The King of England and part of his nobles liked these overtures
very well, and granted our herault as large a safe conduct as he
demanded, and gave him fower nobles of gold for a reward. ...
and the next morning in a village neere to Amiens the Commissioners of both Princes met. . . . The English men after
their wonted manner, first demanded the Crowne, at the least
Normandy and Guienne, but they were no more earnestly
demanded, than stoutly denied. Notwithstanding even at this
first meeting the treatie was brought to a reasonable poynt: for
both the parties desired peace. . . . The King reioyced marvellously at the report that his Commissioners made at their returne,
and sat in Counsell about these overtures of peace: where among
others my selfe was present. Some supposed all this treatie to be
meere deceit and cunning of the English men, but the King was
of a contrary opinion. . . . The King cared not what he did to
rid the King of England out of his Realme, save only that he
would in no wise consent to put any places into the English
mens hands: for rather then he would suffer that, he was fully
determined to hazard all. . . . The King of England to the end
the peace might be fully concluded, came and encamped within
halfe a league of Amiens. The King was at the gate, from whence
he might behold the English men a far off as they came. To say
the truth they seemed but yoong soldiers: for they rode in very
evill order. The King sent to the King of England 300 carts
laden with the best wines that might be gotten: the which
cariage seemed a far off almost as great as the King of Englands
army. Many English men because of the truce repaired to the
town, where they behaved themselves very undiscreetly, and
without all regard of their Princes honour. They came all in
armes, and in great troupes: and if the King our Master would
have dealt falsely with them, so great a number might never so
easily have been destroyed. Notwithstanding he meant nothing
lesse, but studied to make them goode cheere, and to conclude a
sure peace with them for his time. He had caused to be set at the
entry of the towne gate two long tables, on each side of the street
one, furnished with all kinds of delicate meates that provoke

drinke, and with the best wines that might be gotten, and men to wait upon them: of water there was no mention. At each of these tables he placed five or six great fat gentlemen of good houses, therby the better to content them that desired to drinke. . . . After they were within the towne, what house soever they entred into they paid nothing. Further, nine or ten tavernes were well furnished at the Kings charge of all things necessarie: whither they went to eat and drinke, and called for what they would, but the King defraied all: and this cheere endured three or fower daies. . . . The English men (as before I have said) are not so subtile and circumspect in these treaties and assemblies as the French. For (whatsoever men say of them) they go bluntly to worke, but a man must have patience with them and give them no crosse language. . . .

He (Edward iv) was accompanied with the Duke of Clarence his brother, the Earle of Northumberland, and divers other noble men, namely the Lord Hastings his Chamberlaine, his Chauncellor, and others. But there were not past three or fower besides himselfe a parallled in cloth of golde. Further hee ware on his head a blacke velvet cap with a marvellous rich jewell, being a Flower de luce set with stones. He was a goodly tall Prince, but inclined now to be somewahat grosse, and I had seene him before much beautifuller than at this present for sure when the Earle of Warwicke chased him out of England, hee was the goodliest gentleman that ever I set mine eye on. . . . Then the King began the talke and said: Cosin, you are most heartily welcom, there is no man in the world whom I have so much desired to see as you, and praised be God that we are met heere to so good a purpose: hereunto the King of England answered in good French. This talke ended, the Chancellor of England, who was a Prelate and Bishop of Elie, began his oration with a prophesie (whereof the English men are never unfurnished:) which said that in this place of Picquigny an honorable peace should be concluded betweene the Realmes of Fraunce and England. . . . Then was the missal brought forth and opened: upon the which each of the Kings laide one of their hands, and the other upon the true holy crosse, and sware both of them to keepe and observe the articles concluded betweene them, namely the truce for nine yeeres, wherein the confederates of both parties were comprehended, and the mariage of their children to be accomplished in maner and forme as was comprehended in the treatie. After they had both sworne, the King (who had his words at commandement) began to enter into pleasant talke with the King of England: saying that he should come to Paris to solace himselfe there with the Ladies, and that he would give him the Cardinall of Bourbon for his confessor, who would easily assoile him of that sinne, if any were committed. The King of England tooke great pleasure in this talke, and answered with a merry countenance: for hee knew the Cardinall to be a good fellow. After some suchlike speeches passed betweene them, the King to shew that he had authoritie among his men, commanded those that were with him to withdraw themselves, saying that he would commune with the King of England in secret: which they that accompanied the King of England seeing, retired without commandement. After the two Kings had communed a while together, the King called me to him, and asked the King of England if he knew me, who answered, that he knew me well, and named the places where he had seene me, adding, that in times past I had taken paines to doe him service in Calais during the time I was with the Duke of Burgundie. . . . The King returned to Amiens, and the King of England to his campe, whither we sent from the court all kinde of provision necessarie for him, so far foorth, that torches and lights were not forgotten.

COTSWOLD WOOL, 23 November, 1478

The wealth of the wool trade built the great churches of the Cotswolds and Norfolk.

Source: *Cely Papers Merchants of the Staple* 1475–1488, Camden Society, 3rd Ser. vol. i, 1900, p. 11. The headquarters of the Cely business of wool-merchants was at London and Calais.

Further Reading: I. D. Thornley, *England under the Yorkists* 1460–1485, Longmans 1920. E. Power and M. M. Postan, *Studies in English Trade in the 15th Century*, 1933.

Item the xxiiii day of November I have bogwyt of Wyllyam Medewynter of Norlache [Northleach] xl sacke of good cottys-

wolde woll good woll and medell woll of the same xl sacke pryse
the sacke of bothe good woll and medell woll xii marke the refus
woll for to be caste to Wyllyam Medewynter be the woll packer
at the packyng of the forsayd woll at Norlache.

PLAY OF NOAH AT HULL, 1483

The people were very indifferent to the Wars of the Roses and
in spite of them trade and industry grew. Thus in 1449 John Taverner
built a ship of record size at Hull and in 1483 the accounts of the
Trinity House, a guild of master mariners and pilots, contain entries
about a play about Noah, for he was a shipwright. In the text Noah's
wife would be a comic character. The labours of Noah were suitably
chosen to accompany those of St. Joseph on the wall of Carpenters'
Hall, London, and are seen in the Holkham Bible.

Source: G. Hadley, *History of Kingston upon Hull*, 1788.

Further Reading: E. K. Chambers, *The Medieval Stage*, O.U.P. 190 3

To the minstrels, vj d.
To Noah and his wife, j s. vj d.
To Robert Brown playing God, vj d.
To the Ship-child, j d.
To a shipwright for clinking Noah's ship, one day, vij d.
22 kids [faggots] for shoring Noah's ship, i j d.
To a man clearing away the snow, j d.
Straw, for Noah and his children, ij d.
Mass, bellman, torches, minstrels, garland, &c., vj s.
For mending the ship, ij d.
To Noah for playing, j s.
To straw and grease for the wheels, $\frac{1}{4}$ d.
To the waites for going about with the ship, vj d.

EDWARD IV, 1461-83

Edward IV was the son of Richard Duke of York, a descendant
of two of Edward III's sons, both Lionel, Duke of Clarence, and
Edmund, Duke of York. By his queen, Elizabeth Woodville, he had
ten children. When his coffin was opened at Windsor in 1789 his
skeleton measured full six feet three inches.

Source: *The History of King Richard the thirde writen by Master Thomas More one of the undersheriffs of London about* 1513, 1557. A panegyric of Edward IV by one who knew those who saw him, but whose account is perhaps coloured by an excessive desire to contrast his virtues with the vices of Richard III, the villain of the book.

Further Reading: C. L. Schofield, *Life and Reign of Edward IV*, 1928.

This noble Prince deceased at his palice of Westminster, and with greate funerall honoure and heavynesse of his people from thence conveyde, was entered at Windesor. A Kinge of suche governaunce and behavioure in time of peace (for in war eche parte muste needes bee others enemye) that there was never anye Prince of this lande attaynynge the Crowne by battayle, so heartely beloved with the substaunce of the people: nor he hymselfe so speciallye in anye parte of his life, as at the time of his death. Whiche favour and affeccion yet after his decease, by the crueltie, mischiefe, and trouble of the tempestious worlde that folowed, highelye towarde hym more increased. At suche time as he died, the displeasure of those that bare him grudge, for kinge Henries sake the sixte, whome he deposed, was well asswaged, and in effecte quenched, in that manye of them were dead in more then twentie yeares of his raigne, a great parte of a longe lyfe. And many of them in the meane season growen into his favoure, of whiche he was never straunge. He was a goodly parsonage, and very Princely to behold, of hearte couragious, politique in counsaile, in adversitie nothynge abashed, in prosperitie rather ioyfull then prowde, in peace iuste and mercifull, in warre, sharpe and fyerce, in the fielde, bolde and hardye, and nathelesse no farther then wysedome woulde, adventurouse. Whose warres who so well consyder, hee shall no lesse commende hys wysedome where hee voyded, than hys mannehoode where he vainquisshed. He was of visage lovelye, of bodye myghtie, stronge, and cleane made: howe bee it in his latter dayes wyth over liberall dyet, sommewhat corpulente and boorelye [burly], and nathelesse not uncomelye, hee was of youthe greatelye geven to fleshlye wantonnesse: from whiche healthe of bodye in greate prosperitye and fortune, withoute a specyall grace, hardelye refrayneth. Thys faute not greatlye gryeved the people: for neyther could any one mans pleasure, stretch and extende to the dyspleasure of verye manye, and was withoute violence, and over that in hys latter dayes lessyd and wel lefte. In whych tyme of hys latter daies, thys Realm was in quyet and prosperous estate: no feare of outewarde enemyes, no warre in hande, nor none forwarde, but such as no manne looked for: the people towarde the Prynce, not in a constrayned feare, but in a wyllynge and lovynge obedyence: amonge themselfe, the commons in good peace. The Lordes whome he knewe at varyaunce, hym-selfe in hys deathe bedde appeased. He hadde lefte all gatherynge of money (which is the onelye thynge that withdraweth the heartes of Englyshmenne fro the Prynce) nor anye thynge entended hee to take in hande, by which hee shoulde bee dryeven theretoo, for hys trybute oute of Fraunce hee hadde before obtayned. And the yere foregoynge hys deathe, hee hadde obtayned Bar-wycke [Berwick castle 24 Aug. 1482]. And al bee it that all the tyme of hys rayne, hee was wyth hys people, soo benygne, courteyse and so familyer, that no parte of hys vertues was more estemed: yet that condicyon in the ende of hys dayes (in which many princes by a long continued soverainty, decline in to a prowde porte from debonayre behavioure of theyr beginning mervaylouslye) in him grewe and increased: so farre forrthe that in the sommer the laste that ever he sawe, hys hyghenesse beeying at Wyndesore in huntynge, sente for the Mayre and Aldermenne of London to hym. For none other eraunde, but too have them hunte and bee mery with hym, where hee made them not so statelye, but so frendely and so familier chere, and sente venson from thence so frelye in the Citye, that no one thing in manye dayes before, gate hym eyther moe heartes or more heartie favoure amonge the common people, whiche oftentymes more esteme and take for greatter kindenesse, a lyttle courtesye, then a greate benefyte. So deceased (as I have said) this noble kynge, in that tyme, in whiche hys life was moste desyred.

RICHARD III, CROUCHBACK, 1483-5

Attempts have been made by modern historians to show that Richard III was not the wicked uncle which he has been generally painted. The traditional view of him is that of St. Thomas More.

Source: *The History of King Richard the thirde writen by Master Thomas More one of the undersheriffs of London about* 1513, 1557. More was born in 1480, but as he speaks as if present during the last sickness of Edward IV he is thought to have been copying a manuscript by someone else, probably Cardinal Morton.

Further Reading: J. Gairdner, *Life and Times of Richard III*, 1898. P. M. Kendall, *Richard the Third*, 1956.

Richard the third sonne [of Richard Duke of York], of whom we nowe entreate, was in witte and courage egall with either of them, in bodye and prowesse farre under them bothe [Edward IV and George Duke of Clarence], little of stature, ill fetured of limmes, croke backed, his left shoulder much higher than his right, hard favoured of visage, and suche as is in states called warlye [martial], in other menne otherwise, he was malicious, wrathfull, envious, and from afore his birth, ever frowarde. It is for trouth reported, that the Duches his mother had so muche adoe in her travaile, that shee coulde not bee delivered of hym uncutte: and that hee came into the worlde with feete forwarde, as menne bee borne outwarde, and (as the same runneth) also not untothed, whither menne of hatred reporte above the trouthe, or elles that nature chaunged her course in hys beginninge, whiche in the course of his lyfe many thinges unnaturallye committed. None evill captaine was hee in the warre, as to whiche his disposicion was more metely then for peace. Sundrye victories hadde hee, and sommetime overthrowes, but never in defaulte as for his owne parsone, either of hardinesse or polytike order, free was hee called of dyspence, and sommewhat above hys power liberall, with large giftes hee get him unstedfaste frendeshippe, for whiche hee was fain to pil and spoyle in other places, and get him stedfast hatred. Hee was close and secrete, a deepe dissimuler, lowlye of counteynaunce, arrogant of heart, outwardly coumpinable [companionable] where he inwardely hated, not letting to kisse whome hee thoughte to kyll: dispitious and cruell, not for evill will alway, but after for ambicion, and either for the suretie or encrease of his estate. Frende and foo was much what indifferent, where his advauntage grew, he spared no mans deathe, whose life withstoode his purpose. He slewe with his owne handes king Henry the sixt, being prisoner in the Tower, as menne constantly saye, and that without commaundemente or knoweledge of the king, whiche woulde undoubtedly yf he had entended that thinge, have appointed that boocherly office, to some other then his owne borne brother. Somme wise menne also weene, that his drifte covertly convayde, lacked not in helping furth his brother Clarence to his death [in a butt of malmsey, 1478]: whiche hee resisted openly, howbeit somwhat (as menne demed) more faintly then he that wer hartely minded to his welth.

THE BATTLE OF BOSWORTH, 22 August, 1485

Henry Tudor, Earl of Richmond, was the grandson of a Welsh gentleman, Owen Tudor, who married Katherine, widow of Henry V. His mother was Margaret Beaufort who was heir to the claim to the throne of the Beauforts as descendants of John of Gaunt, Duke of Lancaster. He obtained the support of Yorkists as well as Lancastrians by marrying Elizabeth, daughter of Edward IV and sister of Edward V and Richard Duke of York, the two little princes whom Richard III was believed to have murdered in the Tower, though some modern writers have tried to suggest that Richard III was not such a wicked uncle to them. Henry Earl of Richmond landed at Milford Haven on August 7 where many Welsh gentry joined him. Richard III was deserted by the Stanleys at the Battle of Bosworth and the Percies waited to see who should win. The victorious Henry became the king of an England free of dynastic strife. The popular Tudor family had united the country in their own persons.

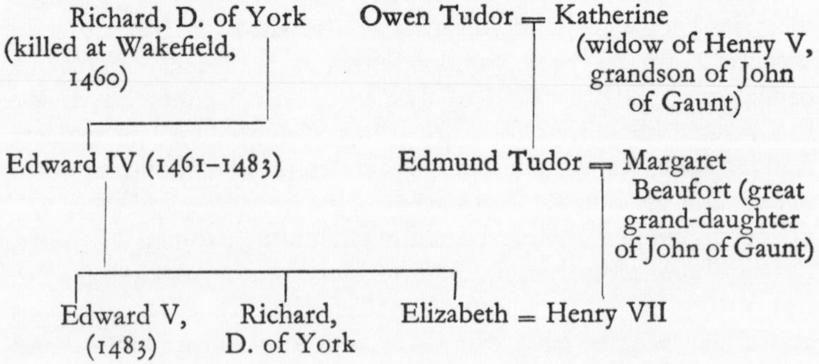
Richard, D. of York
(killed at Wakefield, 1460)
Owen Tudor = Katherine
(widow of Henry V, grandson of John of Gaunt)
Edward IV (1461–1483)
Edmund Tudor = Margaret Beaufort (great grand-daughter of John of Gaunt)
Edward V, (1483)
Richard, D. of York
Elizabeth = Henry VII

Source: Polydore Vergil, *English History*, Camden Soc. xxix, 1844.

Further Reading: Sir C. R. Markham, *Richard III his Life and Character*, 1906.

The report is that king Richerd might have sowght to save himself by flight; for they who wer abowt him, seing the soldiers even from the first stroke to lyft up ther weapons febly and fayntlye, and soome of them to depart the feild pryvyly, suspectyd treason, and exhortyd him to flye, yea and whan the matter began manyfestly to qwaile, they browght him swyft horses; but he, who was not ignorant that the people hatyd him, owt of hope to have any better hap afterward, ys sayd to have awnsweryd, that that very day he wold make end ether of warre or lyfe, suche great fearcenesse and suche huge force of mynd he had: wherfor, knowinge certanely that that day wold ether yeald him a peaceable and quyet realme from hencefurth or els perpetually bereve him the same, he came to the fielde with the crowne uppon his head that therby he might ether make a beginning or ende of his raigne. And so the myserable man had suddaynly suche end as wont ys to happen to them that have right and law both of God and man in lyke estimation, as will, impyeties, and wickednes. Surely these are more vehement examples by muche than ys hable to be utteryd with toong to tereyfy those men which suffer no time to passe free from soome haynous offence, creweltie, or mischief.

Henry, after the victory obtaynyd, gave furthwith thanks unto Almightie God for the same; than after, replenyssyd with joy incredible, he got himself unto the next hill, wher, after he had commandyd his solders, and commandyd to cure [i.e. attend to] the woundyd, and to bury them that wer slane, he gave unto the nobylytie and gentlemen immortal thankes, promysing that he wold be myndfull of ther benyfyttes, all which meane whyle the soldiers cryed, God save king Henry, God save king Henry! and with hart and hand utteryd all the shew of joy that might be; which whan Thomas Stanley dyd see, he set anon king Richerds crowne, which was fownd among the spoyle in the feilde, uppon his head, as thoughe he had bene already by commandment of the people proclamyd king after the maner of his auncestors, and that was the first signe of prosperytie. After that, com-

manding to pak upp all bag and baggage, Henry with his victorious army procedyd in the evening to Leycester, wher, for refressh-
ing of soldiers from ther travaile and panes, and to prepare for
going to London, he taryed two days. In the meane time the
body of king Richerd nakyd of all clothing, and layd uppon an
horse bake with the armes and legges hanginge down on both
sydes, was browght to thabbay of monks Franciscanes at Leycester, a myserable spectacle in good sooth, but not unwoorthy for
the mans lyfe, and there was buryed two days after without any
pompe or solemne funerall. He raigned two yeres and so many
monethes, and one day over. He was lyttle of stature, deformyd
of body, thone showlder being higher than thother, a short and
sowre cowntenance, which semyd to savor of mischief, and utter
evydently craft and deceyt. The whyle he was thinking of any
matter, he dyd contynually byte his nether lyppe, as thowgh that
crewell nature of his did so rage agaynst yt self in that lytle
carkase. Also he was woont to be ever with his right hand pulling
out of the sheath to the myddest, and putting in agane, the dagger
which he did alway were. Trewly he had a sharp witt, provydent
and subtyle, apt both to counterfayt and dissemble; his corage
also hault and fearce, which faylyd him not in the very death,
which, whan his men forsooke him, he rather yealded to take
with the swoord, than by fowle flyght to prolong his lyfe,
uncertane what death perchance soon after by sicknes or other
vyolence to suffer.

INDEX